INDUSTRIAL MEDWAY:
an historical survey

INDUSTRIAL MEDWAY:
an historical survey

J. M. PRESTON

The Industrial Development of the Lower Medway Valley with Special Reference to the Nineteenth and Early Twentieth Centuries

J. M. PRESTON
Borstal Road, Rochester, Kent

This book has been supported and sponsored by the following firms:

BERRY WIGGINS & Co. Ltd., Hoo
C. Townsend Hook & Co. Ltd., Snodland
Rugby Portland Cement Company Ltd., Halling
Joseph Collis Ltd., Strood
G. Wells & Sons Ltd., Strood
Morgan & Co. (Strood) Ltd.
Winget Ltd., Rochester
Palatine Precision Ltd., Rochester
Kimberly-Clark Ltd., Larkfield
Aveling Barford Ltd., Grantham
Lloyds of London
Associated Portland Cement Manufacturers Ltd.
Redland Bricks Ltd., Horsham

Printed litho in Great Britain
by W & J Mackay Ltd, Chatham

Contents

Illustrations

Page

Abbreviations Used in the Text

C.C.R.	Church Commissioners Records.
D.C.R.C.R.	Dean and Chapter of Rochester Cathedral Records.
K.A.O.	Kent Archives Office.
Arch. Cant.	*Archaeologia Cantiana.*
Chatham News	*The Chatham, Rochester and Gillingham News.*
Rochester Journal	*The Rochester and Chatham Journal.*
V.C.H.	Ed. W. Page, *The Victoria History of the Counties of England: Kent.*
A.P.C.M.	The Associated Portland Cement Manufacturers (1900) Ltd.
B.O.C.M.	British Oil and Cake Mills Ltd.
B.P.C.M.	British Portland Cement Manufacturers Ltd.

Acknowledgements

This book is a version of a thesis presented to the University of Kent at Canterbury, and I am indebted to Professor T. C. Barker and Mr John Whyman for their advice and helpful criticism during my research. I am grateful to the librarians at Rochester and Gillingham Public Libraries and at Medway and Maidstone College of Technology Library for their assistance, as I am to the many firms and individuals who have given me useful information and encouragement. I am grateful to Rochester and Maidstone Museums for permission to use photographs from their collections. I would like to thank the firms who have supported this book both morally and financially. My thanks are also due to Mrs Elsegood for producing the typescript. I am also indebted to my wife for her help and encouragement.

Preface

The Lower Medway Valley, particularly the vicinity of the Medway Towns, is now the most highly industrialized part of Kent. How, why and when the transformation from being a part of the rural 'garden of England' took place is the subject of this study. It will set out to show that the bulk of the area, until the mid-nineteenth century, was concerned mainly with agriculture. Superimposed on the agrarian scene was the commerce of the river Medway, flowing strategically from the Weald of Kent into the Thames, from the Kentish industrial centre of the seventeenth and eighteenth centuries to one of the main arteries of English life. The river also provided a fishery destined to disappear with the growth of industry and pollution. The towns owed their existence to non-industrial factors, the river crossing at Rochester with its cathedral, and market, the naval presence at Chatham and Sheerness. Manufacturing industry was represented before 1850 by a scattering of small paper mills, some boat building yards, small brickfields, a scattering of lime kilns, and a chemical works. The study will go on to show that rapid change began to take place from around 1850, with the creation of a new industrial scene between Gillingham and Burham. The major element in the expansion was the demand for building materials for both domestic construction and for civil engineering works. Geologically and geographically the Medway was well fitted to fill the demand, and bricks were produced along most of the Lower Medway. However, the most important factor was the advent of the Portland cement industry. This was brought to the Medway by a fortuitous collection of factors, geological, entrepreneurial, and locational. The building material industries, particularly cement, in turn stimulated the barge building industry to carry away their products, and the engineering industry to meet the demands for plant and equipment from these industries. The engineering industry it will be seen grew up independently of the naval dockyards but did have strong connections with agriculture. The dockyards were very much self-contained units, which, although they saw great development in the second half of the nineteenth century, had more of a social than economic influence on the area. Bricks, cement, barges and engineering were the staple industries from 1850 to the First World War but it will be shown that these four staples were already in decline by 1914 if not by 1900. The process of decline was to proceed, after a boom in some sectors during the 1914–18 War, through the 1920s and 1930s with its accompaniment of unemployment. The decline was due to technological and market changes, which demanded a restructuring of industry in the area. Change had not proceeded far by the Second World War. The local town councils were active in trying to promote new industry even before the First World War, but with marked lack of success. However, lessons learned during the difficult inter war years were fully applied after 1946 leading to relative prosperity once more by the late 1950s. Thus a picture will emerge of industry arising after what is traditionally regarded as the Industrial Revolution, declining after 50 years, languishing in the depressed inter war years, and finally reviving to meet new needs after the Second World War.

The Area

The area which is the subject of this study is taken as the parishes adjacent to the river Medway from Allington Lock, the northern most point of the old Upper Medway Navigation, to Garrison Point, Sheerness. It, therefore, covers the area of the Port of Rochester Authority, formerly controlled by the Medway Conservancy Board.[1] The parishes involved include on the left bank: Aylesford, Snodland, Halling, Cuxton, Strood, Frindsbury, Hoo St Werburgh, Stoke and Grain; on the right bank: Aylesford, Eccles, Burham, Wouldham, Rochester, Chatham, Gillingham, Rainham, Upchurch, Newington, Lower Halstow, Queenborough, and Sheerness.[2]

The area is strategically located, being the Gap in the North Downs. The river Medway flowing through this Gap allowed for transportation of goods by water between the Weald of Kent and Sussex and the River Thames. This, of course, was of great significance in the carriage of heavy or bulky produce of the Weald such as iron, woollen manufactures, timber and agricultural products.

The geology of the area[3] has had considerable influence on local industry, providing the basic raw materials for both bricks and cement. The valley bottom in the Gap, the southern half of Sheppey and much of the Hoo Peninsula comprise alluvial clays furnishing good soils for agricultural purposes. The alluvial clays also provide the raw materials for bricks and cement. The valley dissects the North Downs whose chalk uplands although poor from an agricultural point of view, form the basis of the cement and lime industries. From the east of Chatham between the Downs and the rivers Medway and the Swale is an area of Lower London Tertiary deposits, commonly known as brick earth. This deposit is the basis of the many brickworks, past and present, stretching from Gillingham, through Rainham and Lower Halstow and on to the Sittingbourne area. It was also responsible for the wheat growing of the past in this area and more recent fruit growing activities. The picture then is of a narrow valley between the Downs, the bulk of the industry being located at the northern end of the Gap opening into a wider estuary where the soils allowed for productive farming.[4]

[1] For details see R. Marsh, *The Conservancy of the River Medway 1881–1969* (Rochester, 1971).

[2] See Map I.

[3] See Map IV.

[4] See Ed. S. G. McRae and C. P. Burnham, *The Rural Landscape of Kent* (Wye College, 1973).

PART I

The Lower Medway Valley Before 1850

CHAPTER I

Trade on the Medway, Fishing and Farming

From the earliest times down to the present day one of the major factors influencing activity in the area has been the important route furnished by the Medway for the traffic of goods produced locally and in the Weald to the markets of London, Europe and the World. It has provided a means for the distribution of items not produced locally, such as coal from Tyneside, which were sent up the river to Maidstone and Tonbridge. Access to the reaches of the Medway above Rochester was severely restricted by the various bridges built, the first dating from Roman times. This tended to enhance the importance of Rochester due to the need to tranship cargo from seagoing vessels into barges and lighters for despatch up river, making for the growth of a distributive centre, as well as a convenient point for some processing.

Even before the Medway was made navigable as high as Tonbridge with the authorization of the Upper Medway Navigation in 1740, it was still profitable to drag goods to a wharf on the Medway for shipment. This made possible the carriage of iron goods and timber from the Weald, which, Edward Hasted noted, 'by reason of the badness of the roads' could only otherwise be carried at great expense.[1] John Browne, iron master of Brenchley, can be found in the 1660s transporting guns and gun shot from Yalding to Milhall,[2] where he maintained a depot.[3]

The Wealden iron industry was concerned to a very large extent with the manufacture of munitions. The first cast-iron cannon of English manufacture were made in 1543 at Buxted, Sussex by Ralph Hogge who employed French and Flemish assistants, to provide the requisite skills. At the height of the industry in the early seventeenth century there were 100 furnaces and forge mills in Kent, Sussex and Surrey.[4] The principal villages involved in Kent were Biddenden, Brenchley, Horsmonden, Goudhurst, Hawkhurst, Lamberhurst, Tonbridge, Speldhurst, Ashurst and Cowden.[5] Cannon would have been shipped both to Chatham Dockyard and to the Royal Armouries in London. During the late 1620s and early 1630s cast-iron cannon were shipped to the United Provinces from the large foundries of Kent and Sussex—a time when John Browne was employing 200 men in manufacturing cannon. However, Rhys Jenkins, an authority on iron making, stated that, even in Sussex, which was the chief centre of cannon manufacture in England in the sixteenth century, 'guns never became at any period the largest item of production'. It is quite possible that the Wealden industry provided for the needs of other industries within the South East. Possibly this could include the manufacture of salt pans, a large pan requiring as much metal as a cannon, constant repair and eventual replacement.[6] The copperas industry also required metal vats, pans and boilers, while the shipbuilding industry needed nails, wire for masts, chains and anchors, the latter, according to Prof. Nef, costing in 1618 up to 5 per cent of the value of a vessel.[7] However, the Weald did not share the expansion of the iron industry of the second half of the seventeenth century. By 1740 there were only 4 furnaces in Kent still at work, producing 400 tons of iron per annum.[8] Hasted particularly noted that products of iron in transit were from the mines and furnaces of Sussex.[9] The industry became extinct in Kent in 1796, the main reason being the lack of sufficient timber for the charcoal furnaces.[10]

Timber was another bulky item to be transported from the Weald, and one for which the roads were completely unsuited. The bad condition of the roads is recorded by Daniel Defoe when he described the movement of tree trunks from the Weald to Chatham.

> 'I have seen one Tree on a carriage which they call a Tug, drawn by two and twenty Oxen, and even then 'tis carry'd so little a Way and then thrown down, and left for other Tugs to take up and carry on, that sometimes it is Two or Three Years before it gets to Chatham; for if once the rains come in, it stirs no more that Year, and sometimes a whole Summer is not dry enough to make the roads passable.'[11]

The river then was an ideal means of transport for timber.

The 'timber in the woods is mostly oak and beech . . . in great plenty; and of a very large size fit for the supply of his majesties navy.' wrote Hasted in the 1770s, 'and though (the woods) yearly afford a supply for the Royal Navy of Great Britain, yet in all probability there will be sufficient remaining for the use of it for ages yet to come'.[12] Hasted was only too wrong. The once thickly wooded Weald was being quickly deforested due to the needs of the Royal Dockyards of Chatham, Deptford and Woolwich, local shipbuilding, and the building industry. Wood also served as fuel for iron making (charcoal), brickmaking, salt boiling, dyeing and not least for domestic purposes. The scarcity which began in Tudor times with the emergence of the Dockyards and of the iron industry became critical by the end of the eighteenth century.

Another major item transported by river which was to rise and fall over much the same period was the manufacture of worsteds. This industry was established in the reign of Elizabeth I when French and Flemish refugees set up as weavers at Maidstone, Sandwich and Canterbury and later at Cranbrook and Hawkhurst.[13] Though flourishing in the early seventeenth century, the industry was seriously disrupted during the Civil War. The industry had disappeared by the end of the eighteenth century, apart from one worsted factory at Hawkhurst run by a Mr Winch who employed 100 people. The decline was mainly due to competition from inferior Scottish cloth after 1707, and later from Yorkshire.

Associated with the textile industry was fulling. Flemish skills were used to erect the mills on the fast flowing streams at Cranbrook and on the river Len.[14] At the end of the sixteenth century Lambarde wrote that the stream between Loose and Tovelle (Tovil) in the two miles before it joined the Medway 'beareth thirteene Fulling Milles and one for Corne, which are reputed to earne so many hundreds of pounds by the yeare'.[15] The fullers earth which was used in the mills was to be found in abundance in the parish of Boxley, where in the words of Richard Kilburne 'the bowels of this County are well stored with Fullers Earth'.[16] The estate upon which the fullers earth was found, Groves, was bought by a Mr John Watts in 1702, and this 'ingenious' man 'wrought' this 'famous mine'. The vein of earth lay at a depth of 30 feet and was 7 feet thick. 'There are two sorts of it; the Blue and the Dark Grey.'[17] The decline of textiles and subsidiary fulling was compensated for in trade on the Medway by the conversion of the fulling mills for paper manufacture, and its carriage to London by barge.

The importance of the Medway as a means of communication in the seventeenth century is stressed by C. W. Chalklin in that 'nearly all the manufacturers of North and central Kent made use of the Thames and Medway in the despatch of their products including lime, copperas, paper and worsteds, to London.' Also shipped to London was agricultural produce from Upchurch, Otterham, Rochester and Queenborough.[18] Return cargoes would have included such items as rags for papermaking, and manure for agriculture. The London market was already exerting a considerable influence on the area by the mid-seventeenth century. It was already the greatest centre of consumption in the country with its growing population and consumer wealth based on the presence of the Court, Parliament, the law courts, its growing commercial and financial interests and the port.[19] Also shipped was fullers earth from Rochester to the textile areas, and copperas from Gillingham and Queenborough.[20]

In the eighteenth century the river was being used to carry 'corn, grain, hay, hops, wool, leather, all manner of provisions, coal, lime from chalk dug at Rochester and sent to Essex, Suffolk and Norfolk (for agricultural purposes), quarry stone and all other necessaries and commodities' at an 'easy expense'. A great number of hoys were transporting goods from Maidstone 'freighted for the supply of the London Markets, to which several mills for corn, paper, etc. there and the great quantity of hop-grounds in these parts, do not a little contribute'.[21] To Hasted's list of cargoes, Charles Seymour added timber, apples, cherries and white sand for glass. These could be carried from as far as Maidstone in barges of up to 100 tons burthen.[22] Apart from the obstacle of Rochester bridge, another impediment to traffic was the bridge at Aylesford, described in 1719 as 'a very fair and large stone bridge over the Medway, the arches where of are so high that a large hoy can pass through with her mast lower'd down'.[23]

Another item shipped from the Medway was fish. During his tour Defoe observed that from 'Queenborough, Milton and Feversham, the fish market at Billingsgate is supplied with several sorts of fish; but particularly with the best and largest oysters'.[24] Oysters from the Medway were a great speciality, and not only found their way on to the London market in great quantities, but were exported also to Holland and 'transmitted into Westphalia and other adjacent countries'.[25]

The river was also used for the importation of goods. One important commodity which arrived for distribution up river was coal from Newcastle. Between 1 April 1651 and 12 October 1651 an impost of 2/– per London chaldron[26] on coal raised £109. 7s. 0d. at the port of Rochester,[27] making imports in the region of 1,420 tons for that period. Much of this coal would have been for domestic usage. Other notable imports in the seventeenth century were dairy produce from East Anglia, and bricks from Holland.[28]

Towards the end of the eighteenth century Rochester was obviously a thriving port. Seymour wrote in 1776 'Near 200 sail arrive annually in the port; and the great part of their cargoes, consisting of coals, wine etc. are sent up the Medway to Maidstone, Tunbridge etc.'[29] Rochester in the view of Denne 'may be thought advantageously placed for trade' and added that the 'chief ships which deliver . . . are colliers, wine and east country ships, with various stores for use in the dockyard'. However, he added that 'it does not appear that it [Rochester] ever enjoyed the benefit of any manufacture'. Most of the inhabitants were 'engaged in trade and maritime occupations'.[30] However, a perusal of the Directories for the end of the eighteenth century and the beginning of the nineteenth reveals considerable numbers of people engaged in crafts or trade. These included tailors, shoe and boot makers, cabinet makers, bakers, butchers and the great variety of occupations necessary to a growing community. This view is similar to Hasted's who wrote 'the intercourse of the inhabitants with the Royal Dock, Victualling Office, Navy and other branches of the shipping prove a continual source of wealth and employment to them' and added that 'though there are no particular manufacture carried on here, Rochester was a very busy and populous town'.[31] In the Introduction to his book Hasted observed that 'the seacoast and the rivers Thames and Medway furnish employments so various[32] and lucrative to all ranks of people and cause such an accumulation of trade and riches that not only the adjacent but the most inland parts partake of it.'[33] Of Kent generally Hasted said

> 'There are but few manufactures in this country, as well owing to the great attention paid to agriculture and grazing, as to the great number of easy and lucrative employments in the disposal of government: yet there are some.'

Of those he mentioned only salt making at the Isle of Grain (also made at Stonar in Thanet) was associated with the Lower Medway. The others he thought worthy of mention included muslin at Canterbury, copperas at Whitstable and Deptford, gunpowder at Ospringe, iron furnaces in the Weald, paper at Boxley and iron mills at Dartford and Crayford.[34]

The considerable traffic on the river was therefore one of the major sources of income for the area. Although some of the freight from the Weald was to disappear by the end of the eighteenth century, this was to be compensated for by the rise of new products from the Lower Medway in need of transport, particularly lime and bricks. The steady growth of London would also ensure a stable flow of agricultural products.

Apart from trade on the River, the Medway provided opportunities for fishing. The river abounded in fish! 'below Rochester there are taken the finest and largest smelts that can be, soals, flounders, dabs, thornbacks, maids'.[35] The fishery was long established. Hasted quoted a survey of 1565 which disclosed that Gillingham had 'four Keys', 27 boats and occupied 43 persons 'about fishing', while Lower Halstow had 14 boats and employed

14 people in shipping and fishing.[36] Oysters were dredged from the creeks on the Medway and the Swale. These famed oyster fisheries were controlled by Rochester Corporation in the Medway, and by Queenborough Corporation in the Swale.

The Rochester oyster fishery was governed by an Act of 1729 for the 'better ordering and governing' of the fishery. This allowed an Admiralty Court under the Mayor of Rochester to make rules and orders for the opening and shutting of the dredging season, the quantity taken by each dredgerman on each day, and the preservation of the brood. The mayor could also impose fines. Every person was free to dredge after having served a seven year apprenticeship on payment of a fine of 6s. 8d. and a further payment of 6s. 8d. per year. The company of dredgers bought spat and brood from other areas to lay in the river. The breeding time was April and May, and the spats (spawn) taken in May were cast on a hard bottom till the end of August. The fishermen tried to maintain a hard bed to stop mussels and cockles breeding in the ouse and destroying oysters by occupying places where spats would be cast. They also needed to kill any starfish. Once sown the oysters were not ready for 18 months, the young having to be thrown back. The dredging was done by means of a net with an iron scraper at the mouth which was dragged by a rope from a boat over the beds. The oysters were then stored in special pits with sluices through which the spring tides could flow. The water became stagnant and green in warm weather, and in a few days the oysters gained a tinge which 'renders them of greater value'. They did not obtain full quality and become fit for sale for six to eight weeks.[37]

This fishery was 'a source of great emolument and advantage to the city of Rochester and its neighbourhood'.[38] An Exchange had once existed near Strood Hard, the ground floor of which was used as a meeting place by the dredgermen, and from which one was able to see 100 to 200 boats on the hardway.[39] A note to the census returns for Strood in 1831 stated that 55 males of over 20 years of age were employed in fishing.[40] About this time considerable expenditure was incurred in the upkeep of the oyster fishery which was 'so extensive and important' that in 1833 'a sum of £25,000 was required for restocking the ground with brood alone'.[41] The oyster fishery was to remain prosperous until the 1860s. A report of the auditing of the fishery accounts in July 1860 stated 400 persons were involved in it, '120 of whom are freemen. It appeared that during the last year they had expended nearly £9,000 and that the property within their control is very considerable and is in the course of improvement'.[42]

The floating fishery based on Rochester also flourished until just after 1850, only the freemen of the City of Rochester being allowed to catch fish with a net in the Medway.[43] Up to 1870, 20 or 30 boats, each with a crew of three men, seined for white herring at Rochester between October and December each year.[44] In an article entitled 'Recollections of Old Strood' in 1909, A. Bevans Horsnaill stated that

> 'Old Strood was essentially a fishing town, with its fleet of Bawleys leaving, in company, on Monday mornings with their store of salt for the weeks shrimping and trawling in the lower reaches of the river and outside. Then there was its fleet of dobles for the lighter river work of smelting and dredging which might be seen anywhere up to Hawkwood or Aylesford.'[45]

Gillingham continued to have fishermen, there being in 1831 some 37 males over 20 years of age employed.[46] Hasted said most of the inhabitants of Lower Halstow were also fishermen or dredgermen.[47]

Queenborough was the other important fishing town. It was described by Defoe as 'a miserable, dirty, decayed, poor, pitiful fishing town' the chief business of which 'consists in ale-houses, and oyster catchers'.[48] The oyster fishery under the jurisdiction of Queenborough was in the Swale from Kingsferry to the junction with the Medway. The fishery had been established for centuries, was locally the principal source of employment, and was free and common to every burgess of the borough until 1820. Until 1728 the court leet had power to control the season of fishing as well as the quantity taken, and to order planting of brood. This control was usurped by the Corporation which only allowed freemen to be employed by them, not to fish independently. This was connected with corruption in the unreformed Parliament as a fair proportion of freemen were voters and held government offices.[49] To purchase oyster brood recourse was made to borrowing by way of Corporation bonds, the debt amounting to £14,485 in August 1820, when 70 to 80 people were employed in dredging.[50] The 1831 census returns show that 123 males over 20 years of age were employed in fishing and dredging.[51] However, due to corruption, mismanagement and rising debts, all the fault of the Corporation, the oyster fishery was already in decline. It was eventually leased out to a merchant from 1847 for 21 years at £500 per annum.[52] Floating fish were also caught from Queenborough, trawlers fishing for soles, dabs and shrimps, and seine netting white bait.[53]

Fishing before 1850 was maintained not only by supplying the local market, but particularly by sending its wares to Billingsgate to supply the growing London market, where there was a dramatic growth of population from 1,117,000 in 1801 to 3,227,000 in 1861.[54] Before the growth of the railways provided a speedy link between London and ports like Yarmouth and Lowestoft, fish, salted in barrels, and delivered at Billingsgate quay from the Thames estuary had a greater share of the market. Fishing, apart from directly employing labour also affected the local economy to a degree with its demand for equipment. It required boats, rope, sails, oars, nets and other gear which would have been supplied locally. However, the scale of production, and the number employed in each unit, was so small that little information survives, apart from a few names in nineteenth century directories and in the returns of occupations in the 1841 Census.

Outside the Medway Towns, agriculture remained important, the land use being clear from contemporary descriptions. During her tour in 1697 Celia Fiennes found on the road from Maidstone to Rochester 'a great many fine hopp-yards', and by the road from Rochester to Gravesend 'cherry grounds that are of severall acres of ground and run quite down to the Thames, which is convenient for to convey the Cherries to London'.[55] Cherry and apple orchards were to be found on each side of the Dover road from Rainham to Blean Wood. Rainham by Hasted's time had lost its cherry and apple orchards. It was, however, 'formerly noted for growing the best wheat that this Kingdom produced'. Newington was also mostly planted with apple and cherry orchards.[56] At Lower Halstow the clay land had been improved by spreading lime from Hartlip. At Iwade there was flat marshy pasture 'having vast quantities of sheep continually feeding upon them', which remarkably did not seem to get liver fluke. In Sheppey

> 'the soil of the greater part of the island is an exceedingly stiff clay, by far the largest portion consisting of upland pasture and marshes, the latter being rich and fertile for fatting land. The lands towards the North side, in the parishes of Minster and Eastchurch are very fertile in corn, the enclosures of which are small and surrounded by thick hedgerows of elm'.[57]

In many of the villages agriculture was the most important source of employment before 1850. The returns of the 1831 census show that in Aylesford 149 from 322 males over 20 years were employed in agriculture, in Burham 56 from 92, in Wouldham 43 from 74, in Cuxton 65 from 88 and in Lower Halstow 37 from 67. However, in some villages by 1831, agriculture had ceased to be important, for instance in Frindsbury which had only 107 agricultural labourers from a population of 1856, or in Rainham with 164 from 1,222 or in Upchurch with 74 from 486 people.[58] By

1831, brickmaking was becoming an important source of employment in these areas.

The agricultural produce could be sold in the local markets of Rochester, Chatham, Gillingham, Queenborough or even Maidstone. However, it is clear that the bulk of the produce was shipped by hoy direct to the London markets to exploit the easily accessible and growing market.

The greatest single influence on the area before 1850, both economically and socially, was the employment provided by the State in various military installations. The siting of the Royal Dockyard at Chatham led to the expansion of this village and neighbouring Brompton, while the installation at the mouth of the river created Sheerness. The stationing of regiments of Royal Marines, Engineers and Regiments of the Line at Chatham also provided opportunities for civilian employment, and also generated spending power for local shops and inns. However, the most important establishment was Chatham Dockyard.

[1] Edward Hasted, *The History and Topographical Survey of the County of Kent*, I, (1st Ed., Canterbury, 1778), Introduction, cxxvii.

[2] K. A. O. Browne Mss, TR1295/83 Account dated 29 March 1664.

[3] E. Straker, *Wealden Iron* (1967), 189.

[4] R. Furley, *A History of the Weald of Kent with an outline early History of the County*, II, (Ashford, 1874), 484–5.

[5] E. Melling, *Kentish Sources—Aspects of Agriculture and Industry* (Maidstone, 1961), 93.

[6] J. U. Nef, *War and Human Progress* (1950), 80, 81.

[7] J. U. Nef, *The Rise of the British Coal Industry*, I, (1966), 170–1.

[8] Furley, *op. cit.*, II, 607.

[9] Hasted, *op. cit.*, (1778), I, ccxxiv.

[10] Furley, *op. cit.*, II, 607.

[11] D. Defoe, *A Tour through England and Wales Divided into Circuits of Journies* (Reprinted, from 9th edition, 1968), 128–9.

[12] Hasted, *op. cit.*, I, (2nd Edition, Canterbury, 1797), 268, 297.

[13] Furley, *op. cit.*, II, 480, 486.

[14] Furley, *op. cit.*, II, 329, 606.

[15] William Lambarde, *A Perambulation of Kent* (Reprinted from 3rd edition of between 1596–1640, Bath, 1970), 200.

[16] Richard Kilburne, *A Topographie or Survey of the County of Kent* (1659), 6.

[17] John Harris, *The History of Kent* (1719), 51.

[18] C. W. Chalklin, *Seventeenth Century Kent—a Social and Economic History* (1965), 114–15, 171.

[19] F. J. Fisher, 'The Development of the London Food Market, 1590–1640', *Economic History Review*, v, (1934–5).

[20] Chalklin, *op. cit.*, 178, 179.

[21] Hasted, *op. cit.*, I, (1797), 278.

[22] Charles Seymour, *A New Topographical, Historical and Commercial Survey of the Cities, Towns and Villages of the County of Kent*, II, (Canterbury, 1776), 545.

[23] Harris, *op. cit.*, 32.

[24] Defoe, *op. cit.*, I, (Everyman Ed., 1962) 112–13.

[25] Rev, Samuel Denne, *The History and Antiquities of Rochester and its Environs* (W. Wildash Edition, Rochester, 1817), 293.

[26] Defined by Nef as 26 to 27 cwt.

[27] Nef, *op. cit.*, II, (1966), 401.

[28] Chalklin, *op. cit.*, 172, 181.

[29] Seymour, *op. cit.*, III, 678.

[30] Denne, *op. cit.*, 311–17.

[31] Hasted, *op. cit.*, (1st Edition, 1782), II, 8.

[32] but which, except for such enterprises as the oyster bed, were of a small scale, unrecorded and little known.

[33] Hasted, *op. cit.*, (1778) I, 2–3.

[34] Hasted, *op. cit.*, (1797), I, 270.

[35] Hasted, *op. cit.*, (1778) I, cxxviii.

[36] Hasted, *op. cit.*, II, (1782), 87, 547.

[37] Denne, *op. cit.*, 292–4.

[38] L. Fussell, *A Journey round the Coast of Kent* (1818), 37.

[39] Henry Smetham, *A History of Strood* (Strood, 1899), 50.

[40] Registrar General, *Census of 1831, Enumeration Abstract*, (1833), 264.

[41] Samuel Bagshaw, *History, Gazetteer and Directory of the County of Kent*, I, (Sheffield, 1847), 100.

[42] *Chatham News*, 21 July 1860.

[43] E. M. Hewitt, 'Industries', *V.C.H.*, III, (1932), 433.

[44] Evidence to Sea Fisheries Commission, Rochester 14th November 1878, quoted *V.C.H.*, III, 430.

[45] *Chatham News*, 3rd April 1909.

[46] Registrar General, Census of 1831, *op. cit.*, 263.

[47] Hasted, *op. cit.*, (1st Edition 1778), II, 547.

[48] Defoe, *op. cit.*, (1962), I, 110–1.

[49] W. Ireland, *England's Topographer or A new and complete History of the County of Kent; from the earliest records to the present time, including every modern improvement*, IV, (1828), 138.

The value of Ireland as a source has been called into question by Dr F. Hull, the Kent County Archivist, as an illustrated Hasted. In an article entitled a 'Kentish Historiography', *Archaeologia Cantiana*, LXX (1956), 227–8. Dr Hull wrote 'What is of value comes from Hasted, but there is no attempt to enlarge or expand the earlier work and no evidence either of knowledge of Kent or of original research.' There is in fact a great deal of similarity between the descriptions of Hasted, Ireland and Seymour, and also between Seymour and Denne. It is quite obvious that large sections have been borrowed word for word. However, being written later, there is some additional information included in what little appears on industrial, commercial and agricultural topics. For this reason Ireland, in my view, is a valid source.

[50] R. Goodsall, '*Oyster Fisheries and the North Kent Coast*', *Arch. Cant.* LXXX, (1965), 133–4.

[51] Registrar General, Census of 1831, op cit., 270.

[52] Bagshaw, *op. cit.*, II, 511.

[53] Hewitt, 'Industries', in *V.C.H.*, III, 431.

[54] B. R. Mitchell and P. Deane, *Abstract of British Historical Statistics*, (Cambridge, 1962), 19.

[55] Ed. C. Morris, *The Journeys of Celia Fiennes* (1947), 130.

[56] Hasted, *op. cit.*, (1st Edition 1778), II, 535, 560, 684.

[57] Ireland, *op. cit.*, IV, 21, 114, 118, 226.

[58] Registrar-General, Census of 1831, *op. cit.*

CHAPTER II

The Dockyards, Barracks and their Influence before 1850

The river at Gillingham was first selected as an anchorage in 1547. Its waters were slow running so there was little likelihood of dragging anchors or breaking cables, and the surrounding hills provided shelter from the prevailing winds. The river was rock free and had a mud bottom, and it had a good tide rise which facilitated grounding to carry out caulking, scraping and other operations on the ships' hulls. A storehouse was rented at 13s. 4d. annual rental.[1] The 'station or harborow of the Navie Royall at Gillingham and Chatham' is mentioned by Lambarde.[2]

From being a sheltered anchorage, the yard developed as a result of constant extension of the acreage covered and continual new building. By 1563 Gillingham was the most expensive of the four royal yards, the others being Woolwich, Deptford and Portsmouth, costing £3,700 in that year. It was first officially termed Chatham dockyard in 1567. The yard was then situated below St Mary's Church, Chatham on what later became Gun Wharf. Some of the first works included a mast pond dug in 1570, and a forge and extra store houses erected in 1572. It was in 1586 that the first boat definitely built at Chatham was launched. This was the pinnace *Sunne* of 59 tons burthen, 50 feet overall length and designed for a crew of 30.[3] By 1601 the wage bill for Chatham had risen to £3,600 per annum.

The years 1618 to 1625 saw another expansion. In 1618 a wet dock to take four galleys was constructed from one of the creeks. By 1619 the old yard had become too small for the amount of work allocated to it, so 71 acres of land were leased on the north ward side. This was laid out with three ranges of buildings forming approximately three sides of a rectangle. The south range consisted of officers' houses, the east of a sail loft with more houses, and the north of store houses. The space these ranges enclosed was used for a dry dock, workshops and storage for timber. The space outside was used for a rope walk, rope store and other stores. In 1621 a boat dock with a rope house over was built. In 1623 a single dock was added, and in 1625 a 600-feet long rope house. The site of the original dockyard became an ordnance store in 1666.

Another round of expansion took place between 1685 and 1723. Starting in 1685, two new docks 200 feet by 59 feet were built. In 1686 there followed ten new mast houses, each 112 feet by 17 feet, at a cost of £2,000; also a 660-feet long storehouse was erected, and the yard surrounded by a brick wall. In 1698 a new mast pond with 32 brick arches to keep the masts submerged was built at a cost of £3,200. Following this, the Superintendent's House was constructed in 1703, the Main Gate in 1720, the Ropery in 1719 and the Sail Loft in 1723. By this time the yard covered 61 acres.[4]

The dockyard by the beginning of the eighteenth century was one of the sights of the South East. Travellers such as Celia Fiennes and Daniel Defoe visited Chatham dockyard and described it in glowing terms. Part of Defoe's description runs

> 'the river and its appendices are the most considerable of the kind in the world. This being the chief arsenal of the royal navy in Great Britain. The warehouses, or rather streets of warehouses, and storehouses for laying up naval treasure are the largest in dimension. The rope walk for making cables, and the forges for anchors and other iron work, bear a proportion to the rest, as also the wet dock for keeping masts, and yards of the greatest size . . . all like the whole, monstrously great and extensive and are not easily described. . . . The building-yards, docks, timber yards, deal yard, mast yard, gun yard, rope walks, and all other yards and places set apart for the works belonging to the navy, are like a well ordered city.'[5]

The continual colonial wars of the 18th century provided work for the yard. One of the most famous warships to be laid down at this time was the *Victory* in 1759. The threat of French invasion in these wars led to the construction from 1758 onwards of major defences on the landward side of the dockyard including Chatham Lines and other fortifications.[6] The river approach to the dockyard had, previous to the Dutch attack in June 1667, been defended by gun platforms at Upnor and Gillingham Castles, and forts or gun platforms at Cockham Wood and on the swamp towards Hoo, as well as by 12 guns at Sheerness. The defences were ill-maintained and the success of the attack

> 'gave England such a sense of the consequence of the river Medway, and of the docks and yards at Chatham, and of the danger the royal navy lay exposed to there, that all these doors which were open then, are lock'd up and sufficiently barr'd since that time; . . . for besides all the castles, lines of guns, and

> platforms on each side the river Medway, as we go up, as above; there is now a royal fort built at the point of the Isle of Shepey, call'd Sheerness.'[7]

Apart from ramparts, palisades and a broad ditch running from the Lines to the river at Gillingham, the immediate defence of the yard was completed with the construction of Fort Amhurst in 1779–82. The inner range of fortifications was completed with the construction of Fort Delce and Fort Clarence in 1812[8] and of Fort Pitt in 1819. Barracks were also constructed from 1758 onwards to have five regiments and a battalion of artillery for the defence of the yard.[9] Among the other warlike preparations at Chatham was the collection of weapons at the Ordnance Wharf. This was described by Seymour in 1776 as

> 'situated south of the dockyard between Chatham Church and the river. . . . The guns belonging to the ships in the river are here deposited. Some of the guns weigh 65 cwt. each. Large pyramids of shot are to be seen on different parts of the wharf; there are also capacious storehouses, in which are deposited prodigious quantities of offensive weapons, as muskets, pistols, cutlasses, pikes, pole axes etc.'[10]

The Napoleonic Wars also saw much activity in the yard. The Royal Dockyards were unable to cope with the building programme, many building contracts being put out to private constructors.[11] Chatham dockyard would have undertaken additional maintenance and repair work, besides construction, which at times required working double tides to maintain production. Mr Whyman has found two reports of this, firstly in 1795 when an order was sent to dockyards 'for the workmen to work double tides, and even on Sundays, till the new ships under orders for immediate service are finished', and secondly, a similar order was issued for Chatham workers in 1798[12] During the Wars a total of 14 vessels were built in Chatham yard.[13]

The Wars evidently demonstrated the need for more modern equipment in the yard. Between 1810 and 1813 steam sawmills designed by the elder Brunel were erected on the north-east side of the dockyard, communicating by a tunnel with the mast pond.[14] The sawmills were described in 1838 as being on rising ground 35 feet above water level, standing 90 feet square. The machinery consisted of 8 saw frames, and 2 circular benches with windlasses to feed, driven by a 30 h.p. steam engine. The saw frames took up to 30 saws for plank cutting. The smithery at that time contained 40 forges for making all iron work and anchors up to 5 tons.[15]

In the years 1815–32 forty-six sailing ships were built in the yard. Then in 1833 the first steam engined ship, *Gleaner*, 351 tons with a 130 h.p. engine, was launched. The first steam powered warship was the paddle frigate *Tiger* launched in 1849.[16] The new departures in ship technology demanded new skills, which led to the opening of the Yard Apprentices School in 1843.[17] This was to prove of importance in providing the area with a nucleus of skilled craftsmen on the eve of the expansion of industry in the area.

The expansion of the dockyard was matched by an expansion in employment. Some figures are provided by Admiral Crace.

TABLE OF EMPLOYMENT IN CHATHAM DOCKYARD

1664	324 men	1754	1,188 men
1688	479 men	1758	1,720 men
1712	797 men	1772	1,553 men

Source: Adm. J. G. Crace, *Some notes on the History of Chatham Dockyard* (1946).

One result of anchoring the fleet in the Medway was the opening of a victualling office at Chatham in 1551.[18] This in the late eighteenth century contained a cooperage, houses for pickling, baking, slaughtering and cutting and storage, and a wharf.[19] By 1838 the lease on the premises[20] had expired, and the office had been transferred to Sheerness.[21]

Sheerness began with the construction of a fort in 1572,[22] and was extended into a dockyard in the reign of Charles II.[23] Defoe saw Sheerness as

> 'not only a fortress, but a kind of town, with several streets in it, and inhabitants of several sorts, but chiefly whose business obliges them to reside here: the officers of the ordnance have here appartments, and an office . . . to see to the furnishing of every ship with military stores as need requires. . . . Here is also a yard for building ships, with a dock; the reason for which is to repair any ship speedily that may meet any accident, either riding at the Nore, or in any service at sea near the river.'

The dock was only capable of taking 5th and 6th raters and smaller warships.[24] The Sheerness yard of the nineteenth century was substantially that planned by Sir John Rennie in 1810. Three basins were constructed in the early part of the century. An iron-framed boat shed was constructed in 1861.[25] The activities of victualling, repair and construction of numerous small boats gave employment to between 2,000 and 3,000 artisans and mechanics in 1866.[26]

Among the barracks in the Medway Towns, Kitchener and

Brompton are probably best known. The Kitchener Barracks, originally called Chatham Barracks, were constructed between 1757 and 1778 and originally used as a military hospital and accommodation for infantry regiments. Brompton Barracks, originally called the Artillery Barracks, were built between 1804 and 1806 employing convict labour and French prisoners-of-war to house artillery units for the land ward defence of the dockyard.

Location of the Victualling Office at Chatham.

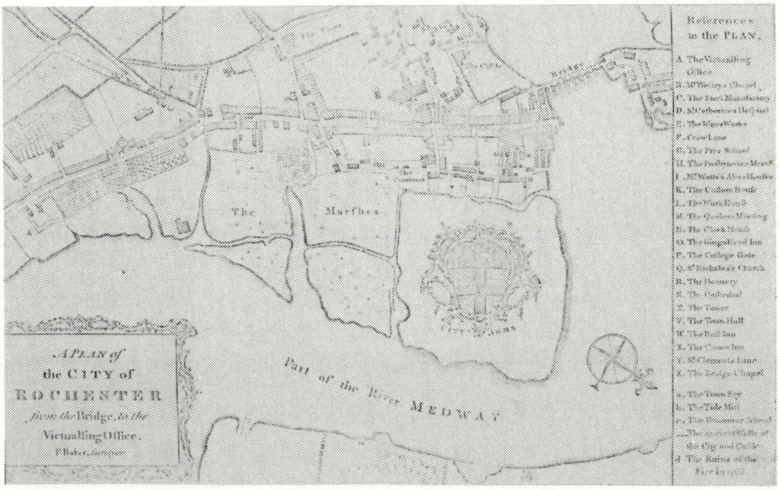

from Rev. S. Denne, *The History and Antiquities of Rochester and its Environs* (Rochester, 1772).

Between 1806 and 1824 there were normally only about four companies of foot artillery. The Royal School of Military Engineering was formed in 1812 as the Royal Engineer Establishment at Chatham to train junior officers and sappers after heavy losses in siege operations during the Peninsular War. The first director was Capt. Charles Pasley, famed for early experiments with cement. The troops originally occupied St Mary's Barracks and billets at Upnor.[27] St Mary's Barracks, erected between 1808 and 1812,[28] were originally intended to house French prisoners of war. The Marine Barracks were erected between 1783 and 1784 between the southern extremity of the dockyard and St Mary's Church.[29]

The naval and military establishments, although involving the greatest capital investment in the area before 1850, did little to promote manufacturing industry. Before 1712, sails and possibly other small items were contracted out for manufacture.[30] Mr Chalklin suggests that leather scuppers, buckets, candles and lanterns may have been made in the Towns. After about 1712 the dockyards became completely self sufficient with their forges, roperies, sail lofts and other workshops. In the construction of the various establishments, the bricks would have been bought from local manufacturers, demand from the dockyard being met from Snodland, Rainham and Upchurch.[31] There is no reason to believe that lime for mortar was purchased outside the valley.

So far as employment is concerned, construction work seems to have provided an occupation for convicts and prisoners of war, more than for civilian workers. However, work in the dockyards did provide employment on a significant scale, and was the basis of the expansion of the Medway Towns. The presence of many army and naval officers would have affected the demand for domestic servants at their homes and required such personnel as mess waiters at the barracks.

Retailing would have been promoted by the spending power of the military personnel. Demand for goods of all kinds to meet household needs would have been satisfied locally in Brompton and Chatham, as well as in the more genteel shops of Rochester. Specialist shops to deal with the services, were also present such as in 1849 James Grover, army clothier of 295 High Street, Chatham, or Samuel Isaacs a military outfitter of High Street, Chatham.[32] Another example at Old Brompton is J. Turner of 75 High Street, an army boot maker.[33] The presence of the services and the large number of men employed in the dockyard also created a demand for beer, a large number of public houses being concentrated in Old Brompton and the Brook area of Chatham, adjacent to the barracks and the dockyard.

The navy supplied every man with one gallon of beer per day[34] which was used as a precaution against scurvy. The naval presence was therefore an important stimulus to brewing in the Medway Towns. The Admiralty had set up brewhouses in some fleet ports, but apparently not at Chatham, and in any case could not satisfy demand during mobilization or war. Professor Mathias comments 'Rich spoils, therefore, awaited the contract brewers of London, Chatham, Portsmouth and Plymouth.' As payments on naval contracts were usually delayed, only a few brewers who had sufficient capital to sustain the delay could be contractors.[35] One such brewer was Bests of Chatham. The second Thomas Best who ran the brewery from 1666 till his death received regular commissions for beer from the Admiralty. One attraction of this trade was the ease with which fraud could be perpetrated, with pursers engaging in paper transactions, signing receipts and sharing the spoils. Between 1707 and 1710, Thomas Best was involved in fraud totalling 3,450 barrels of beer. Another Chatham brewer by the name of Tyhurst was also involved in fraud at the same time.[36] This did not preclude the brewery from further contracts with the Admiralty, and as late as 1749 Bests were doing considerable business with the Victualling Office at Chatham.[37] After this time the Admiralty managed to meet most of its needs from its own new Hartshorne Brewhouse, Tower Hill, London.[38]

A measure of the significance of the Dockyard trade can be found in the interest shown in it by at least one London brewer, Trumans. London brewers generally did not want small country connections which were expensive to service. In this case Trumans in the 1790s supplied Thomas Parry who kept the tap house in Chatham Dockyard. This proved not only a profitable but a convenient arrangement. The beer was delivered by hoy, and the return journey made with cargoes of hops and malt.[39] In 1754 Bests were distributing beer to in the region of 95 public houses in the Medway area and Sheerness, 46 being in Chatham. The value of a public house near the Dockyard is demonstrated by comparing the turnover in 1753 of the 'Sunne in the Wood', Brompton, which was £180 p.a. compared with a typical public house like the 'Crispin and Crispinus', Strood, which was £120 p.a. even though it stood on the Dover road. It was also well worth sending beer the 20 miles to Sheerness, where, in the same year, the 'Three Tuns' near the Dockyard turned over £250.[40] The continued expansion of Bests brewery through the French Wars must obviously have been linked to the growth of activity centred on the Dockyard.

The expansion of population and of housing in the Medway Towns was largely the result of service and dockyard activity, Brompton was growing fairly fast. In 1776, it was

> 'a pretty village above Chatham Dock. There are now about 400 houses standing on the pleasant ascent to this New Town, most of them have been erected within this century.'[41]

Brompton together with the Service establishments were

> 'entirely separated from the Town of Chatham; they were inclosed on the landward side within a line of fortifications preventing the possibility of their union with the Town. There is a considerable number of Houses at Brompton within the Lines, for the most part inhabited by persons connected with the Barracks and the Dockyard.[42]

The expansion of the population of Chatham kept pace with the extensions of the dockyard. The town had a population of about 1,000 in 1600, rising by 1700 to at least 5,000 people.[43] By 1801 this figure had reached 10,505 and by 1851 totalled 21,886.[44]

Rochester, with its inhabitants occupied also with the Dockyard, Victualling Office and Navy,[45] grew from a town of about 3,000 people[46] in 1664 to 5,645 in 1801 and 11,385 in 1851.[47]

There would appear to be little doubt about the overwhelming social and economic influence of the Dockyard and the military installations on the Medway Towns and Sheerness areas. Chatham, Rochester, Gillingham and Sheerness were the main centres of population. The agricultural and fishing villages of the valley had as yet no economic significance. This difference in importance is demonstrated by the population figures for the first half of the nineteenth century.

See Table.

In the early eighteenth century Defoe had commented:

> 'Rochester, Stroud and Chatham, are three distinct Places, but contiguous, except the Interval of the River between the two first, and a very small Marsh or Vacancy between Rochester and Chatham.'[48]

In 1818 Fussell made a similar comment:

> 'Strood, which together with Rochester and Chatham being in a manner contiguous, may be considered as forming one large town.'[49]

POPULATION OF VILLAGES AND TOWNS OF LOWER MEDWAY VALLEY 1801–1851

Parish	1801	1811	1821	1831	1841	1851
Aylesford	912	875	1,136	1,301	1,344	1,487
Burham	144	158	236	287	380	518
Snodland and Paddlesworth	312	350	438	518	500	625
Wouldham	165	159	176	247	284	343
Cuxton	202	195	384	298	376	374
Frindsbury	1,066	1,489	1,562	1,856	2,142	2,258
Halling	249	202	346	431	448	550
Lower Halstow	121	158	220	221	297	344
Newington	507	526	629	730	734	731
Rainham	722	877	1,030	1,222	1,175	1,115
Upchurch	243	285	414	456	520	407
Queenborough	545	805	881	786	634	772
Strood	2,344	2,504	2,704	2,722	2,834	2,937
Hoo St Werburgh	550	710	960	910	930	1,000
Rochester	5,645	6,566	8,066	8,718	9,797	11,385
Chatham	10,505	12,652	14,754	16,485	18,962	21,886
Gillingham	4,135	5,135	6,209	6,734	7,640	9,321
Minster in Sheppey	4,139	5,838	7,597	7,922	8,684	11,082
(including Sheerness Ville)[50]	1,422	1,165	817	61		

Source: G. S. Minchin, 'Population', *V.C.H.*, III, 358–70.

Rochester, Chatham, Strood, Gillingham and Minster in Sheppey (Sheerness) over the period 1801 to 1851 showed sustained growth in their populations reflecting the importance of these towns as centres of trade and employment. The villages in the valley, as yet untouched by industry to any extent, had a fluctuating population growth rate, some parishes even showing a decline in numbers over some decades. By 1851, nine of the thirteen parishes of the valley (excluding the Medway Towns and Sheerness) had fewer than one thousand inhabitants.

Chatham was

> 'joined to the city of Rochester by a row of houses standing on a rising ground called St Margaret Bank which command a pleasing view of the winding course of the Medway, the buildings belonging to Chatham dockyard and a variety of interesting objects on the opposite bank of the river, which rises into several irregular eminencies agreeably interspersed with trees and hamlets.'[51]

Some general impressions of the Medway Towns can be drawn from contemporary writers. Chatham with its dockyard and Strood with its fishery were socially distinct from the more genteel Rochester with its cathedral and clergy. The whole parish of Chatham was

> 'very extensive running for two or three miles to the southward; a small part of it is within the Liberties of the City of Rochester. There is a row of Houses a short distance out of the Town on Chatham Hill. The rest of the parish is entirely agricultural containing a small village at Luton, and a few other scattered houses."

The dockyard, barracks and other military and naval establishments were at Brompton separated from Chatham by the fortifications of Chatham Lines. At Brompton there was

> 'a considerable number of Houses for the most part inhabited by persons connected with the Barracks and Dockyard."

The houses at the eastern end of Chatham towards Gillingham at Cage Lane and on Chatham Hill were mostly small

> 'it is certainly the poorest part of the Town, and inhabited chiefly by labouring people.'[52]

Chatham, apart from the Dockyard and its shops had

> 'a very considerable market on Saturdays which is well supplied with meat and other articles from the adjacent country. The Market Place is very commodious and situated on the north side of the High Street near the town centre.[53]

Strood was equally as poor as the Cage Lane, Chatham Hill area, with its 'principal street, like all the rest,—narrow all illpaved, and the buildings . . . irregular and mean.'[54]

Rochester, was socially different, and boasted 'houses fit for residence of small genteel families' and some 'commodious shops',[55] together with 'three capital and spacious inns', Assembly Rooms in Free School Lane, the Phoenix Circulating Library and Reading Room, a theatre in Canterbury Road built in 1791 and a commodious floating salt water bath with 'every accommodation for bathing on very reasonable terms'.[56] Rochester was a market town, making its retailing more comprehensive. It also derived benefit from being situated on the road to Dover, along which there was a continual flow of traffic.[57] Its hostelries had originally grown up due to its position on the Pilgrim's Way, and to the promotion of St William as a counter attraction to the Rood of Grace at Boxley Abbey. In the eighteenth century it was preferable to break a journey in Rochester than stay in squalid Chatham. There were also some proposals to convert the whole Medway Towns area into a watering place, with the added attractions of the short distance from London, the saline water, fresh air, the scenery of the Medway valley, the fortifications, the castle and cathedral, the military manoeuvres, and horse races on Chatham Lines.[58] The castle and cathedral at Rochester were later said to be 'objects of attraction during the summer months to thousands of excursionists who help to support the "credit" of the "ancient city",'[59] but this was in the age of the railways, and of the beginnings of pollution of the Medway. However, there is no reason to alter for the beginning of the nineteenth century the view expressed by Prof. D. C. Coleman for the age of the Later Stuarts that Rochester was of little economic significance except as it was linked to the Dockyard, fishing and trade on the Medway.[60] In the words of Hasted, there were 'no particular manufactures carried on here'.[61]

[1] Adm. J. G. Crace, *Some notes on the History of Chatham Dockyard* (1946), 1.

[2] W. Lambarde, *A Perambulation of Kent*, (reprint Bath, 1970), 311.

[3] Crace, *op. cit.*, 2–4.

[4] Crace, *op. cit.*, 6, 8, 10–13.

[5] D. Defoe, *A Tour through the Whole Island of Great Britain.* (Everyman Edition, 1962), I, 105, 108.

[6] Crace, *op. cit.*, 13.

[7] Defoe, *op. cit.*, I, (1948), 108–9.

[8] J. Presnail, *Chatham—The Story of a Dockyard Town*, (Chatham, 1952), 156, 175.

[9] Crace, *op. cit.*, 13.

[10] C. Seymour, *A New Topographical, Historical and Commercial Survey of the Cities, Towns and Villages of the County of Kent*, I, (Canterbury, 1776), 239.

[11] See below,

[12] J. Whyman, *A Sketch of Economic Development in Kent, 1600–1900* (unpublished MSS), 40.

[13] Crace, *op. cit.*, 64–5.

[14] *Ibid.*, 15.

[15] Wright's, *Topography of Rochester, Chatham and Strood* (Chatham, 1838), 73.

[16] Crace, *op. cit.*, 65–8.

[17] *Ibid*, 15. Another educational establishment which had been influenced by the area's connection with the navy and shipping was Sir Joseph Williamson's Mathematical School Rochester which opened in 1709. It's function was to be

> 'the instructing and educating of such youth there (Rochester) who were or should be the sons of the freemen, these towards the Mathematics and all other things which might fit and encourage them for the sea service and arts and callings leading and relating there to.'

See Ed. D. Flower, *A Short History of Sir Joseph Williamson's Mathematical School Rochester* (Privately published, Rochester, 1951), 22–4.

[18] Presnail, *op. cit.*, 70.

[19] E. Hasted, *The History and Topographical Survey of the County of Kent*, II, (Canterbury, 1782), 73.

[20] See Map.

[21] Samuel Lewis, *A Topographical Dictionary of England*, III, (5th Edition, 1844), 656.

[22] Crace, *op. cit.*, 3.

[23] Hasted, *op. cit.*, (1st Edition, 1782), 654.

[24] Defoe, *op. cit.*, (1962), I, 109–10.

[25] P. Banbury, *Shipbuilders of the Thames and Medway*, (Newton Abbott, 1971), 104–5.

[26] *Post Office Directory of Kent*, (1866), 1118.

[27] Royal School of Military Engineering, *Open Day Booklet*, 1972, 8, 13, 17.

[28] Presnail, *op. cit.*, 178.

[29] *Ibid.*

[30] Crace, *op. cit.*, 12.

[31] C. W. Chalklin, *Seventeenth Century Kent—a Social and Economic History* (1965), 144, 147.

[32] Williams, *Directory embracing the following Towns: Rochester, Chatham, Brompton, Maidstone, Dover, Margate, Broadstairs, Ramsgate etc. giving a complete alphabetical list of all the principal inhabitants in the above towns* (1849), Chatham, 12, 15.

[33] Simpson's, *Rochester, Chatham, Strood and Brompton Directory* (1865), 45.

[34] Presnail, *op. cit.*, 140.

[35] P. Mathias, *The Brewing Industry in England 1700–1830* (Cambridge, 1959), 195–6.

[36] Mathias, *op. cit.*, 198–9.

[37] V. Salmon, 'James Best, Brewer of Chatham 1744–1782', *Cantium*, Vol. 4. No. 3, Winter 1971/1972, 98.

[38] Mathias, *op. cit.*, 200.

[39] *Ibid*, 148.

[40] Salmon, *op. cit.*, 98.

[41] Seymour, *op. cit.*, I, 87.

[42] Parliamentary Papers—Boundary Reports. Kent to Somersetshire. Reports from Commissioners on Proposed Division of Counties and Boundaries of Boroughs, II, Part I, (1823), 19.

[43] Chalklin, *op. cit.*, 31.

[44] G. S. Minchin, 'Population'. *V.C.H.*, III, 358–70.

[45] Hasted, *op. cit.*, (1778) II, 8.

[46] Chalklin, *op. cit.*, 31.

[47] *V.C.H.*, III, 358–70.

[48] Defoe, *op. cit.*, 1, 105.

[49] L. Fussell, *A Journey round the Coast of Kent* (1818), 35.

[50] Demolished by 1841 and formed part of the Dockyard.

[51] Fussell, *op. cit.*, 37.

[52] Parliamentary Papers. *Boundary Reports. Kent to Somersetshire. Reports from Commissioners on Proposed Division of Counties and Boundaries of Boroughs*, Vol. II, Part I, 1823, 19.

[53] Seymour, *op. cit.*, I, 241.

[54] Fussell, *op. cit.*, 35.

[55] Seymour, *op. cit.*, III, 677.

[56] Denne, *op. cit.*, 311–17.

[57] Seymour, *op. cit.*, III, 677.

[58] Wright, *op. cit.*, 85, 117–18.

[59] Black's, *Guide to the South Eastern Counties of England, Kent* (Edinburgh, 1861), 100.

[60] D. C. Coleman, *The Economy of Kent under the Later Stuarts* (London Ph.d. thesis, 1951), 236.

[61] Hasted, *op. cit.*, (1782), II, 8.

CHAPTER III

Industry Before 1850

I. DEFUNCT AND DECLINING INDUSTRY

Although the pre-1850 scene on the Lower Medway was dominated by trade, agriculture, fishing and employment in the Dockyards, there was a scattering of industry along the river. The industries were characterized by small production and few employees,[1] and with the exception of lime and brick making and boat building, not really typical industries of the valley. Some of these small industries, notably salt making and warship construction in private yards had disappeared before 1850, while others, including papermaking, copperas, oil-seed crushing and distilling were in decline.

Salt making was one industry which disappeared early, the precise date not being recorded. Equally when the works were set up on the Medway is not recorded. Efforts were apparently made under Cecil 1563–71 to establish a coastal salt industry, with the help of German artisans, to reduce Britain's dependence on imports from France and Spain.[2] The growth of population in London and other towns in the sixteenth and seventeenth centuries is a likely reason for salt pans being set up on the Medway, helping to meet the greatly increased demand for salt as a preservative for fish and meat. However, at that time, most of the coastal pans were concentrated around the mouths of the Tyne and Wear, and on the Firth of Forth, where they could utilize abundant supplies of cheap inferior coal.[3]

One of the two sets of salt pans which once existed on the Isle of Grain lies beneath the site of the British Petroleum oil refinery. These were described in 1669 as consisting of

> '10 boyling panns and 60 acres of outworks with a leaden trough in the middle of those boyling panns 1½ feet deep and 8 feet broad and 80 feet long. A leaden cysten of 3 foot deep and 16 foot square. Store houses to hold 200 weighs of salt,[4] one store house 40 foot long, 26 foot broad and 16 foot high. The outwork

> consist of 600 brine pans of 3 foot square every such pann having 2 other panns to flood through so that these are in all 1800 of those panns.'

It was proposed to borrow £1,000 upon these works to develop the plant.[5] The works were well situated to receive brine from the Medway, and also fuel in the form of timber from the Weald or later coal from Tyneside. The fact that a leaden cystern was used probably meant the use of wood fuel, coal not being used till after the substitution of iron boiling pans. These works were small compared with those in the North, where Prof. Nef cites the existence of iron boiling pans 20 feet or more square and 5 or 6 feet deep, and where as early as 1589 one capitalist claimed to employ 300 men at works on the Wear and to have invested the equivalent of $200,000.[6] With 4 men employed per boiling pan, the Isle of Grain works must have given employment to in the region of 40 men.

Map showing the location of the Copperas, Salt, Paper and Oil Seed Crushing Industries before 1850.

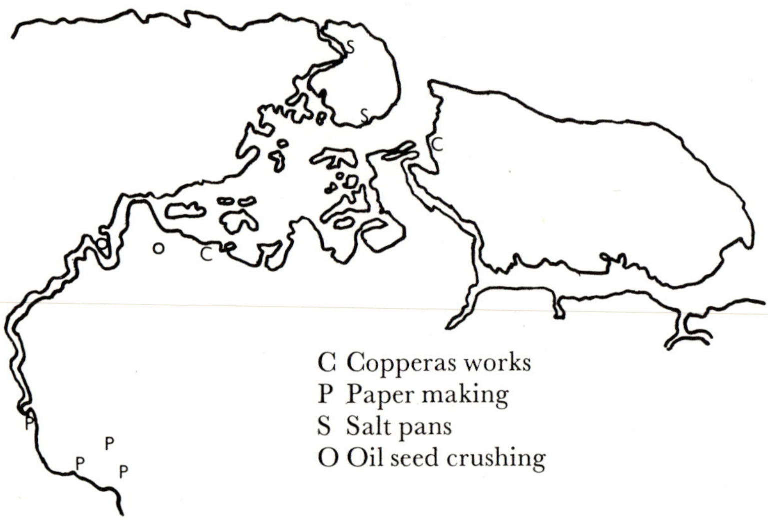

These salt pans apparently produced insufficient salt to meet local demand from the fishery, for preservation of meat and vegetables and for domestic consumption. Until 1700 salt was imported direct to Rochester from Spain and France, and thereafter brought from Newcastle in coastal vessels.[7]

These salt pans which gave their name to Saltpan Reach in the

River Medway,[8] and marked on a map of 1725,[9] and referred to by Hasted in a description of the Isle of Grain.

> 'There is a good estate in that part of this island next the River Medway, which consists of several farms, lands and salt works, the principal of which is called Wallend Farm. The salt works . . . are on the south east side next to the Medway . . . belonging to Mr Davenport.'[10]

A second salt works was erected on the Isle of Grain about one mile from the Thames on the North Yantlet Creek sometime before 1750. Here George Mason of St James, Grain, had leased land and salt marshes and 'carried on work of making salt'. Mason had erected 'severall pans and other works for the making of salt on the said lands and premises and erected and built several store houses, sheds and buildings there on for the more convenient carrying on the trade and business of salt making'. Mason lacked working capital and borrowed from a Mr Robert Wilford of Bridlington, Yorkshire including the sum of '£40 to buy coals and other necessaries to enable him to carry on the said salt works'. When Mason's indebtedness reached £227. 3s. 8d., Wilford took over the lease and then sold the 'salt works, salt pans, boyling pans, kilns, coppers, dwelling houses, storehouses, outhouses, sheds and all other erections, buildings and implements in trade whatsoever now standing lying and being on said lands' to Robert Cart of Rochester.[11]

When production of salt ended on the Isle of Grain is uncertain. Both sets of pans are marked on a map of 1805,[12] but only the North Yantlet pans appear on a map by W. Faden of 1810.[13] Ireland in 1828 mentioned that

> 'there are two sets of salt works, or salt pans, as they are called, one situated close to the water at the southern boundary of the island; the other on Mr. Davenports estate of Wallend . . . close to the Medway.'[14]

As Ireland's work is to some degree suspect the works might already have been out of production. The Tithe Assessment for Grain in 1842 gives the condition of both sets of pans as 'pasture',[15] perhaps denoting a long standing change of use.

The Grain salt pans would have suffered as a result of being less favourably situated in relation to fuel than their North East coast sea salt competitors. However, competition from rock salt discovered in 1670 in Cheshire was effectively ruining sea salt makers by the 1750s. The advantage was that whereas sea salt water required 6 tons of coal to make one ton of salt, the Cheshire 'wiches' required only one ton of coal per ton of salt,[16] which together with nearby coal measures meant a cheaper product. Pan owners in the south of England could not compete.

The rise and fall of warship building in private yards is more easily traced. During the eighteenth century and up till the end of the Napoleonic Wars, Britain was continually involved in war. The demand for warships could not be met by the government dockyards, resulting in the construction of many smaller warships being contracted out to private yards. Tenders were accepted on the basis of a set price per ton, plus a bonus for completion within a specified time.[17]

Although the most prosperous time for these yards was between 1793 and 1815 at least four yards operated before that time, each building one or more ships. Sedger and Hogben of Chatham launched H.M.S. *Assistance*, 50 guns, in 1747, while Thomas Seward of Rochester launched H.M.S. *Maidstone*, 28 guns, in 1758. Greaves and Nicholson had a yard at Frindsbury where two ships were launched, H.M.S. *Maleager*, 32 guns, in 1785 and H.M.S. *Bellerophon*, 74 guns, in 1786.[18] The *Bellerophon* was designed by Sir Thomas Slade who also designed the *Victory*. Work on her commenced in May 1783 and she consumed 3,000 loads of oak brought down the Medway from the Weald. A 3rd rater of 1,613 tons, her main claim to fame was not battle but the surrender of Napoleon I to her captain after the battle of Waterloo.[19] The fourth yard was that of Sir John Hennicker also of Frindsbury, who constructed five warships between 1758 and 1774.[20] The yard continued to function into the 1780s.[21]

One or other of the yards at Frindsbury was put up for auction in 1790. The property to be sold was a freehold and leasehold estate 'known by the name of the Quarry House Farm and Shipbuilders Yard, delightfully situated in parish of Frindsbury'. There were the usual farm buildings plus 76 acres while

> 'In the Shipbuilders yard there has lately been built ships of war of 74 guns, and other vessels and is as commodious as any private yard in the Kingdom either for builders or timber merchants, with a good rope walk, and every suitable convenience to it'

Also included was Quarry House.[22] By 1808 Thomas Levett of Northfleet had acquired the lease of the house and estate, and tried to turn the property to commercial use. In 1809 part of the estate was let to John Nicholson for use as a dock, and another part to John Pelham for use as a shipbuilders yard.[23] Nicholson appears to have been in business on his own account as well as in partnership with Edward Greaves, and launched three small ships, H.M.S. *Dispatch*, 16 guns, in 1795, H.M.S. *Staunch*, 12 guns, in

1797, and H.M.S. *Monkey*, 12 guns, in 1801. John Pelham built eight warships between 1807 and 1815, the largest being H.M.S. *Romney*, 58 guns, launched in 1815.[24] Joseph and Thomas Brindley were also associated with Quarry House, and secured the lease in 1814,[25] and had also leased Manor Farm, Frindsbury from November 1810 to 1823.[26] One of their main preoccupations was quarrying and lime burning, but they also were the largest single private warship constructors on the Medway. Their yard stood some distance east of the site of the old oil mills at the mid-point of the Frindsbury shore of Chatham Ness. The Brindleys who were nephews of Lord Nelson[27] also owned a yard at Lynn in Norfolk. From their three large ship-building slips[28] twenty warships were launched. Three small ships were launched in 1794. Apart from 1812, one or more launchings took place every year between 1804 and 1814, and three 3rd rater 74 gun battleships, one of which was the *Aboukir* of 1807,[29] which heeled over on launching, the timbers being used to build Aboukir House for the Misses Brindley.[30] During the wars the Brindleys employed 51 shipwrights and apprentices. Their shipbuilding activities came to an end according to C. Knight as a result of penalties exacted by the Admiralty for late delivery.[31]

One more small yard existed at Frindsbury, operated by Wilson

A Map showing the location of private warshipbuilding yards, and Chatham Dockyard

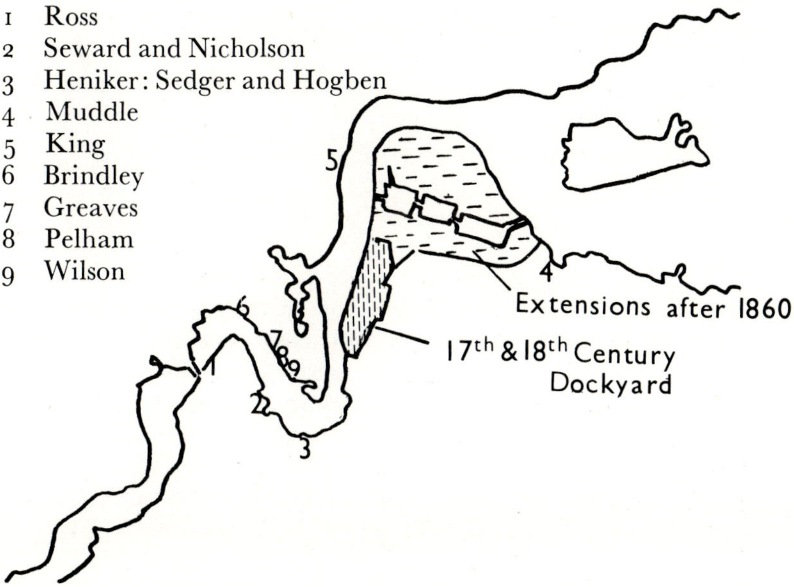

and Company who launched four small vessels between 1794 and 1797. At Upnor John King had a yard which between 1808 and 1814 launched 16 ships. This total included five brigs launched in 1808, and two 74 gun 3rd raters, H.M.S. *Poitiers* in 1809 and H.M.S. *Mulgrave* in 1812.[32]

At Acorn Wharf, Rochester, a shipyard was owned by Charles and Mary Ross. Before the French Wars, Charles Ross had built merchant vessels including several for the Hudsons Bay Company.[33] His interest in warships appeared to begin in 1791 when he rebuilt the French frigate *Le Amiable*. In 1797 H.M.S. *Albatross* a sloop of war was launched, followed by a gap till 1806 when the 38 gun frigate H.M.S. *Resistance* was launched, followed in 1807 by the similar H.M.S. *Spartan*. In 1808 Charles Ross died,[34] but his wife Mary carried on to build H.M.S. *Vigo* (1810) and H.M.S. *Stirling Castle* (1812) both 74 gun 3rd raters, two 32 gun frigates Tamais and Eridanais, three gun brigs, three gun boats, one lighter and one bomb ship H.M.S. *Fury* which was later left by Capt. Parry on an Iceberg in Fury Bay.[35]

One further yard existed which did some Admiralty work. This small yard had a long history dating from the beginning of the seventeenth century when David Duck an officer in the dockyard contracted to repair ships there. The yard was associated with the Pett family from about 1604 to somewhere around 1680, when the Muddle family took over the site, later used as the Gillingham Cement Company wharf. Ships built here were small, such as the lighter *Deptford*, 105 tons built for the Admiralty 1780–1. The vessel which cost £1,195. 5s. 9d, took Edward Muddle one year to build. This was followed by further lighters in 1782, 1792 and 1801, and a 54 ton victualling vessel *Mary* in 1802. The yard employed few men, only four shipwrights and two apprentices being at work in 1804 when there were no Admiralty orders. In 1808 a gun boat for the Scheldt expedition was launched, and the 10 gun brig *Opossum*.[36] No further Admiralty work was carried on here, although they may have continued to build small boats after this.

Warship building in private yards came to a permanent end with the termination of the Napoleonic Wars. Over the period of the French Wars a total of 70 vessels were launched by private builders for the Admiralty compared with 14 launched in Chatham Dockyard, which included four 1st rater battleships. The privately produced total was made up of:

7—74 gun 3rd rate battleships
1—58 gun 4th rate battleship

4—38 gun frigates
4—36 gun frigates
2—32 gun frigates
2—26 gun frigates
4—20 gun ships
10—18 gun ships
3—16 gun brigs
9—12 gun brigs
9—10 gun brigs
4—gun boats
4—gun brigs
1—sloop of war
1—bomb ship
1—transport
1—victualling ship
1—cutter
1—lighter
1—mooring lighter

The disparity in building performance was probably caused by the Dockyard having to undertake maintenance and repair work, for the fleet anchored at the Nore.

Launchings per year for private yards were:

1793	0	1801	2	1809	7
1794	4	1802	1	1810	5
1795	1	1803	0	1811	2
1796	1	1804	2	1812	7
1797	4	1805	2	1813	7
1798	0	1806	2	1814	6
1799	0	1807	3	1815	1
1800	0	1808	10		

Three other vessels were launched after 1808 from the yard of Mary Ross, but dates are uncertain.

Before 1808 the private yards would have posed little competition for labour to the Dockyard. However, in peak building years employment in these yards must have reached perhaps a few hundreds. With this degree of activity in the area, something approaching a boom of prosperity must have hit the Medway Towns, if only affecting the brewers!

Some industries of long standing were already in decline in the first half of the nineteenth century, although none of them were typical of the Medway as a whole. The paper mills above Snodland really formed part of the industry centred upon Maidstone, oil seed crushing was represented by a mill at Frindsbury and another at Gillingham, while copperas was represented by the one surviving factory at Queenborough.

Papermaking came to Kent in 1588 when John Spilman established the first successful papermill at Dartford. Spilman, a German, employed about 600 men, many also Germans, in his white papermaking enterprise[37] where he utilized a disused iron works, converted at a cost of between £1,400 and £1,500, the two wheels driving the hammers for beating the cloth and the stamping machinery formerly driving the blast furnace bellows.[38] Other mills were established using German and later Huguenot skills,[39] so that by 1690 there were about 100 mills in the country,[40] and the industry was firmly established in Kent.

The technology involved in papermaking was quite simple, the only substantial pieces of equipment needed being beating or stamping machines to break down the raw material, rags, until all fibres were separated. The rest of the processing was done by hand.[41] In Kent, the decline of the clothing industry left in its wake numbers of redundant fulling mills whose machinery proved ideal for conversion to papermaking uses.[42] However, the mills that were to grow up along the streams around Maidstone were not on the scale of Spilman's Dartford mill. Dr Shorter stated that production was carried on in characteristic small units where the number of workmen ranged from 6 to 15.[43] Among the fulling mills converted for papermaking was Old Turkey Mill, Boxley, which together with two mills at Sandling was converted by George Gill, before passing in 1739 into the hands of James Whatman, famed for his high quality writing paper.[44] Gill was originally connected with the Dartford Mill before becoming one of the major papermakers of the 1670s and 1680s. The first reference to a mill at Sandling dates from 1671.[45]

Apart from the advantage of having redundant mills on streams convenient as a source of power, the area around Maidstone had other advantages for papermaking. The water from springs, wells or streams in the area was free from mud, pollution or mineral content which would discolour the paper. The Medway provided a convenient means of communication between the principal source of raw materials and principal market, London, and the manufactories. Locally the worn out gear from sailing vessels provided a source of raw materials for inferior wrapping papers. An advertisement of 1765 offered for sale at Chatham

> 'Paper stuff in Ropes, Hammocoes, and Canvas in Rags, Bolt rope, Refuse ends, Nets, Buntin and Ground Tres.'[46]

The Maidstone papermaking district was represented below Allington Lock by four mills, Cobtree Manor, Pratling Street, Forstal and Snodland. Cobtree Manor and Pratling Street mills could well be those referred to by Hasted as 'two mills are situated on the western side of the parish (Boxley) near Aylesford . . . and are used for making an inferior kind of merchandize'.[47] Cobtree Manor Mill can be traced from 1700 when it was in the possession of various members of the Dean family. In 1781 it passed to papermakers named Wise, Charles Wise becoming bankrupt in 1824. It passed through the hands of two partnerships, those of Henry Allnutt and John Wilson, and Henry Allnutt and Thomas Smith[48] before leaving off work in 1838.[49]

Pratling Street mill first appeared in 1816 when Thomas Stroud was master papermaker. From 1821 until his bankruptcy Charles Wise also occupied this mill. John Lavender succeeded in 1825 to be followed by Joseph Moreton in 1832, a white papermaker. John Mason was the next occupier, but by 1846 the mill was in the hands of Samuel Salkeld Knight, a mill board maker.[50] The mill changed hands in 1847, Thomas Compere the occupier.[51] The mill had only one beating machine in 1851[52] when Compere became bankrupt.[53] After this date millboards were made at the site by Goerge Mason until about 1860.[54]

Forstall Mill probably dates from 1671. John Hillier was papermaker here from 1712 to 1724, whereafter the mill was occupied by members of the Russell family until 1816 when Clement Taylor Russell became bankrupt. He was followed by William Trindale, in 1821 John Pine, and 1824 Charles Wise, perhaps contributing to his bankruptcy. In the 1830s George Fowle, a white papermaker was occupier.[55] In 1840 the mill was in the hands of John Lavender when it was described as the 'only manufactory' of Aylesford.[56] The mill left off work soon after this time.

These three mills were obviously small concerns, water-powered, with little machinery, making hand produced vat paper. The frequent changes of occupier, and several bankruptcies demonstrate an inability to compete with the more highly capitalized mills, and machine made paper. Local competition would have come from such large mills as Balston's Springfield Mill, Maidstone, which was the first mill to be steam powered in Kent using a Boulton and Watt engine when work started in 1806.[57] The number of Fourdrinier type papermachines in use was increasing, which, although they cost about £1,000 each, could produce 5 to 7 times the amount of paper as labour force could by hand.[58]

TABLE OF NUMBER OF MACHINES IN USE IN GREAT BRITAIN COMPARED WITH NUMBER OF VATS

Year	*Machines*	*Vats*
1805	6	760
1835	89	540
1840	191	380
1850	267	200

from A. D. Spicer, *The Paper Trade* (1907), 249–50.

The production of paper made by machine also increased dramatically.

TABLE OF PRODUCTION OF PAPER (IN TONS)

Year	*Hand made*	*Machine made*
1805	16,502	557
1810	14,278	4,793
1820	12,675	8,873
1825	13,670	16,518
1840	9,937	33,463
1855	4,164	70,336

From A. D. Spicer, *The Paper Trade* (1907), 158.

Further although Forstal mill was situated adjacent to the Medway, Cobtree Manor and Pratling Street are isolated having neither direct access to the Medway, nor the use of a main road. The mills fit A. D. Spicer's three factors to explain the decline in the number of mills, the introduction of expensive machinery of unlimited capacity, competition from capitalistic firms benefitting from economies of scale, isolation from cheap means of transport.[59]

The mill at Snodland was far more advantageously placed than the others, standing by a small stream which provided pure water and motive power, and adjacent to a wharf on the Medway. Several views as to the origins of this mill have been put forward. One asserts that there was probably a mill at Snodland as early as 1600 employing Flemish craftsmen.[60] However, according to Dr Shorter, the first reference to a paper maker at Snodland is to James Smith, buried 1705.[61] Also some doubt exists as to the use to which the site of the mill had been put before the manufacture of paper. One assertion is that the building was used as a gun factory in the reign of Henry VII.[62] In *Snodland and its History* (1928) 'the compiler of these notes has seen it stated that this mill was at one time, as far back as Henry VII, used as a solid iron shot factory, but cannot find authority for this statement'.[63] The most likely explanation was that guns produced in the Weald were proofed at Snodland by Ordnance Officials before being sent on to London or to the navy at Chatham.[64] The most likely previous use was that of a corn mill, which were also frequently converted.[65]

The mill was probably owned by a local family named May and leased between 1755 and 1780 to Jasper Crothall, and from 1782 to 1807 to Isaac Wenman.[66] In 1807 the mill and estate were put up for sale comprising 72 acres and

> 'a substantially erected Paper Mill, advantageously situate for water carriage on the Bank of the Medway, near Snodland . . . with a wharf, 6 cottages, and numerous outbuildings, in excellent repair.'[67]

The mill was destroyed by fire in December 1807, but was rebuilt and passed through several occupiers till it was in the possession of William Joynson from 1824 to 1832.[68] Joynson also operated a mill at St Mary Cray which was a highly capitalized unit employing 12 steam engines and two paper making machines.[69]

The property came into the hands of Messrs Drawbridge and Thomas Spong, coal merchants of Millhall, Aylesford who ran a coal wharf adjacent to the mill at Snodland. The mill they leased out, together with the 6 cottages. Reuben Hunt, a papermaker of Wooburn, Bucks., took a 21 year lease from 1 January 1834 at a rental of the considerable sum of £220 per annum. In the lease were important provisions dealing with the modernization of the mill which must have been important in maintaining its competitive position. Hunt was to erect

> 'with all convenient speed two cast iron rag engines with a steam engine of 10 h.p. . . . also to erect a four feet paper engine with drying cylinders driven by a 4 h.p. steam engine.'

The new capital was to total £1,500, the introduction of the machine being crucial to survival.[70] When Hunt assigned his lease to John Clark in July 1838, the mill was well equipped with machinery including 4 rag beating machines and 1 paper machine and steam engines. The valuation of the mill for insurance purposes at this time was £2,500.[71] After mortgaging the mill and plant for £2,000 in July 1840 to London stationers,[72] Clark, who apparently lacked capital, was declared bankrupt in September 1840.[73] The lease of the mill was assigned in July 1842 to John Cole, a paper stainer from Chelsea,[74] who in turn in September 1842 assigned the lease to Henry Holden, described as a gentleman of Fulham.[75] By 1852 this modern well equipped mill was in the hands of a William Wildes.[76]

Snodland mill survived as a white paper factory isolated from the rest of the Maidstone paper district largely due to its very accessible location in relation to its sources of raw materials, to its main market, London, to a source of power and clean water. The insistence in the lease of the mill on investment in modern machinery was also a crucial factor.

Another untypical industry which was well on the way to extinction by 1850 was the production of copperas. Two factories were in operation on the Lower Medway in the eighteenth century, a little known one at Gillingham, and a well-known factory at Queenborough. Copperas was used as a dye for woollen cloth and hats, in tanning, for making Spanish brown paint, and for ink.[77] The manufacturing process was relatively simple. Stones containing iron pyrites were picked from the beaches, placed in wooden reservoirs for ripening from five to six years. On degeneration the liquor was drawn off to boiling pans, where evaporation took place and copperas crystals were formed and collected.[78] Markets for copperas would have been found locally for the textile industry of the Medway, and, of course, in London, served by river barge. Copperas was shipped from Queenborough, Rochester and Gillingham.[79]

Little information exists on the Gillingham works, the sole mention being by Seymour in 1776 when he said of Gillingham 'here are also Copperas Works'.[80] On a map of 1742 copperas beds are marked in the vicinity of Grange, Gillingham, together with a cluster of buildings. Access to the Medway was via 'Copperas House Creek'.[81] The marsh area is still known as Copperhouse Marsh. These works were most likely very small employers of labour, and one can only assume had little impact on the local economy.

The Queenborough works are better known. They were probably the first chemical works to be set up in Britain. In 1579 Lambarde wrote

> 'Being at this Castle (Quinborow) I found there, one Mathias Falconar (a Brabander) who did (in a furnesse that he had erected) trie and drawe very good brimstone and Copperas out of a certain stone that is gathered in great plenty upon the Shoare unto Minster in this Isle.'[82]

Although the first works were set up here, a patent for making copperas was originally granted in 1565 to Cornelius Stephenson of Whitstable, where eventually six houses were situated, making the Whitstable works the most important in the area.[83]

Prof. Coleman's view that copperas was one of the more capitalized industries and one of the most important users of coal in the area[84] is borne out by a description of 1634.

'Here [Queenborough] was a most ingenious copperas work erected. A square plot of ground, about an acre, the earth hath been taken all away, and a kind of stone brought from Essex shore, which, falling into the sea, is tempered by salt water; which stone, by rain and sun, is beaten and reduced to soil; this ground is clayed in the bottom, and is made a fair bottom. Betwixt every bed is a trough made with three deane [deal] boards, bored full of holes; this is digged over every summer, the bottom laid highest and the top lowest. This trough receives and conveys away all the liquor and moisture which doth flow from that soil in rainy and moist weather; old barrels, into which these troughs lead, are prepared and placed in the earth, in clay, which receive the moisture, out of which the liquor is conveyed into divers great cisterns of boards, two bayes of buildings, all which are laid and set in clay, out of which it runs into a great tub, placed in another spacious house, and near unto a mighty cistern of lead, wherein this liquor is boiled. Under this cistern are fire furnaces, a partition 'twixt them; these furnaces spend half a cauldron of coals a day, and this leaden cistern will last four years. There is half a barrel of old iron boiled in this liquor, which is consumed to dirt. When it is sufficiently boiled, it runs through a leaden pipe into lead cisterns; the copperas matter thickens and adheres to birch twigs, or bushes, which they hang upon overcross poles, into the cisterns. It is worth £5 a ton; one boiling will yield three or four ton.'[85]

The coal consumed was an inferior Newcastle grade known as 'pan coal', of which 300 tons were used in 1634.[86]

Apart from the iron pyrites stones being brought in from Essex, stones were to be found along the shore beneath the cliffs between Minster and Warden where erosion by the sea washed out the material. Hasted said the cliffs were

'let out to the different proprietors of the copperas works who employ the neighbouring poor to collect pyrites upon the beach, which they deposit in heaps until a sufficient quantity is procured to load a vessel to carry it away.'[87]

This was the most labour consuming part of the operation, and would have provided more employment than the actual works, especially bearing in mind that stones were also shipped to Blackwall and Deptford,[88] the latter works being considered by Prof. Nef as being the most important after the Civil War.[89] Whitstable had its own supply of pyrites stones washed from the cliffs at Herne

Bay, and the collection of these 'used to afford occupation to a considerable number of fishermen'.[90]

As to the ownership of the works, Harris in 1719 had noted 'a good Copperas Work which belongs to several persons.[91] It would appear that the land, one acre, on which the works stood belonged to the Queenborough Corporation, and grants of a share in the works also were linked with grazing rights and a share in the oyster fishery. Among the early partners was a John Johnson, haberdasher of London, in 1602.[92] This can be seen in a lease of 1737 when Sir Christopher Hales leased to Philip Trahern.

> 'all that his full fifth part and all other the shares, parts and purports of him the said Sir Christopher Hales be the same more or less than the description above said of and in One Moiety of half part of all those Copperas Works or places for making copperas and in all the storehouses, cisterns, beds, coolers and other buildings . . . and of land containing an estimated one acre more or less.'

The lease, which was for 14 years, apart from giving a list of moveable equipment which had to be given up at the end of the lease, also gave directions as to scale of production. Trahern was to lay in 6,000 bushels of copperas at the rate of 2,000 in each of the first two five year periods, and 2,000 in the final four years.[93]

Copperas manufacture from the mid-eighteenth century tended to move to more favourable sites near the coalfields such as at Newcastle-upon-Tyne, whence it was exported in large quantities. Further competition came in 1808 when Macintosh, Knox and Co. started a factory at Campsie, Stirlingshire to utilize a very pyritous alum shale, found in coal measures, for production of both alum and copperas.[94] Already by 1825, at Whitstable 'owing to the cheapness of the article in the North of England and elsewhere the works have been for some time disused'.[95] The Queenborough works, however, lingered on eventually coming into the hands of a local businessman, Josiah Hall, by 1847.[96] He carried on the works on a limited scale[97] largely owing 'to the dearth of material'.[98] By the nineteenth century the works cannot have been of any real significance in the economy of the area.

Oil seed crushing was another industry which appeared in the area. As the bulk of the raw material, cotton, rape, hemp and linseed, was imported from the Baltic and Egypt, it was natural that the industry should be set up at ports and on navigable rivers on the east coast, Hull, holding a fairly central position on the east coast, had the biggest concentration of mills. Others appeared on the Thames, and at such ports as Dover where 'the River Dour, with its cornmills, oil seed crushing mills and papermills was for many centuries a great aid to Dover's commerce and industry'.[99]

Oil seed mills variously employed stamp mills, rollers, mill stones, screw and stamper presses for crushing and extracting oil.[100] These processes could be equally adapted to water, wind and steam powered mills, all of which were to be found on the Medway. The water mill was at Maidstone, operated on a shift system, and 'made a great quantity of linseed oil' from seed imported from Archangel.[101] The wind oil mill is marked on a map of 1832 in open land between Brompton and Gillingham,[102] which presumably was of the stamp mill variety. Between 1833 and 1838 the mill was in the hands of F. B. Elvy.[103] Later the mill, which stood in Mill Road, New Brompton, came into the hands of Stephen and Edward Morgan[104] who remained in occupation until the mill was struck by lightning and destroyed by fire somewhere around 1852.[105]

The steam-powered mill stood on the banks of the Medway on a site measuring 2 rods 20 perches below Quarry House, Frindsbury on land owned by the Church Commissioners.[106] In 1838 when the mill was in the hands of David Samuel it was described as

> 'very eligibly situated at Frindsbury, on the Medway, worked by a large steam engine, where linseed is crushed, making the well known and requisite article of Linseed Cake, on which farmers mainly depend on for food during the winter months, and Linseed Oil, the only oil which can be used for Paint, on account of its drying properties, giving constant winter employment to twenty five or thirty men.'[107]

The mill was advertised for sale in 1841 when it was equipped with four hydraulic presses.[108] However, oil seed crushing would not appear to have been a business in great demand on the Medway at this time. The factory became disused, and the warehouses, workshops and Boulton and Watt engine were adapted by George Burge Snr. and I. C. Johnson for the production of Portland cement in 1851.[109] The industry cannot be said to have added a great deal to the pre 1850 economy of the area.

Distilling was another of the minor industries which appear to decline. Gin drinking, an urban vice which one might expect in a town like Chatham, had been discouraged by Gin Acts of 1743, 1744, 1751, 1753 and 1756.[110] However, despite official opposition, and competition from rum, four distillers can be identified in Rochester and Chatham. There was a Walter Prentice distilling in Rochester in 1798.[111] Cazeneuve Jacob Troy, the builder of Troy Town, Rochester, operated a distillery between at least 1793[112] and 1803.[113] Troy was also described as 'an eminent wine merchant in Chatham'.[114] A third, one Nichols distilled in Chatham in 1803.[115] The fourth concern was longer lasting, but first appeared in a directory for 1826 by which time the other three had disappeared. A change of taste towards the new lighter beers may have been the reason for their closure. However, early in the nineteenth century distilling in the Medway towns was probably overshadowed by the distilling of Maidstone Geneva which had achieved international fame by the end of the eighteenth century. The Maidstone gin distillery was set up in 1789 by George Bishop, and met a considerable demand for its product till its closure in 1818.[116] This closure allowed room for the establishment at St Margarets Bank, Rochester of Boys, Winch and Co., distillers and rectifiers by 1826.[117] By 1840 the business was in the hands of Richard Winch, of Rochester Distillery which Pigot described as 'extensive'.[118] Again there is no reason to believe that this industry had any beneficial effect on the area.

The industries which died out or were declining before 1850 were not typical of the Lower Medway area as a whole, but isolated examples which grew up according to special circumstances, war, local pockets of raw materials, or as in the case of paper spill over into the area from an adjoining district. However, there were to grow up a range of industries before 1850 which were more typical of the whole Lower Medway, which were based on raw materials found along virtually the whole length, or on demand created by the expanding industries. These were to be lime burning, brickmaking and barge building. Brewing for other reasons prospered in the Medway Towns.

[1] C. W. Chalklin, *Seventeenth Century Kent—a Social and Economic History* (1965), 156.

[2] J. U. Nef, *Rise of the British Coal Industry*, I, (1966), 175.

[3] J. U. Nef, *The Conquest of the Material World*, (Chicago, 1964), 137.

[4] According to Prof. Nef a weigh of salt was equivalent to 1 ton. Nef. *op. cit.*, II (1966), 374.

[5] K.A.O. Clayton MSS., U214, E7/22.

[6] Nef, *op. cit.*, (1964), 137.

[7] D. C. Coleman, *The Economy of Kent under the Later Stuarts* (London Ph.d. thesis, 1951), 126.

[8] W. Coles Finch, *The Medway River and Valley* (1929), 193.

[9] 1725 map British Museum P15439 K16 31–2.

[10] E. Hasted, *The History and Topographical Survey of the County of Kent*, II, (Canterbury, 1772), 90.

[11] K.A.O. V145 T44. Assignment of lease 9 May 1749.

[12] John Stockdale, *A Map of Kent from the Best Authorities* (Piccadilly, 26 March 1805)

[13] W. Faden, The County of Kent shewing the line of the intended Medway

and Thames Canal (1810). The marking of such information as salt pans varied from one map maker to another, and is not necessarily a good guide to the destruction of a works. Mudge in his 'General Survey of England and Wales' O.S. 1801 marks only the Medway works.

[14] W. Ireland, *England's Topographer or A new and complete History of the County of Kent; from the earliest records to the present time, including every modern improvement*, IV, (1828), 161.

[15] K.A.O. CTR 314 A/B. Tithe Map and Assessment.

[16] Nef. *op. cit.*, I, (1966), 178, 207.

[17] C. Knight, *Shipbuilding at Gillingham* (Reprinted from *Chatham News* 1938), 16, 17.

[18] P. Banbury, *Shipbuilders of the Thames and Medway* (Newton Abbott, 1971), 152, 149.

[19] A. H. Waite, 'Great Ships of Kent—H.M.S. *Bellerophon*', *Kent Life*, Vol. 9, No. 7, (July 1970), 40.

[20] Banbury, *op. cit.*, 149.

[21] J. Presnail, *Chatham, the Story of a Dockyard Town* (Chatham, 1952), 166.

[22] Note from Edwin Harris to Henry Smetham quoting *Kentish Gazette*, 24 August 1790.

[23] A. A. Arnold, 'Quarry House on Frindsbury Hill', *Arch. Cant.* XVII, (1887), 179.

[24] Banbury, *op. cit.*, 150, 151.

[25] Rev. S. Robertson, 'Quarry House on Frindsbury Hill', *Arch. Cant.* XVI, (1886), 288.

[26] *Church Commission*, File 5815, 45.

[27] Banbury, *op. cit.*, 126.

[28] H. Smetham, *History of Strood* (Strood, 1899), 345.

[29] Banbury, *op. cit.*, 126.

[30] Smetham, *op. cit.*, 345.

[31] Knight, *op. cit.*, 17, 18.

[32] Banbury, *op. cit.*, 155, 149–50.

[33] W. C. Finch, *The Foords of Rochester* (Rochester, 1917), 7.

[34] E. Harris, *A Trip down the Medway* (Rochester, 1897), 4.

[35] Finch, *op. cit.*, (1917), 7.

[36] Knight, *op. cit.*, 8, 11, 14, 16, 17, 18.

[37] F. W. Jessup, *A History of Kent with Maps and Pictures* (1958), 106.

[38] Nef. *op. cit.*, (1964), 125.

[39] Jessup, *op. cit.*, 106.

[40] A. H. Shorter, *The Historical Geography of the Papermaking Industry in England* (London, Ph.d. thesis, 1954), 85.

[41] Good descriptions of all papermaking processes appear in A. Dykes Spicer, *The Paper Trade* (1907).

[42] E. Melling, *Kentish Sources—Aspects of Agriculture and Industry* (Maidstone, 1961), 91.

[43] A. H. Shorter, *Paper Making in the British Isles—An Historical and Geographical Study* (Newton Abbott, 1971), 15.

[44] Hasted, *op. cit.*, (1782), II, 132.

[45] Shorter, *op. cit.*, (1971), 19, 29, 50,

[46] *London Gazette*, 16 April 1765. Quoted Shorter, *op. cit.*, (1954), 429.

[47] Hasted, *op. cit.*, (1798), II, 132.

[48] A. Shorter. 'Paper Mills in the Maidstone District', *The Paper Maker and British Paper Journal* (April 1960), 62.

[49] Shorter, *op. cit.*, (1954), 336.

[50] *The Paper Maker and British Paper Journal* (April 1960), 62.

[51] Samuel Bagshaw, *History, Gazetteer and Directory of the County of Kent*, I, (Sheffield, 1847), 254.

[52] *The Paper Maker and British Paper Journal* (April 1960), 62.

[53] Shorter, *op. cit.*, (1954), 336.

[54] *The Paper Maker and British Paper Journal* (April 1960), 62.

[55] *The Paper Maker and British Paper Journal* (April 1960), 62.

[55] *Ibid.*

[56] Pigot, *Directory of Kent* (1840), 243.

[57] T. Balston, *William Balston, Paper Maker* (1955), 39.

[58] Shorter, *op. cit.*, (1954), 108–10.

[59] A. D. Spicer, *op. cit.*, 4–5.

[60] V. E. Morant, *The Historical Geography of Maidstone* (London, M.A. thesis, 1948), 207.

[61] *The Paper Maker and British Paper Journal*, March 1960, 62.

[62] *Historical Jottings of the Parish of Snodland: forming a complete history of the village from the earliest period to the present time.* (Snodland, 1894), 10.

[63] C. de P. Wall, *Snodland and its History 550BC to AD1928* (Snodland, 1928), 21.

[64] Coleman, *op. cit.*, 184.

[65] Melling, *op. cit.*, 91.

[66] *The Paper Maker and British Paper Journal*, March 1960, 62.

[67] *Times*, 25 April 1807. (Quoted J. Whyman, MSS. *Sketch of the Economic Development of Kent*)

[68] *The Paper Maker and British Paper Journal*, March 1960, 62.

[69] Shorter, *op. cit.*, (1971), 111.

[70] K.A.O. Q/RD2 2/1–13. Lease Drawbridge and Spong to R. Hunt 1 January 1834.

[71] K.A.O. Q/RD2 2/1–13. Assignment of lease R. Hunt to J. Clark July 1838.

[72] K.A.O. Q/RD2 2/1–13. Assignment of mortgage to Revell and Spicer, 13 July 1840.

[73] *Paper Maker and British Paper Journal*, March 1960, 62.

[74] K.A.O. Q/RD2 2/1–13. Assignment of lease Clark to Cole, 13 July 1842.

[75] K.A.O. Q/RD2 2/1–13. Assignment of lease Cole to Holden, 1 September 1842.

[76] *Post Office Directory of Kent* (1952), 1106–1852.

[77] M. Hewitt, 'Industries', *V.C.H.*, III, 398.;
R. H. Goodsall, 'The Whitstable Copperas Industry', *Arch. Cant.* LXX (1956), 142–3.

[78] Chalklin, *op. cit.*, 154; Nef, *op. cit.*, (1966), I, 210.

[79] Chalklin, *op. cit.*, 179.

[80] C. Seymour, *A New Topographical, Historical and Commercial Survey of the Cities, Towns and Villages of the County of Kent*, II, (Canterbury, 1776), 401.

[81] T. Bryant, '*A plan of the River Medway and Creeks adjacent taken in 1742*' (rough copy by C. Knight—Gillingham Library).

[82] W. Lambarde, *A Perambulation of Kent* (Reprinted from 3rd edition of between 1596–1640, Bath, 1970), 227–8.

[83] Goodsall, *op. cit.*, 142, 143.

[84] Coleman, *op. cit.*, 171.

[85] Sir William Brereton, *Travels in Holland, the United Provinces, England, Scotland and Ireland*, (Printed for the Chetham Society, 1844), 2–3.

[86] Nef, *op. cit.*, (1966), 210.

[87] Hasted, *op. cit.* (1778), II, 645.

[88] K.A.O. U487 E1 Folios 10, 17, 25. 'Schedule of deeds by Dame Dorothy Franklin of lands in Minster of St. John Hayward Knt. deceased and in the hands of John Walsall, 1712'; Chalklin, *op. cit.*, 154.

[89] Nef, *op. cit.*, (1966), I, 210.

[90] A. O. Collard, *The Oyster and Dredgers of Whitstable* (1902), 36.

[91] J. Harris, *The History of Kent* (1719), 244.

[92] K. A. O. Qb/L7 Translation of Lease of Copperas Works.

[93] K. A. O. U36 T688 Lease Hales to Trahern dated 1 December 1737.

[94] Singer, Holmyard, Hall and Williams. *A History of Technology*, IV, (Oxford, 1957), 251.

[95] Goodsall, *op. cit.* 142.

[96] Bagshaw, *op. cit.*, 511.

[97] Black's *Guide to the South Eastern Counties of England—Kent* (Edinburgh, 1861), 463.

[98] William Miller, *Jottings of Kent, being a series of Historical Ecclesiastical and Statistical Sketches* (2nd Edition, 1864), 131.

[99] J. B. Jones, *Annals of Dover* (Dover, 1916), 418.

[100] For processes see H. W. Brace, *A History of Seed Crushing in Britain* (1960).

[101] Seymour, *op. cit.*, II, 547.

[102] Parliamentary Papers. Boundary Reports—Kent to Somerset. Reports from Commissioners on Proposed Division of Counties and Boundaries of Boroughs, Vol. II, Pt. I, (1832), 19.

[103] Brace, *op. cit.*, 111.

[104] Pigot's, *Directory of Kent*, (1840), 261.

[105] *Chatham News*, 2 July 1892, 8c.

[106] Church Commissioners, File 37842; File 5815.

[107] Wright's, *Topography of Rochester, Chatham and Strood* (Chatham, 1838), 142.

[108] Brace, *op. cit.*, 109.

[109] H. Smethan, *History of Strood* (Strood, 1899), 345. Church Commission F37892.

[110] M. W. Flinn, *British Population Growth 1700–1850* (1970), 41.

[111] *Universal-British Directory* (1798), 334.

[112] *Universal British Directory* (1793), 657.

[113] W. Finch, *A Historical Sketch of the County of Kent* (1803), 148.

[114] S. Denne, *The History and Antiquities of Rochester and the Vicinity* (Rochester, 1817), 313

[115] Finch, *op. cit.*, 149.

[116] J. W. Bridge, 'Maidstone Geneva, An Old Maidstone Industry', *Arch. Cant.*, LXV, (1952), 79–84.

[117] Pigot's, *London and Provincial New Commercial Directory* (1826), 646.

[118] Pigot's, *Royal, National and Commercial Directory* (1840) 35, 352.

II. INDUSTRY PROSPERING AND EXPANDING BEFORE 1850

The years before 1850 were to see the rise of two industries which were to have the greatest effect on the Lower Medway in the second half of the nineteenth century, lime burning and brick-making. Linked with these, barge building, to provide the necessary transport facilities before the railway age, begins to assume some importance, and later to be of crucial importance to the cement industry. To provide for the increasing number of thirsty labouring men in the area, brewing remained prosperous.

Before the coming of the railways, areas like the Lower Medway were protected from competition from the big London brewers because it was only economical to market beer within a six-mile radius of the brewery. London brewers therefore generally shunned small country connections which were expensive to service.[1] In 1803, William Finch recorded six brewers in Rochester and Chatham.[2] The number reached a height in 1840 of fourteen brewers including one at Aylesford and another at Gillingham,[3] before falling back to eleven in 1852.[4] Other brewers existed at Sheerness. There were in all probability more brewers than those listed in the local directories, the criteria for inclusion not being at all clear. Bests Brewery, the biggest in the Medway Towns does not for instance appear in the Universal British Directory for either 1793 or 1798. However, a good proportion of those missed out and also of those included in the directories were probably publican brewers, in business in a small way providing their own house with perhaps some further local connections. The directories do indicate a steady turnover among the small brewers. Only among the larger plants did any permanence of ownership appear, in the cases of Pope of Gillingham Street, Gillingham; Daniel Coulter, Pump Lane, Rochester; William Wood, New Brewery, Frindsbury Road, Strood; William Lane, East End Brewery, Chatham; Messrs. Shepherd, Troy Town Brewery; Messrs Hulkes, Lion Brewery, High Street, Chatham; and Messrs Best, High Street, Chatham.

Bests Brewery was by far the largest in the Medway Towns, with a history stretching back to the mid-seventeenth century.[5] The business saw its greatest expansion while under the control of James Best Snr from 1744 to 1782. His assets in 1745, when he entered a partnership to be dissolved in 1763 with Samuel Waring one of his senior clerks,[6] were slightly over £12,000.[7] At his death in 1782 the value of the plant was just under £60,000. His output was increased from 15,000 barrels in 1755 to 23,000 barrels in 1772. Part of this success at least was due to James Best's interest in the latest techniques of brewing porter about which he corresponded with leading London brewers. Best was probably the first brewer in the Medway Towns to use a thermometer. The result was that between 1765 and 1774 Bests paid twice the Excise duty of all other local brewers put together.[8]

James Best Snr. had been involved in two mergers, the first in 1751 when he took over a brewhouse from a Mrs Waite and the second in 1767 when he bought the business of a Colonel Frederick.[9] As early as 1754, Best had been delivering to 95 public houses, in the Medway and Sheerness areas, 46 of them being in Chatham,[10] but only three the Kings Arms and the Angel, Rochester, and the Jolly Sailor, Chatham, could be definitely linked with the brewery.[11]

By 1782 Bests had probably reached their expansion potential in the Medway, Sheerness and Gravesend areas, and as a result decided to enter the export market for beer.[12] There was a demand for beer in the West Indies and India, accessible as markets due to cheap freights as many ships sailed outward bound in ballast. A strong brew was necessary to offset heat and ship's movement. Other attractive markets were Cork, Dublin and Waterford in Ireland.[13] However, the venture, which was entered into in a rather half-hearted way by the family, was wound up in 1786 after only two trips to Ireland, Madeira and Antigua.[14] James Best Jnr proceeded instead to tie in houses. By 1793 he had acquired 65 freehold and 16 leasehold houses, some as far away as Gravesend and Sheerness.[15] The attempt to secure outlets for beer was a process which was going on nationally, half of all houses being tied by 1800.[16]

In 1795 the brewery was inherited by James, Richard and George Best, who ran the business into difficulties due to their extravagance, but who did in 1799 instal a Boulton and Watt engine. From 1801 to 1807 the brewery was run by the family solicitors Messrs William and Edward Twopenny.[17] The value of the concern had fallen to just under £44,000 in 1807.[18] James Best then gained possession till 1828, when it passed to his nephew Col James Best, the brewery still being one of the largest in Kent. After his death in 1849, the Best family decided to give up any personal interest in the management of the brewery,[19] with the result that the business was leased to Edward Winch of the Sun Hotel, Chatham from 30 August 1851.[20]

Brewing in general would, therefore, appear to have prospered in the Medway Towns before 1850. It still had a very good market locally in the many serviceman based in the area, and in the many labourers employed in the dockyards. As yet it was not feeling the competition later to be felt as a result of cheap railway transport creating breweries on a national scale. Neither was the industry yet having its outlets squeezed as a deliberate policy on the part of the licencing magistrates which was later to affect the structure of the brewing industry.

Brickmaking was an area of activity where considerable expansion was taking place before 1850. The Lower Medway Valley was favourably situated for this industry, with a fairly wide distribution of brick earth from Aylesford to beyond Lower Halstow and with a suitable location for the easy importation of coal or wood fuel. The industry had a local market created by the construction of the dockyard at Chatham, and the subsequent growth of the town.

It would appear that the industry grew up in the seventeenth century. This was largely the result of an acute shortage of timber and rapidly rising prices which forced a change to brick as a building material. Coal fuel was also introduced about the same time, but this created certain problems as up to 25 per cent of the bricks were lost in the firing process due to gaseous coals burning too fiercely in the kilns and causing the bricks to fuse.[21] It was necessary to apply heat gently at first to drive off water vapour before applying a fierce heat, otherwise the bricks became distorted as well as fused.[22] This problem was overcome towards the end of the seventeenth century by the use of a mixture of coal ashes, with street sweepings or clay known as 'Spanish' which often replaced coal in the kilns.[23] The Medway brick industry was well placed to receive large quantities of ash and refuse from London which could serve as a return cargo for the barge trade. This mixture was used in clamp burning which was well established in the London area by the eighteenth century,[24] and adopted fairly widely on the Medway. This particular process consisted of the hand moulded, green bricks being built up in special close formation on a layer of fuel placed on a floor of fired bricks, and being covered over with discarded bricks and earth. The bottom layer of fuel was ignited by small fires started in special flues in the base. This in turn ignited the 'Spanish' mixture mixed with the clay of the green bricks. The clamp was then allowed to burn itself out.[25]

Clamp burning was usual among the manufacturers of yellow London stock bricks, a staple product of the Medway brickmakers, and among the smaller seasonal brickmakers as little capital was involved in fixed plant. However, some difficulty resulted from this method of firing as there was no control over the fire once lit, and in a strong wind the whole clamp could be lost. Usually about 10 per cent of the bricks were lost, and the proportion of best bricks produced was low.[26] The bricks from nearest the fire were the hardest and of best quality, these were the 'stocks'.[27]

During the seventeenth century local demand for bricks absorbed the output of the Kentish brickmakers, and considerable quantities of bricks were imported through Rochester from Holland. Demand from the dockyard was considerable, Chalklin quoting 208,000 bricks and tiles being bought from Kentish makers between 1664 and 1667 for building storehouses and walls.[28] Brick-making operations were scattered about the valley, presumably serving nearby building sites, and mostly with a very small output before the nineteenth century. Such works at various times included one in 1669 at West Court, two miles from Rochester and 'within halfe a mile from the waterside' consisting 'a Brickill and Lymekill with a good house 120 foote long to make bricks in',[29] or another brick-kiln situated in the Old Palace Yard at Halling in 1786 in which bricks were burnt for building in Halling.[30]

In the town areas builders probably burnt their bricks on site, which was a fairly common practice where clay was available, as in the Medway area, clamp burning requiring little capital, and resulted in cutting out brickmakers' profit margins, royalties and high transport costs.[31] In 1828 William Ireland observed that 'Troy Town, standing at the back of Rochester, which has sprung up within the last thirty years, occupies a space of ground formerly used as brickfields'. This was most likely a case of on site production and it is also likely that the bricks required for the 400 or so houses recently built (1828) in Brompton[32] were burnt from the abundant brickearth on site. Builders it would appear often had their own small brickfields worked on a seasonal basis to supply their own needs, an example being James Watchurst, bricklayer, of Rainham who leased part of Cuxton brickfield from 1800–39.[33]

The big expansion of brick making on the Medway occurs with the growth of London particularly at the beginning of the nineteenth century when hundreds of millions of bricks were transported by barge to the building sites.[34] The population of Greater London rose from 1,117,000 in 1801 to 2,685,000 in 1851[35] creating a great demand for residential accommodation. Between 1820 and 1850 there was a marked expansion of shipments of especially yellow stock bricks with the building of docks, warehouses, railways and other industrial plant.[36] The expansion reflects the national trend in brick output as shown in decennial averages of production.

DECENNIAL AVERAGE PRODUCTION OF BRICKS
(IN MILLIONS)

	1790–9	1800–9	1810–19	1820–9	1830–9	1840–9
Bricks	661	779	859	1217	1278	1593
Index	100	118	131	184	193	241
% Increase		18	11	40	5	25

From H. A. Shannon, 'Bricks—a trade index 1785–1849'.
In Carus Wilson, *Essays in Economic History*, III, (1962), 192.

This also accords with H. A. Shannon's theory that the difference in the rate of growth of population, between 1817 and 1849 at 1.366 per cent per annum, and the rate of increase in brick production over the same period, at 1.796 per cent, represented acceleration in industrial building.[37] Production in the second quarter of the nineteenth century in the Rochester area does show a remarkable upswing as reflected in the brick excise collected at the Rochester centre before 1849.

INDEX OF PRODUCTION OF BRICKS
(ROCHESTER EXCISE CENTRE) 1830–1848

1830	1832	1834	1836	1838
100	79	92	138	138
1840	**1842**	**1844**	**1846**	**1848**
195	173	221	333	191

From H. A. Shannon, *op. cit.*, 194–5.

Unfortunately the actual statistics of the number of bricks made no longer exist.

Relatively little information exists on the operation of individual brickfields before 1850. However, 21 brickmakers are listed by Bagshaw in 1847, scattered from Sheerness, Bobbing and Lower Halstow through the valley to Aylesford, the biggest concentration, six, being at Frindsbury.[38] The population of Frindsbury had grown by roughly 80 per cent between 1801 and 1831, from 1066 to 1856, a note in the 1831 Census Abstract stating "brickmaking is extensively carried on in the Parish of Frindsbury to which the increase of population is attributed'.[39]

The only production figures that appear to survive relate to three sites on Manor Farm, Frindsbury, which were owned by the Dean and Chapter of Rochester Cathedral, two at Whitewall Creek, the other at Ten Gun Field, Upnor. Brickmaking had taken place on the latter site at least since 1800[40] and Accounts of production were kept from 1828 to 1864 for excise duty pruposes and also for assembling royalties.

Year†	*Whitewall Creek*				*Ten Gun Field*		*Total*
	Brickmaker	No.	Brickmaker	No.	Brickmaker	No.	No.
1828	Barton	1,206,800	Hankey	755,900			1,962,700
1829		636,690		452,142			1,088,832
1830	Everist	1,716,150	Field	1,018,650	Little	1,193,450	3,928,250
1831		1,647,475		489,100		1,233,300	3,369,785
1832		NA		NA		NA	3,361,825
1833		844,675	Larkin	824,525		0	1,689,200
1834		2,420,925				441,175	2,852,100
1835		7,988,000				971,000	8,959,000
1836		7,935,035				795,300	8,730,335
1837		7,774,100			Baker	1,590,775	9,294,875
1838		4,439,700				2,466,400	6,906,100
1839		6,001,300				2,258,750	8,260,050
1840		8,702,000				2,612,000	11,314,000
1841		7,969,500				2,357,000	10,326,500
1842		8,216,500				3,002,400	11,218,900
1843		8,157,000				2,456,000	10,613,000
1844		11,450,000				2,621,000	14,071,000
1845		7,980,300				2,524,000	10,504,300
1846		4,502,423				2,230,416	6,732,839
1847		—				2,652,000	2,652,000
1848		—				2,314,000	2,314,000
1849		—				2,365,000	2,365,000
1850		—				2,413,324	2,413,324

Compiled from Dean and Chapter of Rochester Cathedral Records.
Eb1/1 to Eb1/48 Statements of Brick Production at Manor Farm, Frindsbury.

* 10% of gross production was allowed for wastage.
† The season ran from October to October so 1828 refers to October 1828 to October 1829.

Manor Farm was one of the more important brick making areas in the valley before 1850, at its height in 1844 producing 1 per cent of the nation's output. The greatest expansion on this site came in 1835 after Henry Everist, who was probably the biggest brickmaker in the area, contracted to make 8 million bricks for a Mr Nicholson. Where the bricks were to be used is unknown but they were to be moved by water as Everist proposed to dredge a creek at Whitewall to provide a second wharf at the cost of £30 and to spend £15 per annum on maintaining two wharves.[41] Manor Farm lost its importance when Everist concentrated production at Strood, producing approximately 3,000,000 bricks at One Field,[42] Temple County and 4,743,884 bricks at Temple City in the 1845 season.[43] The move was probably dictated by the gradual exhaustion of brickearth deposits in the Whitewall area, a process complained of as early as 1809.[44]

The general impression of the years to 1850 remains one of growing interest in brick production together with a growth of employment and production.

Parallel with the growth of the brick industry there also occurred an expansion in the production of lime. Limestone occurs in abundance in the Medway valley, and had long been exploited. In fact it was used for a variety of purposes, in block form for building in place of brick or stone, as lime for mortar or plaster, as whitewash for decorative purposes, as an agricultural dressing and fertilizer, and as ballast for vessels leaving the port of Rochester unladen. As far as the latter point is concerned the original quarry on Chatham Ness marked on maps of 1698 and 1742[45] was adjacent to a 'Ballast Wharf'. This was an ideal site to service vessels lying below Rochester Bridge.

Lime burning assumed an increased importance during the seventeenth century with changes in building materials generally and specifically as a result of the regulation of building materials in London after the Great Fire. The Kent lime industry also benefitted from growing agricultural demand from neighbouring countries. Prof. Nef commented that

> 'lime kilns were not only set up in towns, but were scattered in increasing numbers over the countryside. For lime was also wanted in ever greater quantities to nourish arable land, now that the advantages of artificial fertilization were beginning to be understood.'[46]

The Medway not only had the basic raw material for lime burning, but also was suitably placed for the importation of coal, the universal fuel, of which half a ton was required to burn a chaldron of lime.[47] A scattering of kilns can be traced, for instance one at Chatham dockyard in 1623 when lime was made on the site during extensions,[48] or the 'lyme kill' at West Court, Rochester in 1669.[49]

However, Mr Chalklin considers the Gravesend and Northfleet areas to have been the most important for lime burning in Kent in the seventeenth century, being well situated to serve both the London building and the Essex agricultural markets.[50] Defoe described the trade in lime and chalk from the Erith, Greenwich and Northfleet area

> 'in which places the chalk hills come close to the river, and from thence the city of London, the adjacent counties, and even Holland and Flanders, are supply'd with lime, for their building, or chalk to make lime, and for other uses.
>
> 'From these chalky cliffs on the river side, the rubbish of the chalk, which crumbles away when they dig the large chalk for lime . . . and which they must be at the charge of removing to be out of their way, is bought and fetch'd away by lighters and hoys; and carry'd to all the ports and creeks in the opposite county of Essex, and even to Suffolk and Norfolk, and sold there to the country farmers to lay upon their land, and that in prodigious quantities; . . . they fetch it by land-carriage ten miles, say fifteen miles, up into the country'.[51]

An example of a continuously burning lime kiln by the riverside at Gravesend is cited by Sir William Brereton for as early as 1634.[52]

Lime burning on the Medway had expanded considerably by the second half of the eighteenth century when lime from chalk dug near Rochester was being carried by water to Essex, Suffolk and Norfolk.[53] By 1828 Ireland could state that lime was transported 'to the most distant parts of the country'.[54] He also cited one local example of lime being used to improve the soil at Lower Halstow where the clay land was spread with lime from Hartlip.[55] By the early nineteenth century lime burning was carried on in the vicinity of Chatham Hill, Frindsbury, Borstal, Wouldham, Burham, Cuxton and Halling. Samuel Lewis wrote that 'chalk pits in the neighbourhood (of Cuxton) supply the material for lime'[56] and that at Halling 'Chalk abounds, and the works for burning it into lime provide the chief occupation of the inhabitants; the lime used in building Waterloo and New London bridges was brought from Halling.'[57] Snodland was

> 'noted for its extensive lime works established about the year 1820. The metropolis which was at one time principally supplied from Dorking in Surrey, now receives an immense quantity from this place.'[58]

In 1831 the chalk pits of Snodland had employed 26 labourers over 20 years of age, those of Wouldham 19 and above 40 labourers were employed in the pits of Halling.[59] The 1851 Census showed that Burham had 33 chalk diggers, mostly originating from surrounding rural villages and probably former agricultural labourers, and 8 lime burners.[60]

Many of the lime works were very small consisting of a single kiln together with a chalk pit. This would have included all the lime burners and whiting manufacturers to be found in business in the parish of Chatham in 1847: Richard Austin, John Denny and Alfred Richardson at Chalk Pit Hill; John Batchelor at Chatham Hill; David Ward and Henry Honeyset at Beacon Hill.[61] This also applied to Blue Bell Hill where there have been chalk pits and kilns for 200 years,[62] three separate pits being worked in 1849.[63]

The more important works were situated by the riverside which facilitated the easy transportation of the lime. Among these were the Chalk Pits on Chatham Ness where in the 53 years between 1756 and 1810 Philip Boghurst excavated 354, 545½ tons of chalk, an annual average of 6,689 tons. J. and T. Brindley[64] the warship builders excavated 52,380 tons between 1810 and 1817 when their lease was acquired by the Thames and Medway Canal Co.[65] Chalk was also excavated from the Quarry, Chatham Ness, and the Cliff, Upnor on land owned by the Dean and Chapter of Rochester Cathedral. The lime was burnt at what became Frindsbury Lime Works on Chatham Ness which was operated from 1842 on by the

CHALK DUG AT MANOR FARM, FRINSBURY 1837–1849

	Chalk Pit (tons)	*Cliff* (tons)	D.C.R.C.R. reference
July-Nov. 1837	1,547	170	Eb1/4
Nov 1837-Nov 1838	1,496	311	Eb1/16
Nov 1838-Oct 1839	4,302	1,011	Eb1/18
1840–1841	1,918	87	Eb1/20A
Oct 1841-Oct 1842	4,398	–	Eb1/21A
Oct 1842-June 1843	1,722	51	Eb1/21D
Oct 1842-Oct 1843	2,633	51	Eb1/24A
Oct 1843-Oct 1844	4,165	–	Eb1/25E
1844–1845	6,943	70	Eb1/26A/B
15 Nov 1845- 20 April 1846	13,000	2,000	Eb1/28A
Oct 1846–1847	17,500	3,400	Eb1/29A
1847–1848	17,242	1,893	Eb1/30C
1848–1849	22,348	1,600	Eb1/31A

Compiled from Dean and Chapter of Rochester Cathedral Records.

firm of Coles and Sankey,[66] who were also limeburners at Wouldham.[67] The only figures for the consumption of lime available relate to these works, and show a sharply rising trend from the late 1830s.

Upstream at Borstal the Tuff family had a lime kiln, gravel pit and chalk pit on five acres of ground at Brambletree Wharf,[68] while across the river at Cuxton, William and John Cutbush of Maidstone and Edward Jarvis, a lime merchant of Yalding, started a lime works at Whornes Place in 1799. They had originally bought one acre of chalk for £1,200 from the Earl of Romney. The business went better than expected and a second acre was acquired in 1801 and more kilns erected.[69] This thriving lime works was from 1832 leased by Thomas Boorman of Brighton.[70] Further upstream at Halling Thomas Poynder and William Medlicott worked a lime kiln on the riverside just below Halling church and another slightly upstream of the site later occupied by Lee's Lime Works. These were supplied from two pits on the hill behind the works.[71] In 1846 these works were purchased by William Lee, and were rapidly extended during his ownership.

William Lee had been a lime burner at Burham, on the opposite bank, from 1826 to 1846[72] on three acres of land later to become the site of the West Kent Cement Works, with a chalky hole (Margetts Pit) below Scarborough Terrace, Burham. Nearby, adjacent to the site of the Roman Temple was the lime kiln and works of Edward Davis,[73] supplied from two small pits above Wouldham Hall (later part of Peters Pit). In Wouldham was to be found John Lindridge's one acre pit at School Farm Lime Works, later the site of the Wouldham Cement Company's pit and nearby behind Ravens Knowle was the works of Coles and Sankey.[74]

Lime burning was obviously an expanding industry with a continuing demand almost assured by the growth of London's population, by industrial developments and by enlightened agriculture. To cater for the carriage of both lime and bricks to their markets it was necessary to have an adequate barge and barge building industry. This already existed to some extent as a result of the trade to the London market in agricultural produce from Kent. A distinctive style of barge had been developed for use on the Thames and Medway, the spritsail barge.[75]

The most common spritsail design was the topsail barge which could be used for river and coastal work. These were usually about 80 feet long and capable of carrying a cargo of between 70 and 120 tons. These barges faced problems while working above the Thames bridges when the bargemen were forced to lower the rigging and row. There were also what were known as 'stumpies', river barges without topsails of restricted dimensions to negotiate bridges and canals. Stumpies were usually about 70 feet long with a cargo capacity of 70 to 80 tons. They, being relatively small, manoeuvrable, shallow draughted boats, were easily managed by a crew of two. Specialized designs for different uses evolved. Some were stack barges known as 'stackies' which had a shallower draught and wider deck than usual. It was customary to fill the hold with mangel-wurzel or corn and to stack between 35 and 55 loads of hay on top.[76] To manage one of these barges the mate would sit on top of the stack calling out steering instructions to the skipper whose vision was entirely blocked. The shallow draught was necessary for operation from shallow creeks and farm wharves on upper reaches of rivers.[77] The stack barges were mainly used in transporting the huge quantities of fodder and bedding needed in London in the days of the horse before 1914. Others were brick barges built with squarer sections to facilitate loading, known as 'brickies'. These varied in size though boats with a cargo capacity of 100 tons or 40,000 bricks were common.[78] Stumpy barges were generally favoured for brick transport as they were very manoeuvrable in narrow creeks and on the congested Thames. Return cargoes usually consisted of refuse from London rubbish dumps for use in the brickfields.

Barge making did not require a great deal of fixed capital. A barge could be built on any hard bank which sloped down towards the river.[79] It was not necessary for a barge maker to have his own forge and sail loft as most items such as masts, sails, rope, spars, blocks, oars and metal accessories could be bought in from specialist manufacturers. Barges were built entirely by hand with hand tools, planks being sawn in a pit at the yard, and masts, spars and other timber work being shaped with an adze. The one essential piece of equipment was a boiler to heat the planks for shaping the bows of the barges. The barge builders were highly skilled craftsmen who worked almost completely by eye. A purchaser would state his requirements as to type and tonnage required, and working without plans, although rarely a half model was constructed, the constructor could produce a boat within a ton or two of that required.[80] As well as not requiring a great deal of fixed capital, the early barge yards would have been small employers of labour.

The last point seems to be borne out by the fact that very few barge makers are listed in early directories, and very little information is available about them. The earliest name to appear is that of R. Horsnaill, shipbuilder of Strood in 1803,[81] who had slipways adjacent to the grain stores near the old tide mill where he apparently built barges.[82] Edmund Geer Watson had a wharf at

Acorn Wharf, Rochester, from 1809, from which he launched barges.[83] Another little known shipwright was William Crook of the Common, Rochester, who was building at least between 1823 and 1840.[84] One of the longest surviving firms, that of John Curel was founded in 1819 at Frindsbury on a site near the later Phoenix Cement Works.[85]

However, although little is known about these yards it is clear from the directories that there was a considerable expansion in barge building in the 1840s, which coincided with the expansion of the lime and brick industries. There were at least fifteen builders operating at various times between 1840 and 1849 compared with a possible five in the 1820s.

Closely allied to barge building must have been the construction of fishing boats for the local fishing industry thriving before 1850. Two types of boats were built for fishing on the Medway in the nineteenth century, the double ended doble and the bawley.[86] The doble was usually less than 25 feet long, decked fore and aft, and with a fish well amidships with holes in the bottom of the hull to allow in water to keep the fish alive. The boat was usually rigged with a small sprit sail and jib. They were mainly used for river work, seining for smelt or dredging for oysters.[87] Bawleys were bigger boats which worked in the Medway and Thames estuaries going out for a week at a time, trawling and shrimping.

Like the barges, fishing boats were made with hand tools by what were virtually one man businesses. Few names of fishing boat makers come to light probably because their businesses were insignificant. Fishing boats were probably among the 'boats of all sorts' built by Messrs Tassell of Taylors Lane, Strood and among the barges and 'other craft' built on Robert Horsnaill's slips at Strood. Alexander Ring of Canal Road Strood was a well-known builder of dobles and bawleys,[88] during the 1840s and 1850s. However, there must have been a steady market for fishing boats at Strood and Queenborough while oyster dredging and fishing still prospered before 1850.

Among the most important of the makers of gear for boats were the sailmakers. These would appear to have been most numerous as independent businesses, before 1850, five being mentioned in a directory of 1826,[89] and ten in a directory of 1849.[90] These again would have been relatively small businesses. E. G. Watson was one of the best known sailmakers having in the 1830s premises at 25 High Street, Chatham, backing on to Joslyn's Wharf where he had a laying ou troom for sail making[91] at Acorn Wharf he also had barge premises 'the ground floor was used for mast and oar manufacture, and the upper floor the sail loft'. Another known sailmaker was Sam Bullard of Old Foundry Wharf, who also carried on business as a brewer's agent.[92] Others included Bladen's sailmaking establishment in Strood which was cleared away to make room for Aveling and Porter's factory[93] and Richard Taylor's sail loft in Frindsbury above Strood Dock.[94]

Equally small businesses probably typified the block, mast, pump and oar makers, thirteen of whom appear in directories between 1793 and 1840. Ropemaking was also essential to the craft on the Medway. The rope walks were most likely small affairs, the ropes hand made, and the only building necessary a store house. From the directories the greatest number of ropemakers, eight in all, were at work in the Medway Towns in 1849.[95]

Taking the Medway scene in 1850 a picture emerges of a group of related or interdependent industries growing up from especially the late 1830s and through the 1840s which were to lay the basis for the industrialization of the valley, particularly the Medway Towns and the Medway gap areas, soon after the mid-point of the century.

[1] P. Mathias, *The Brewing Industry in England 1700–1830* (Cambridge, 1959), xxii, 148.

[2] W. Finch, *A Historical Sketch of the County of Kent* (1803).

[3] Pigot's *Royal, National and Commercial Directory* (1840).

[4] *Post Office Directory of the Six Home Counties* (1852).

[5] E. Melling, *Kentish Sources—Aspects of Agriculture and Industry* (Maidstone, 1961), 121.

[6] R. A. Keen, 'Messrs Bests, Brewers of Chatham', *Arch. Cant.*, LXXII, (1958), 172–5.

[7] Melling, *op. eit.*, 121.

[8] V. Salmon, 'James Best, Brewer of Chatham 1744–1782'. *Cantium*, Vol. 3, No. 4, Winter 1971/2, 95–8.

[9] Keen, *op. cit.*, 176.

[10] Salmon, *op. cit.*, 95–8.

[11] Melling, *op. cit.*, 121.

[12] V. Salmon, 'Beer Exporting from Chatham in the 18th century,' *Cantium*, Vol. IV, No. 3, Autumn 1972, 55.

[13] Mathias, *op. cit.*, 172, 153.

[14] Salmon, *op. cit.*, (Autumn 1972), 57.

[15] Melling, *op. cit.*, 121.

[16] J. Vaizey 'The Brewing Industry', in Ed. P. Lesley Cook, *Effects of Mergers* (1958), 400.

[17] Keen, *op. cit.*, 176–8.

[18] Melling, *op. cit.*, 121.

[19] Keen, *op. cit.*, 178.

[20] K. A. O. U480 T42 Lease of Bests Brewery to Edward Winch 1851.

[21] J. U. Nef, *Rise of the British Coal Industry*, I, (1966), 161, 217.

[22] Information from Col. Dean V.C., Newington Brickworks Ltd.

[23] Nef, *op. cit.*, 217.

[24] N. Lloyd, *A History of English Brickwork* (1934), 23.

[25] The Brick Development Association, *How Bricks are made*, 10–11.

[26] B. Butterworth, *Clay Building Bricks*, National Building Studies, Bulletin I (HMSO 1948), 45.

[27] Lloyd, *op. cit.*, 18.

[28] C. W. Chalklin, *Seventeenth Century Kent—a social and economic history* (1965), 144, 147.

[29] K. A. O. U214/E7/21 Clayton Mss.

[30] K. A. O. U522 T65 Counterpart Lease W. Dalison to Edward Maynard 1786.

[31] H. Hobhouse, *Thomas Cubitt, Master Builder* (1971), 312.

[32] W. Ireland, *England's Topographer or A New and Complete History of the County of Kent*, IV, (1828), 338, 349.

[33] K. A. O. U565 Addnl. Mss. T168A Assignment of lease J. Watchurst to J. Muddle 18 November 1839.

[34] Information from M. Tyrrell, Technical Director, Redlands Brick Ltd.

[35] B. R. Mitchell and P. Deane, *Abstract of British Historical Statistics* (Cambridge, 1962), 19.

[36] Information from Mr Tyrrell.

[37] H. A. Shannon 'Bricks—a trade index 1785–1849' in Ed. Carus Wilson, *Essays in Economic History*, III, (1962), 196.

[38] S. Bagshaw, *History Gazetteer and Directory of the County of Kent* (Sheffield, 1847).

[39] Registrar General, Census of 1831, *Enumeration Abstract* (1833), 264.

[40] D.C.R.C.R. Eg2/15/1.

[41] D.C.R.C.R. Eb1/8.

[42] D.C.R.C.R. Eb1/26 A3b.

[43] D.C.R.C.R. Eb1/27F.

[44] D.C.R.C.R. Eg2/15/1.

[45] Photocopy in Gillingham Library of British Museum, Kings Mss, Ref. 44. Map, *From a survey and description of the principal harbours, with their accommodations and conveniences for erecting mooring securing and refitting the Royal Navy of England* (1698).

T. Bryant, *A Plan of the River Medway and Creeks adjacent taken in 1742.*

[46] J. U. Nef, *op. cit.*, I, 187.

[47] *Ibid.*, I, 205.

[48] J. Presnail, *Chatham, The Story of a Dockyard Town* (Chatham 1952), 98.

[49] K. A. O. Clayton Mss U214 E7/21.

[50] Chalklin, *op. cit.*, 148.

[51] D. Defoe, *A Tour through England and Wales divided into Circuits of Journies*, I, (reprinted from 9th edition, 1948), 99.

[52] Sir W. Brereton, *Travels in Holland, the United Provinces, England, Scotland and Ireland* (Printed for the Chetham Society, 1844), 1–2.

[53] E. Hasted, *The History and Topographical Survey of the County of Kent*, I, (Canterbury, 1778), ccxxiv.

[54] W. Ireland, *England's Topographer or a new and complete History of the County of Kent*, I, (1828), 101.

[55] *Ibid*, IV, (1829), 19.

[56] S. Lewis, *A Topographical Dictionary of England*, I, (5th Ed., 1844), 734.

[57] *Ibid*, II, 377.

[58] Bagshaw, *op. cit.*, I, 276.

[59] Registrar General, Census of 1831, *op. cit.*, 264.

[60] *Census Enumerators Returns for Burham*, 1851.

[61] Bagshaw, *op. cit.*, I, 141.

[62] Information from Messrs Sandford Ltd.

[63] K.A.O. U886 R9 Plan of the Preston Hall Estate. Surveyed under the direction of Frank Giles by I. J. West 1849.

[64] Pit sited near mouth of canal and canal basin.

[65] D.C.R.C.R. LA3156; LA3/62/1 24 January 1819.

[66] D.C.R.C.R. Eb1/23.

[67] *Post Office Directory of the Six Home Counties* (1852), 1085.

[68] K.A.O. CTR 305B. Tithe assessment.

[69] K.A.O. U565 E171 Darnley Mss. Lease Romney to Cutbush and Jarvis dated 1 September 1802; D.C.R.C.R. LA3/79/1.

[70] K.A.O. U565 E8. Darnley Mss Draft Lease 31 August 1832.

[71] K.A.O. CTR 165A/B. Tithe Map and Assessment 5 June 1843.

[72] Information from Mr F. Parker.

[73] K.A.O. CTR 52. Tithe Map and Assessment 2nd May 1842.

[74] K.A.O. CTR 405A/B. Tithe Map and Assessment 19 April 1842.

[75] These were a refinement of the hoys used in the Thames and Medway.

[76] E. J. March, *Spritsail Barges of the Thames and Medway* (Newton Abbott, 1970), 23, 30, 31, 36.

[77] Information from Mr O'Shea, Curator of the Dolphin Barge Museum, Sittingbourne.

[78] F. S. Cooper and J. Chancellor, *A Handbook of Sailing Barges* (1955), 29.

[79] March, *op. cit.*, 25, 26, 127.

[80] Information from Mr O'Shea.

[81] W. Finch, *An Historical Sketch of the County of Kent* (1803), 157.

[82] *Chatham News*, 3 April 1909.

[83] E. Harris, *The Riverside* (Rochester, 1930), 15.

[84] Pigot's *Directory* (1823), (1845).

[85] J. Rochard, *Historical Chatham and Rochester* (Chatham, 1894), 48.

[86] E. J. March, *Inshore Craft of Britain—In the Days of Sail and Oar*, II, (Newton Abbott, 1970), 29.

[87] D. Coombe, 'The Medway Doble', *Kent Life*, Vol. 9, No. 2, February 1970, 54, 55.

[88] *Chatham News*, 3 April 1909.

[89] Pigot, *Directory*, (1826).

[90] Williams, *Directory embracing the following Towns: Rochester, Chatham, Brompton, Maidstone, Dover, Margate, Broadstairs, Ramsgate etc. giving a complete alphabetical list of all the principle inhabitants in the above towns* (1849).

[91] F. Sanders, *A Business History of Chatham High Street*, I, Mss. (1961), 31.

[92] Harris, *op. cit.*, 4, 15.

[93] *Chatham News*, 3 April 1909.

[94] K.A.O., CTR 150B, Tithe Assessment, April 1844.

[95] Williams, *op. cit.*

PART II

Industry 1850–1900

Introduction

The period 1850 to 1900 witnessed an intensified industrialization of the Lower Medway Valley. The biggest single change was the introduction of Portland cement to the area. The industry was about the only one which could be regarded as typical of the valley as a whole, with works lining the river from Queenborough to Aylesford. The cement industry transformed many of the villages especially in the upper reaches of the area, including Eccles, Burham, Wouldham and Snodland, as can be seen from the population figures.

THE POPULATION OF THE CEMENT VILLAGES
1851–1901

	1851	1861	1871	1881	1891	1901
Aylesford	1,487	2,057	2,100	2,719	2,979	2,676
Burham	518	755	1,172	1,353	1,680	1,725
Snodland	625	1,078	1,844	2,826	3,188	3,133
Wouldham	343	433	818	1,268	1,373	1,272
Halling	550	760	836	1,306	2,095	2,454
Frindsbury	2,258	2,219	3,092	3,815	5,091	5,454

Figures taken from *Victoria County History*, III, (1932), 358–70. G. S. Minchin, 'Population'.

In the book *Historical Jottings of the Parish of Snodland* the question is posed 'When did Snodland begin to improve? 'The answer given is 'When the railroad was put here they began to build' with the result that 'there are cement and lime works, with tall chimneys smoking away; and thousands of people in Snodland where there used only to be hundreds.'[1] At the same time the valley was becoming disfigured and scarred by the huge quarries being hewn from the chalk.

The brick and associated clay industries also prospered over most of this time, serving not only the expansion locally, but also the great London market. This industry like cement was scattered along the valley, stretching from Lower Halstow to as far as Aylesford, and having a similar effect on the growth of villages.

THE POPULATION OF BRICK MAKING VILLAGES 1851–1901

	1851	1861	1871	1881	1891	1901
Lower Halstow	334	399	508	721	653	675
Newington	731	854	1,013	1,038	968	1,072
Upchurch	407	468	777	1,121	1,218	1,129
Rainham	1,155	1,422	2,082	2,719	3,082	3,693
Hoo St. Werburgh	1,000	1,065	1,260	1,322	1,400	1,655

Figures taken from *Victoria County History*, III, (1932), 358–70. G. S. Minchin, 'Population'.

The need to shift the great quantities of cement and bricks produced a barge building industry which thrived in the Medway. The biggest centre of production was in the Medway Towns, but specialist barge builders existed from Queenborough to Aylesford, and many of the cement and brick manufacturers from time to time owned their own barge yards at places such as Lower Halstow, Upnor, Burham and Snodland. The brick and cement industries were also on a sufficiently large scale to encourage the development of an engineering industry largely, but not wholly, based upon supplying requirements for mills, engines and other plant. This industry was established in Rochester and Strood.

Another major development of these years was the massive expansion of Chatham dockyard. This had a marked effect on the development of Chatham and Gillingham, with a particularly rapid growth in the latter.

POPULATION OF THE MEDWAY TOWNS 1851–1901

	1851	1861	1871	1881	1891	1901
Strood	2,937	3,915	4,186	5,395	7,796	10,006
Rochester	11,385	12,311	12,806	14,254	15,611	17,613
Chatham	21,886	24,650	26,184	26,525	31,594	36,944
Gillingham	9,321	14,608	19,936	20,644	27,872	42,643

Figures taken from *Victoria County History*, III, (1932), 358–70. G. S. Minchin, 'Population'.

The Medway Towns saw a return of oilseed crushing among the industries to be highly localized in the centre. Mineral water manufacture and carriage building were among the industries which grew up to serve the affluent urban area. Brewing in the Medway Towns continued to flourish, but followed national trends with a concentration of production into the hands of bigger brewers.

Elsewhere in the valley isolated industries flourished. Fertilizer and glue production came to Queenborough to replace the old copperas works. Tar distillation grew up as incidental to gas works at Queenborough and Snodland. The paper works at Snodland continued to prosper throughout the period. There was even an attempt to set up a factory at Snodland to make bleaching powder by electrolysis.

The only real story of failure before 1900 concerned fishing with the virtual destruction of the oyster fishery, and pollution killing the floating fish. The brick industry was facing increasing competition by the 1890s, but was far from finished as an important influence.

The period 1850–1900 was one, taken overall, of expansion in trade, in employment and incomes, in the range of industries represented as well as in the physical size of the built up area and population of the region.

[1] J. Woolmer, *Historical Jottings of the Parish of Snodland* (Snodland, 1894), 45–6.

CHAPTER IV

The Rise of the Portland Cement Industry

The fifty years after 1850 were to see the development of the Medway Gap and the Medway Towns into a truly industrial area with the biggest concentration of industry in Kent. This industrialization was the result of the growth of four related industries; Portland cement, bricks, engineering and barge building. Of these four by far the most important before 1900 was the Portland cement industry which became the largest employer of labour in the area.

Cements were developed as a result of demand for a hydraulic cement (water resistant or capable of setting under water), for the growing number of civil engineering projects, harbours, lighthouses and the like, which were being undertaken in the eighteenth century. The breakthrough came in 1796 when James Parker of Northfleet discovered that he could make a hydraulic cement from nodules of argillaceous limestone (septaria).[1] The septaria was to be found at Sheppey and Whitstable[2] where it was washed from the Tertiary clay beds, and deposited along the Essex coast.[3] Parker took out Patent 2120 of 1796,[4] and set up his 'Roman' cement factory at Northfleet. The process consisted of 'reducing to powder certain burnt stones or argillaceous productions called "nodules" of clay, and using that powder with water so as to form a mortar or cement stronger and harder than any mortar or cement now prepared by artificial means.'[5] 'Roman' cement, although weak from a structural point of view, was water resistant. Its importance is seen in the rise of a 'Roman' cement industry on the Thames Estuary, on the Medway and an industry at Harwich, which survived into the 1860s. Harwich became the main centre of Roman cement production under James Frost. Between 1812 and 1845 over one million tons of septaria were removed from the foreshore at Harwich. In 1845 the government under Peel prohibited digging within 50 feet of the cliffs at Harwich as they feared a shortage of materials as a result of the railway boom. Subsequently material was obtained by dredging until the product was superseded by Portland cement.[6]

In Kent, apart from the Northfleet works, a 'Roman' cement factory was established at Faversham in 1816 by Mr Samuel Sheppard. Faversham was well situated to receive supplies of septaria from Sheppey, and also stone dredged from the Essex coast. In 1848, the works were taken over by Mr C. J. Hilton who entered a partnership with Mr J. A. Anderson, making Roman cement and plaster of Paris. However, the production of Portland cement began here in 1849.[7] The references to 'Roman' cement manufacture on the Medway all date from after 1845 and the discovery of Portland cement. Queenborough, being adjacent to the supply of stone, had its works, where 'Roman cement is [1861] manufactured extensively from the septaria.[8] To what extent Roman cement was made on the Medway cannot be gauged, and references to production of Roman cement higher up the river could possibly be a confusion of terms. The *Post Office Directory of Kent* for 1866 states that at Lower Halling 'the manufacture of Portland and Roman cement is carried on on a very extensive scale' and names Thomas Weekes as a Roman cement manufacturer. Also at Frindsbury 'the manufacture of Portland and Roman cement is carried on extensively', and here William Tingey was cited as a Roman, as well as Portland, cement manufacturer.[9] There is no further evidence on the subject of Roman cement.

In 1811 Frost patented a cement made from limestone and clay ground together in wet condition. However, his calcining temperature was too low, and the resultant product was inferior to Parker's cement. In 1822 Frost patented (no. 4679) his 'British' cement. The process employed a higher burning temperature, driving off more of the CO_2 gas, and producing a more successful cement.[10] In Frost's British cement the blue clay from the Medway, containing silicate of alumina, was an important ingredient.[11] British cement was made by Frost at Swanscombe, the works being taken over by J. Bazley White in 1827.[12]

Portland cement as a term first occurred in the specification of a Patent, No. 5022 (21 October 1824), granted to Joseph Aspdin, a bricklayer of Leeds.[13] The patent related to 'An improvement in the modes of producing artificial stone and which I call "Portland cement" ',[14] the name being derived from the resemblance to Portland stone. Joseph Aspdin does not appear to have made true Portland cement, 'nor was his mode of manufacture identical with that which has been generally adopted'.[15] The cement made at Aspdin's works at Wakefield set up in 1825 seems to have differed in that it was not burnt at a high enough temperature to vitrify the mixture of chalk and clay into a clinker for grinding .[16]Joseph's son William Aspdin was one of the earliest makers of genuine

A Map of the basic geology of the Lower Medway in relation to the siting of cement works and brickfields.

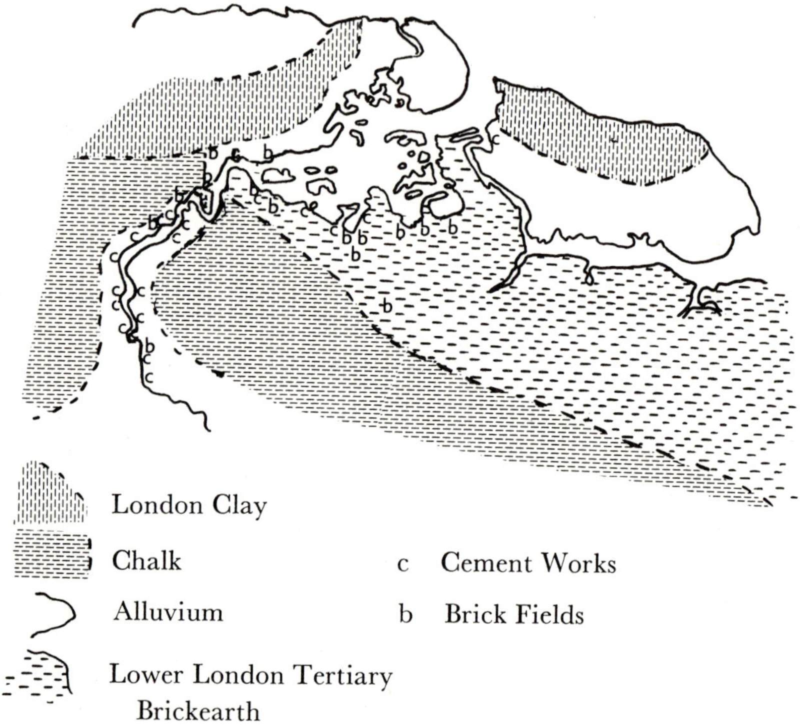

Portland cement. He set up a factory at Northfleet, trading with partners as Maude, Jones and Aspdin, and subsequently as Robins, Aspdin and Co. He shared with Messrs J. Bazley White the distinction of having been the founders of the Portland Cement manufacture in the London district.[17] There was great secrecy over Aspdin's process, and in the competition between the two firms. Aspdin's products were more in demand, being used for instance for Brunel's Thames Tunnel in 1838 and later by the Metropolitan Board of Works for the London Drainage Canal 1859.[18] I. C. Johnson (1811–1911), who became Works Manager for White's at Swanscombe in 1838 when the firm was producing Roman cement, British cement and Keene's plaster, began research to produce a cement comparable with Aspdin's.[19] The answer to the problem was discovered accidentally by Johnson in 1845 who experimented with grinding vitrified clinker which was usually discarded after burning. The resultant satisfactory cement led him to realize the necessity to burn the material at a sufficiently high temperature for it to vitrify into a clinker.[20] Whites' put I. C. Johnson's cement into production in 1845, advertisements in *The Builder* from April 1845 describing J. B. White and Sons of Millbank, Westminster, as manufacturers of Roman and Portland cement.[21]

I. C. Johnson decided to leave Whites and set up his own manufactory. This he did in 1851 on the Medway at Frindsbury, where he set up the first Portland cement works on the river.[22] However, he was not the first cement manufacturer at Frindsbury. Richard Cork was listed in 1847 as being a 'patent fuel and cement manufacturer',[23] but what manner of cement was involved is not known. Within a very short time after 1851 numerous lime works had been converted or completely new works were set up to produce cement along the banks of the Thames and Medway, and cement production became the staple industry of the area.[24] Producers on the Medway were able to utilize the blue clay of the river with its high content of silica and alumina which had been used by Frost, and the value of which had been ascertained by Major General Sir Charles Pasley (lecturer on architecture at the Royal Engineers School, Chatham) who in 1830 had performed experiments in cement making.[25] Abundant supplies of suitable limestone occur within easy reach of the riverside between Rainham and Aylesford.

I. C. Johnson's works were situated at the old oil mills (formerly David Samuel's) and at what was probably Cork's patent fuel factory on the riverbank on Chatham Ness. The mill, with its Old Boulton and Watt steam engines, was converted for cement production,[26] the works being 'substantially constructed in brick'.[27] The position on the Ness at Frindsbury was ideal, with abundant supplies of chalk from the spur behind, and almost unlimited quantities of blue Medway mud close at hand. With a wharf on the Medway below the bridge these works were well placed to receive fuel and cheaply transport their cement.[28] For this venture Johnson formed a partnership with George Burge who was an engineer and had been engaged under Telford in building St Katharine's Docks, London, as well as building railways[29] and also had been the contractor for Herne Bay Pier.[30] Production commenced on the 1 May 1851.[31] However, I. C. Johnson severed his connection with the Frindsbury works in 1853, when he took a lease on some chalk and marshland at Cliffe from about June 1853, where he made cement under the title of Johnson and Poynter. The works eventually came into the hands of Francis and Co.[32] This would account for the statement by Henry Smetham that Mr George Burge was 'the enterprising owner and moving spirit in this innovation'.[33] Production at this pioneer plant was extremely limited. Henry Smetham gave a figure of production in 1899 when he estimated that 'At the time the first cement works was erected, its total output was from 50 to 60 tons per week'.[34] This figure can be checked from the records of the Dean and Chapter estate for chalk digging.

CHALK DUG BY MESSRS. BURGE AND CO.
OCTOBER 1851 TO OCTOBER 1858

Year	Chalk dug (tons)
October 1851– October 1852	2,974
22 October 1852–22 October 1853	1,700
22 October 1853–22 October 1854	2,748
October 1854– October 1855	1,867
1855– October 1856	1,400
October 1856– October 1857	1,236
October 1857– October 1858	742.5 (550 yrds. at at 1.35 tons per yard)

Compiled from D.C.R.C. Eb1/33, Eb1/34, Eb1/35A, Eb1/36A, Eb1/37/c, Eb1/38A, Eb1/39.

To the tonnage of chalk one-third the weight of clay was added, the usual ratio being 3:1 in cement production. If 40 per cent is deducted for weight reduction during firing, and a few weeks allowed for the works being halted by weather conditions in the winter, the works show a decline in production from the figure mentioned by Smetham to in the region of 15 tons per week in 1858.

In response to the changes taking place on the Thames and at Frindsbury, the lime burners on the Medway began to turn to cement production. Among these was William Lee of Snodland, though it is doubtful that he began to make cement as early as 1848 as stated by Wall in 1928.[35] The firm, however, became famed for the quality of their cement.[36] Nearby at Cuxton, Boorman, Wild and Co. began to make cement in the early 1850s,[37] the works being carried on by Thomas Weeks from 1864.[38] Other works sprang up in the vicinity of existing lime works, or on completely new sites. These included a small cement works at Burham dating from about 1854. These were built alongside Thomas Cubitt's brickworks, and were conveniently situated to supply Cubitt's building operations in London.[39] At Wouldham village Thomas Freen and Co. were making cement in the early 1850s, becoming bankrupt in 1855.[40] Further upstream at Wouldham Hall, William Peters was making cement at the Greystone lime works by at least 1858,[41] using the quarry previously dug by the lime burners Davis and Hayman. At Brambletree Wharf, Borstal, cement works were set up in 1852 by Edwin Hollick.[42] Charles Formby was in business at Halling by 1858,[43] and in the same year the Upnor works of Messrs Hilton, Anderson and Co. of Faversham commenced production.[44] By 1860 the firm of Messrs Lark Fletcher and Co. was established by Strood Dock, Frindsbury.[45] By 1865 there were eleven active cement works on the Medway.[46]

The general method of making the cement at these early works can be seen from Edwin Harris' description of the works at Strood Dock which had a capacity of about 160 tons per week.[47]

> 'Many years ago a fairly large cement and lime burning works stood on this site. . . . There were a number of conical shaped kilns in which the cement was baked; these kilns were nearest the mouth of the basin. Beyond these the ground had been dug out in the form of dripping pans, and from the works ran a number of wooden gutters, in an inclined direction towards these dripping pans. The cement, in a liquid form ran down these troughs, looking like pure milk. When one of these squares was full, the fluid was diverted to another. This was left for several days until it began to harden; its colour used to change, with dust and soot, until it became a kind of ashen grey. As it dried cracks and fissures were observable on the surface. Then, men, with puddler's spades, dug out these pans and loaded into wheelbarrows, which were wheeled on planks into the kilns. Fires were lighted, and the cement baked until the fires dried out; it was then taken to the grinding mills and ground into fine powder.'[48]

Before running into the slurry backs the clay and chalk were washed together in a wash-mill. In the backs the slurry dried between six and eight weeks before the firing.[49] The burning was done in the original bottle or beehive kilns at a temperature of 1400° centigrade.[50] In loading the kiln faggots were arranged on bars at the bottom to start the fire, and alternate layers of coke and dried slurry heaped on top, the thickness of the layers gradually decreasing till the kiln was filled. The kiln was then fired, the whole contents burning through with the heat fairly evenly distributed through the kiln, and when the burning had ceased the clinker had to be allowed to cool before unloading could take place. As these were intermittent kilns with distinct charging and drawing operations, the whole firing occupied five to six days.[51]

> The clinker was ground by millstones[52] when it was of 'great importance to reduce the cement to a fine state of subdivision, and to exclude all "core" or hard particles by sifting. . . . All

> cement was benefitted by spreading it in thin heaps on the floor of the warehouse; this operation being termed "purging" the cement.'[53]

The ground cement was usually packed in casks or sacks by hand, being shovelled from the warehouse floor, before being wheeled on hand trucks to the loading bays. Despatch to markets was then by barge from the cement works' own wharves.

Digging the chalk was 'formerly carried out by small armies of men with great personal exertion and at considerable risk'.[54]

Edwin Harris in 1930 described at Frindsbury

> 'former times when I have seen men, with a life-line fastened round their bodies, securely tied to an iron crowbar driven into the ground at the top and some few yards from the edge of the chalk cliff. There would be several men working at different heights quarrying the chalk, which would sometimes crumble beneath their feet.'[55]

The quarry face was worked at a fairly steep slope for a height of 30 to 100 feet. The bottom of the face was worked to a narrow outlet, at which a truck was placed. The chalk, which was loosened with pointed bars, rolled down the slope and was guided into the truck. It was possible for a man to dig 3 tons of chalk per hour.[56] The chalk was usually transported to the works by narrow gauge railway which was the cheapest method. For instance land for a tramway was leased by the Wouldham Patent Portland Cement Co. in 1856 to provide a link between their pit and their works at Wouldham which were 1,380 feet apart.[57] Later, however, chalk was sometimes pumped through 6-inch pipes as a wet slurry,[58] which seems to have been the case at a large quarry without cement works adjacent to Wouldham Rectory. This quarry was connected to a dock and wharf on the Medway by tramway with nine sidings[59] alongside which ran a 6-inch diameter cast iron pipeline.

Clay was dug from the river Medway. Many thousands of tons of mud were removed from Upchurch marshes by barge to the cement works.[60] The clay diggers beached their barges on the saltings on a falling tide, loaded at low tide with a special wooden spade known as a 'fly tool', and floated off at high tide.[61] Digging took place on such a large scale as to worry Rochester Corporation, later after 1881 the Medway Conservancy Board and the Admiralty. Walled areas were breached to allow in the mud barges, water was able to flood over a wider area reducing the velocity of the flow of the river and causing silting. Some idea of the scale of digging can be gained from the operations around the turn of the century of the biggest mud contractor on the Medway, S. J. Brice and Sons of the Point Barge Yard. Between 1881 and 1911 he dug 1,356,000 tons from East Hoo Creek and between 1881 and 1907, 557,000 tons from West Hoo Creek, apart from being active elsewhere on the river.[62] Some works however substituted Gault clay for mud.[63] digging from nearby pits, as in the case of the Burham works.

Transportation of the cement to market was in the early years exclusively by means of water. All the cement works on the Medway were situated with their own wharves on the riverside. Most of the cement companies owned barges or fleets of barges, which helped to keep the barge building industry on the Medway in a healthy state until the early years of the twentieth century. Some works even had their own barge yards. The cement manufacturers therefore had a vested interest in keeping the river in good condition. William Lee took a leading part in the movement to establish the Medway Conservancy Board which was finally achieved in 1881.[64] Five of the six conservators appointed in 1881 were cement manufacturers; William Lee; Henry Peters of Wouldham Hall; John A. Anderson, a partner in Hilton, Anderson and Co. of Halling and Upnor; A. D. Robertson of Wouldham Cement Co.; and William Porter, who, apart from being a partner in Aveling and Porter, was also a partner in the Burham Cement Company.

The other main ingredient in the early cement industry was labour. The main qualification was a tough physique to stand the hard, heavy work and uncomfortable conditions. At the beginning it was only the low paid agricultural labourers who were attracted into the industry.[65] This situation was to change as cement manufacturing slowly developed into a far more scientific industry.

The preceding information indicates by and large the position reached by 1870. There were a number of the original works active on the Medway, but they were all small and 'total output did not exceed 1,000 to 1,200 tons per week. During the next ten years there was but a very small addition to the quantity made'.[66] Among the factors involved in the further development and prosperity of the industry were the reliability of the product, technical developments, competition from other areas, the building cycle and the attractiveness of the industry to capitalists.

Portland cement was not immediately a great success, largely due to the fact that it varied greatly in quality. This resulted from rule of thumb methods being used in the slurry mixing and in the amount of fuel used. In the early years little scientific knowledge was applied. Progress in the chemical analysis of compounds formed during burning was made by Le Chatelier in France.[67]

Considerable debate ensued as to what tests should be applied to cement, much of the work in testing cement, however, being conducted between 1859 and 1871 by Mr John Grant for the Metropolitan Board of Works.[68] The Frindsbury firm of Lark and White took part in these tests in the 1860s, and Burham Cement Company supplied 938,000 bushels between 1859 and 1865, more than twice the amount supplied by all the other thirteen firms invited to participate. The firm, then trading as Webster and Co., secured contracts to supply the cement for about two thirds of the total required for Grant's South London Drainage Scheme.[69] The tests appear to have put a seal of approval on cement as a building material.

The early lack of interest in Portland Cement was demonstrated by Mr E. A. Bernays in a paper read to the Institute of Civil Engineers in May 1880 in which he described his experiences in the extension of Chatham Dockyard.

> 'When these works were commenced, in 1867, so little confidence was placed in Portland cement that that material was not even mentioned in the contract specifications; grey stone lime, blue lias lime, and pozzolano being specified for all descriptions of mortar and concrete. Soon afterwards, however, it was found desirable to substitute Portland cement for the above materials. For all ordinary concrete it was ascertained that a mixture of one part of Portland cement with twelve parts of shingle gave a better result at the same or less cost than the concrete provided for in the specification, to be composed of one part of Warwickshire blue lias lime to six parts of shingle. The Portland cement used throughout the Admiralty works had been of good, but not costly, character.'

Upwards of 50,00 tons were used on the project.[70]

In 1880 the recognized tests for Portland cement were: its weight per bushel; the fineness to which it was ground; its colour; its tensile strength. It was recognized that variations in the strength of the cement would occur with different mixtures of raw materials, the use of too much clay for instance producing a quick setting cement which would contract. Over or under burning would also affect setting times.[71] However, uniform cement was only possible when the chemistry of cement was known. Writing in 1898 W. R. Craske commented

> 'Perhaps the principal cause of the rapid growth of the trade during the last few years is the greater care exercised in the manufacture and the consequent improvement in the quality. Twenty years ago there was not a works in England using

chemical tests for the analysis of the raw material and slurry; now an elementary knowledge of chemistry is to be found in every testing room, and but very few makers fail in testing their slurry as it leaves the wash mill several times a day. Our German competitors are largely responsible for this departure, as they realized earlier than we the importance of making a really reliable article.'

Apart from early consumer resistance being overcome by improved quality, greater reliability resulted in that

> 'Engineers began to find that Portland cement . . . could be safely used for many purposes that had not hitherto been thought of, and that it was the cheapest building material known where great resistances were required.'[72]

Apart from its hydraulic qualities and strength for such things as foundations, its value as a fireproofing substance began to be recognized. It also opened new possibilities as a cladding for buildings with iron and steel frameworks.[73]

Nor in its early years according to W. R. Craske was the trade

> 'looked upon with favour by capitalists, as many mistakes had been made in the erection of the works then in operation, and a large amount of money had been sunk in experiments that had proved to be failures.'[74]

The combination of poor quality cement and inappropriate plant could well have been factors in the difficulties of some of the pioneer firms. Thomas Freen and Co. of Wouldham became bankrupt in 1855, and the firm which succeeded it at the village site, the Wouldham Patent Portland Cement Co. formed by a group headed by George Burge, and incorporated with a capital of £20,000 in 1857,[75] was wound up by a resolution at an Extraordinary General Meeting, 20 September 1859.[76] An attempt in 1859 to take over the Burham brick and cement interests from the executors of Thomas Cubitt by a 'Burham Brick, Lime, Pottery and Cement Co. Ltd', failed because the £100,000 capital needed was not subscribed.[77] The small works of about 160 tons per week output which stood to the north east of the Canal basin, and which were totally destroyed in or about 1880,[78] had a frequently changing ownership. In July 1860 they appear under the title of Messrs Lark and Fletcher and Co.,[79] in 1864 as 'Lark and Parrock of the Medway Cement Works, Strood', at which time the firm had 'obtained the contract to supply the French Government with cements etc. for use in Government Works'.[80] In 1865 the firm appeared as 'Lark and

White',[81] in 1867 as 'James Lark',[82] in 1871–3 as 'W. H. White and Co.',[83] and finally in 1877 as 'Weston and Co.'[84]

As far as technical change was concerned, modifications were made to plant 'with a view to improve the quality and to reduce the cost of labour, fuel, wear and tear, etc.'. According to W. R. Craske the

> 'first radical change was introduced by the late Mr Goreham of Northfleet, who found that by mixing the raw materials with about 1/10th of the quantity of water generally used and passing the slurry through mill stones to reduce the chalk to the requisite fineness, it could be pumped direct to the drying floors and thus avoiding the use of settling backs. This effected a considerable saving in labour and also allowed the manufacturer to turn raw material into finished cement within fourteen days, the time previously being from three to four months and often longer.'[85]

An alternative to passing the wet slip through mill stones was in use by 1880 which employed a rubbing surface of metal plates which surrounded the wash mill.[86] Closely following these changes I. C. Johnson

> 'closed the tops of the kilns and built in place of the high domes long chambers into which wet slurry was pumped to a suitable depth, and through which the heat from the burning clinker in the kiln passed, and which were so regulated that enough slurry was dried each time of burning to reload the kiln, thus making the process continuous. By utilizing the waste heat from the kilns the drying floors were not required, and the coal used in heating them was then saved.'[87]

These chamber kilns, which were usually designed to produce about 30 tons of cement at each charge still used considerable amounts of fuel and labour,[88] consumption being eight to nine cwt of coke per ton of cement.[89] By 1898 Clarke commented that

> 'other kilns of the same type, especially those designed by Mr G. Burge and Mr G. Batchelor, have to a large extent superseded Mr Johnsons, but the object of all has been the same, and the long chambers have been adhered to'[90]

The Batchelor kiln, which was similar in principle to the chamber kiln, instead of having a single drying floor had at the rear of the kilns a series of slurry drying chambers in the form of two or three arched floors one above the other, with usually one big chimney serving a whole block of kilns.[91] Good quality cement was produced in kilns of this type.

Further technical development took place in grinding plant about which W. R. Craske said

> 'No detail in the works has called forth as much inventive ingenuity as the grinding plant, and in no department has there been so much money wasted on fruitless experiments. In the old days all the grinding was done with French burr stones of a similar character to those used for grinding wheat, but made of burrs especially selected for hardness and soundness. While engineers were satisfied with cement ground sufficiently for 80% to pass through a sieve with 1,600 holes per sq in, the need for machinery was not felt, but in the course of time it was found that the finer the cement was ground the greater was the strength of the mortar or concrete made with it, and it became necessary to erect mills that would do the work with less wear and tear and taking less power to drive the mill stones. The number of mills that have been introduced, tried and generally thrown on the scrap heap is legion, but those invented by our townsmen, Mr J. Collis and Mr P. J. Neates, and two or three that had their origins in Germany have proved successful, and are rapidly superseding stones. At the present time engineers' specifications for fineness vary from 90% through a sieve having 2,500 holes per square inch to 95% through one having 5,600 holes, and in a few instances a still greater degree of fineness is demanded. The difference between the most coarsely ground cement of the present day and the best that was current a few years ago will explain some of the difficulties that have had to be faced in the erection of suitable milling plant.'[92]

Improvements in the technology of cement making were to some extent the result of increased competition. In the 1850s and 1860s the industry had been localized on the Thames and Medway with all their natural advantages and the draw of the London market. With a monopoly of Portland cement production the area had been 'supplying the world with cement'. The basic materials for cement manufacture are fairly widely distributed with the result that

> 'the great cement producing centres in England found their trade abroad contested by a growing local manufacture and the exports to many foreign markets were continued at such prices as to be barely remunerative.'[93]

By 1880 cement was being manufactured in other areas; at Folkestone, at Harwich, Newcastle on Tyne, and Stockton-on-Tees a local blue clay which contained 'the requisite proportions of silica and alumina' was used with chalk 'imported generally from the Thames'. Cement was made at Rugby and in Somersetshire and elsewhere from blue lias formations.[94]

Cement being a cheap bulky material, its price was greatly affected by transport costs, leading to price advantages for local producers in overseas markets. France quickly started to produce Portland cement at Boulogne. Germany and the United States rapidly developed their own industries, the lucrative American market being completely lost.[95] A variety of materials were used in cement production abroad. At Rio de Janiero coral lime and river mud were used; at Madras lime produced from sea shells; and in the neighbourhood of Neufchatel and Devres in France a natural cement earth was found 'which much resembles grey chalk in appearance' which contained 'the exact proportions of lime, silica and alumina for the production of a high-class cement.'[96] In face of this competition in foreign markets export prices declined, the average value per cwt. (f.o.b.) falling from 4.12 shillings in 1848 to 2.43 shillings in 1870. After 1886 the price remained below 2 shillings for the rest of the century, the lowest point being 1.62 shillings in 1895. However, the effects of this competition were not severe until at least the 1890s and more particularly after 1900.

The fortunes of the cement industry before 1900 in England, which were reflected in price levels, were more related to expansion of capacity in the industry, the state of industrial activity and the building cycles, than to foreign developments. The price level held at 30 pence per bushel from 1854 to 1860, when it fell to 28 pence and remained at about that level till 1867. For the next twenty years to 1887 the price did not fall below 30 pence. The price then fell to 28 pence, touched 24 pence in 1893–5, before recovering to 30 pence per bushel in 1899.[97]

Two indices of residential house building can be used to compare developments in the cement industry. These are

A. An Index of House-Building in London 1856–1916 (1900–9=100)

and

B. An Index of House-Building in 34 Towns 1856–1923 (1900–9=100)

	A	B		A	B
1856	18.9	40.2	1879	99.6	65.8
1857	25.7	36.4	1880	115.0	63.6
1858	26.6	39.0	1881	120.7	60.6
1859	31.4	34.2	1882	107.5	62.7
1860	34.6	34.6	1883	97.4	62.7

	A	B		A	B
1861	31.6	34.6	1884	85.0	63.1
1862	42.6	44.5	1885	72.7	58.8
1863	50.9	49.3	1886	56.5	57.5
1864	48.8	46.6	1887	57.6	60.3
1865	55.2	41.0	1888	57.3	61.2
1866	61.6	42.3	1889	54.6	60.9
1867	63.0	50.0	1890	50.4	58.1
1868	70.1	53.9	1891	55.8	60.6
1869	53.9	59.0	1892	51.7	64.3
1870	46.3	65.8	1893	59.2	65.8
1871	40.1	69.2	1894	59.4	69.8
1872	51.6	71.9	1895	60.6	68.8
1873	35.5	62.6	1896	77.98	82.0
1874	35.8	69.6	1897	85.5	99.8
1875	46.2	92.2	1898	114.6	120.8
1876	59.7	100.2	1899	126.3	119.6
1877	66.5	95.0	1900	116.0	107.0
1878	79.0	81.6			

From B. Weber, 'A New Index of Residential Construction and Long Cycles in House-Building in Great Britain, 1838–1950', *Scottish Journal of Political Economy*, June 1955, 131–2.

The indices diverge before about 1886.

Peaks—London	1868		1881	1899
Peaks—Elsewhere		1876		1898
Troughs—London		1873		1890
Troughs—Elsewhere			1886	

However, with improvements in the quality of cement and with increased demand for it in the country generally reaching a peak in 1876,

> 'more interest (was) taken in the trade by persons looking for safe investments, and the flood of commercial prosperity about 25 years ago (1873) caused a large influx of capital, which was the means of erecting six or eight works on the Medway, and the enlargement of most of the old ones.'[98]

Entry to the industry was easy for anyone with a basic knowledge of cement and a small amount of capital. Raw materials were in abundant supply and factory sites plentiful.

The upswing of the indices of the 1870s is obviously related to a spate of new cement factories. Among the new works was the Halling Manor Lime and Cement Works set up in 1878,[99] as an addition to the works of Messrs Hilton, Anderson and Co. at Upnor and Faversham, and from whose pits the latter works were supplied with chalk.[100] In 1874 the Gillingham Portland Cement Co, Ltd, of Danes Hill, Gillingham appeared.[101] The Company was formed by George Burge Jnr in association with William Morgan (an accountant) and C. R. Cheffins, a civil engineer. Burge erected the works which were based on continuous chamber kilns of the type patented by him in 1872, and acted as works manager. A few years later the company was joined by Frank Chapman (a son in law of William Tingey who had taken the Crown Works in 1867) who had a good knowledge of the export trade.[102] Among the works enlarged in the mid-1870s were those of Thomas Weekes, who replaced Boorman, Wild at Whornes Place, Halling. In 1876 he rented a further acre of land to erect four or five kilns, a drying floor and engine house.[103]

A firm contemplating entering the manufacture of cement was the West Kent Gault Brick and Cement Co. incorporated in 1873, in which the leading figure was William George Margetts, a stock-broker of 7 Warnford Close, Throgmorton Street, who had bought the lease of the Aylesford and Burham brickfields in February 1872.[104] A new lease was being negotiated in August 1876, it being clear that the new company intended to manufacture cement. The company's solicitor was asking in this month to be able to see the lease granted to Messrs Peters with reference to the conditions to the supply of chalk,[105] and a letter sent with the returned and approved draft lease mentioned 'plans of the intended new works'.[106] The lease allowed for the manufacture of cement, and for the erection of convenient plant and buildings.[107] Chamber kilns were subsequently built at Aylesford, but the site although having access to clay, had no chalk.

The biggest concentration of cement works was to be along the chalk spur at Frindsbury. After the original works, Crown, the next to be opened were the Phoenix in 1877. George Burge Jnr with John McGowan formed the Phoenix Portland Cement Company in 1868,[108] and started to erect works on land leased from the Church Commission by William Tingey. However, it would appear that it was not until 1877 that the works were 'satisfactorily completed'.[109] The other five works in the area were opened about or just after the peak of the London building index in 1881. The Globe, which appears to have been opened in 1880 was operated initially by its constructor in association with George Burge Jnr, and later with Frederick Barron.[110] The Bridge works were also constructed by William Tingey, opened in 1885 and the business sold to the Bridge Portland Cement Co.[111]

William Tingey also built three more works on land leased from the Bridge Wardens. He sublet the Beaver Works to McLean and Co Ltd, from 1884,[112] and obtained powers to sublet to the same firm the 600 feet above the Beaver Works with factory and buildings standing for 80 years from 1884—this was the Beehive Works.[113] In April 1893 the Beaver was under the guidance of a Mr Clark as Secretary, and George Burge and a Mr Meadows as Directors, while the Beehive had George Burge as Manager.[114] The last works erected on the Ness were the Quarry, which were opened in 1888 and sublet to Chas. Cheffins, William Morgan and Tingey's son in law, Frank Chapman, but the cement boom had passed by this time.[115] Although some of these works were to change hands several times, control over them was basically kept by William Tingey Snr and Jnr, Frank Chapman, George Burge Jnr and their associates, like Charles Cheffins.

Other works also started up around the peak year of 1881. John Adams of Strood obtained a lease on part of Wickham Farm, Strood for the erection of cement works,[116] part of the capital for which he raised by mortgaging the works.[117] He had managed by 1890–1 to erect a few static chamber kilns which produced about 150 tons per week and employed about 60 men and paid about £100 in weekly wages.[118] In 1882 a cement works was established at Queenborough by Josiah Hall,[119] who was also the owner of the copperas works. Clay was excavated from a pit nearby, but chalk was brought by barge from Gillingham, possibly from the quarry at Sharps Green.[120] The works had eventually four kilns and an output of approximately 400 tons per week.[121] Also in 1882 works were set up by George Burge Jnr and Frederick Barron at Otterham Quay, Rainham.[122] Lastly, in 1883 a Mr E. Robson Cummin, an engineer of Gravesend leased the site of the former Cuxton brickfield[123] where six static kilns were set up.[124]

The rapid expansion of capacity on the Medway was followed by a trough in the building cycle reaching an overall low in 1890. The result was that many of the cement works ran into financial difficulties. At the Wickham Works, Strood, John Adams ran into trouble in January 1887, when goods at the works were to be sold 'under distress for rent',[125] while in the following month his mortgage was foreclosed.[126] After several changes of hand the works came into the possession of the Reliance Portland Cement Works Ltd in 1890.[127] This firm was liquidated by Court Order in March 1894. The neighbouring cement works at Cuxton was the only one to disappear completely on its liquidation. The Medway Portland Cement Co. Ltd, had been formed in 1885 by E. Turner, a barrister, Thomas Grover, a contractor, and A. R.

Robinson, a civil engineer, to take over Cummins works. The firm became bankrupt in 1891,[128] and the works closed permanently.

The only works to be opened during the depression were the Borstal Manor. A newspaper report on a meeting of Rochester Town Council in early 1893 stated 'The works committee has approved plans of a Cement Works at Borstal, for Mr J. L. Spoor'.[129] Upwards of £20,000 were expended on the plant and buildings by 1894 when Spoor became bankrupt and the works were sold up by the Sheriff.[130] His creditors were his mortgagers A. E. Greville, a solicitor of Towcester, and J. B. Martin, who had recently become involved in the Wickham Works, the Stevens Cask and Barrel Co. and E. J. and W. Goldsmith the barge owners.[131] These works eventually about 1898 came into the hands of W. R. Craske, quoted in this work.

One effect of the depression in cement was a certain concentration of ownership. The Globe and the Bridge works appear to have been in the control of J. B. White from 1895.[132] In 1896 White's absorbed the Quarry Works while taking over its parent company the Gillingham Portland Cement Co.[133]

The last four years of the century were ones of relative prosperity for the cement industry with the building cycle reaching a peak in 1898–9. Expansion of capacity continued at the older established works. In June 1895 Lord Darnley had consented to Trechmann Weekes of Halling erecting 3 or 4 more kilns.[134] The Wickham Works under J. B. Martin were much expanded. He joined with E. J. Vivasour Earle to form a new company Martin, Earle and Co. Ltd.[135] By 1899 production had reached 2,000 tons per week, giving employment to over 800 men and with a weekly wage bill of over £1,000. By that date nearly £500,000 had been expended on the premises, wharf and associated engineering works. The wharves stretched for a half a mile, being the most extensive on the Medway, and often had as many as 25 barges alongside, loading and unloading. The Company also possessed a large ship, costing £9,000, which received loads of cement below Rochester Bridge from barges and lighters.[136] In the 1890s Peter's Wouldham Hall Works which employed in the region of 1,000 men[137] was still being equipped with Batchelor kilns, the tall chimney shafts not being demolished till the 1939–45 war.[138] These would have been in addition to the '18 large beehive kilns, with chimneys belching forth flames and smoke'[139] described around the turn of the century.

The Burham Works also saw some expansion. A Mr Arthur Higgins who retired from A.P.C.M. in 1958 recounted that when he joined the Burham Company in 1888, the firm operated 36 Chamber kilns producing 1,000 tons of Portland cement per week and 24 lime kilns producing about 950 tons of Lump Quick Lime per week, and also produced 20,000 bricks per day with a labour force of 2,000.[140] By 1898 the works were one of the finest in the country producing 1,500 tons of high quality cement per week from 45 static kilns.[141] These compared well with the works in the Quarry area which, in 1899, were employing 'a total of 750 hands, and producing together an average output of 3,900 tons of cement per week'.[142] The seven factories there consisted of a total of 152 chamber kilns of different types, with about 30 chimneys.[143]

Peter's Bros. Wouldham Hall Cement Works taken about 1900.

Later additions in the form of the tall chimneys of Batchelor Kilns at the north end of the works. Sailing barges and lighters so essential for transport from the east bank cement works are much in evidence along the wharf. Faintly in the distance to the north rise the tall chimneys of Lees Lime Works and Halling Manor Cement Works.

The century ended on a bright note for the cement industry which by now had established itself as the most important industry on the Medway and the biggest single employer of labour. In 1898 W. R. Craske tried to estimate the influence of the industry locally. He wrote

> 'The statement that 15,000 tons of cement are made every week on the Medway, and that the direct wages paid in connection therewith is about £6,000 per week gives but a very inadequate

Peter's Bros. Wouldham Hall Cement Works taken about 1900.

Illustrated is a row of seventeen early bottle kilns dating from the late 1860's, but still at work.

Photographs reproduced by courtesy of Maidstone Museum

idea of the amount of money it puts into circulation. The carriage of this quantity from the works to the places where it is used, distributed or transhipped for longer voyages gives constant employment to over 200 barges, and fully another 100 can be added to this number that are employed in carrying to the works coal, coke, clay and other materials used in the manufacture. These 300 barges earn a gross freight of about £2,000 per week, one moiety of which is paid to the crew as wages, and the other moiety is largely reduced by the amount paid by the owners for repairs of which a large proportion goes for shipwrights wages. Add to this a further sum for building new barges, and it will be readily seen to what a large extent the barge building trade has profited by the growth of the cement industry.

The great wear and tear on machinery in cement works has called into existence several engineers' shops employing a large number of men that are almost entirely dependent upon it for work, and building and allied trades have received an impetus that is due to the same cause. If from some cause all cement works were to close down immediately, it may be fairly estimated that the working classes in Rochester and the neighbourhood would lose purchasing power to the extent of £10,000 per week. What this would mean to the tradesmen—is impossible to overestimate.'[144]

[1] N. Davey, *A History of Building Materials* (1961), 104.

[2] *Victoria County History*, III, (1932), 398. E. M. Hewitt, 'Industries'.

[3] Davey, *op. cit.*, 104.

[4] V.C.H. *op. cit.*, 398. Hewitt.

[5] A. C. Davis, *Portland Cement* (2nd edition, 1943), 4, 6.

[6] Davey, *op. cit.*, 107.

[7] A. C. Davis, *A Hundred Years of Portland Cement*, 1824–1924, 66.

[8] Black's, *Guide to the South Eastern Counties of England, Kent* (Edinburgh, 1861), 463.

[9] *Post Office Directory of Kent* (1866), 996, 1094, 1101.

[10] Davey, *op. cit.*, 106.

[11] Davis, *op. cit.*, (1924), 47.

[12] Davis, *op. cit.*, (1943), 6.

[13] *The Builder*, 22 May 1880, 643a.

[14] Davis, *op. cit.*, (1943), 1.

[15] *The Builder*, 22 May 1880, 643a.

[16] Davey, *op. cit.*, 106.

[17] *The Builder*, 22 May 1880, 643a.

[18] M. Bowley, *Innovations in Building Materials* (1960), 86–7.

[19] Information from Mr Parker.

[20] Davis, *op. cit.*, (1924), 47–52.

[21] Information from Mr. Parker.

[22] Davis, *op. cit.*, (1924), 53.

[23] S. Bagshaw, *History, Gazetteer and Dictionary of the County of Kent*, I, (Sheffield, 1847), 327.

[24] Davis, *op. cit.*, (1924), 56.

[25] *V.C.H.*, III, 398.

[26] H. Smetham, *History of Strood* (Strood, 1899), 345.

[27] Ecclesiastical Commission, File 37842, 24.

[28] J. Preston, 'When Medway was Cement River', *Medway, The Quarterly Journal of the Medway Chamber of Commerce*, No. 94, Autumn 1973, 8.

[29] Information from Mr Parker.

[30] C. Dendy Marshall, *A History of the Southern Railway* (1968) 325.

[31] Information from Mr Parker.

[32] K.A.O. U565 E9 Darnley Mss.

[33] Smetham, *op. cit.*, 345.

[34] Smetham, *op. cit.*, 347.

[35] C. de Rochfort Wall, *Snodland and its History 55 BC to AD 1928* (Snodland, 1928), 22.

[36] Information from Mr Parker.

[37] K.A.O. U565 E8 Darnley Mss. Draft lease to Boorman Wild 1854.

[38] K.A.O. U565 E8 Darnley Mss. Draft licence to assign 19 August 1864.

[39] H. Hobhouse, *Thomas Cubitt, Master Builder* (1971), 315.

[40] Information from Mr Parker.

[41] J. and J. F. Phippen, *A Directory for Rochester, Chatham, Strood and their vicinities* (Rochester, 1858), 79.

[42] Information from Mr Parker.

[43] Phippen, *op. cit.*, 75.
[44] Information from Mr Parker.
[45] *Chatham News*, 28 July 1860.
[46] Preston, *op. cit.*
[47] Smetham, *op. cit.*, 347.
[48] E. Harris, *The Riverside* (Rochester, 1930), 41.
[49] *The Builder*, 22 May 1880, 643.
[50] Davis, *op. cit.* (1943), 96.
[51] Davis, *op. cit.*, (1943), 97, 98.
[52] *V.C.H.*, III, 398.
[53] *The Builder*, 22 May 1880, 643.
[54] Davis, *op. cit.*, (1943) 17.
[55] Harris, *op. cit.*, 43.
[56] Davis, *op. cit.*, (1943), 35.
[57] K.A.O. U1730 T1/1. Lease Lay to Wouldham Patent Portland Cement Co. 26 November 1857.
[58] Davis, *op. cit.*, (1943), 40.
[59] O.S. 2nd Edition 2″ to 1 mile. Sheet XIX/9.
[60] *V.C.H.*, III, 133.
[61] R. Marsh, *The Conservancy of the River Medway, 1881–1969* (Rochester, 1971), 55–6.
[62] Marsh, *op. cit.*, 41, 53, 56.
[63] *The Builder*, 28 February 1880, 246a.
[64] Marsh, *op. cit.*, 2, 20–2.
[65] Davis, *op. cit.*, (1943), 17.
[66] W. R. Craske, 'The Cement Industry—Its Rise and Progress on The Medway', *Chatham, Rochester and Brompton Observer*, 7 May 1898, 8c.
[67] Bowley, *op. cit.*, 89.
[68] *The Builder*, 22 May 1880, 643.
[69] Information from Mr Parker.
[70] *The Builder*, 22 May 1880, 643.
[71] *The Builder*, 28 February 1880, 246.
[72] Craske, *op. cit.*, 8d.
[73] Bowley, *op. cit.*, 87.
[74] Craske, *op. cit.*
[75] Information from Mr Parker.
[76] K.A.O. U1730 T1/3 Assignment of lease to Campbell and Howard 1 January 1863.
[77] Information from Mr Parker.
[78] Smetham, *op. cit.*, 347.
[79] *Chatham News*, 28 July 1860.
[80] *Chatham News*, 13 February 1864.
[81] Simpsons, *Rochester, Chatham, Strood and Brompton Directory* (1865), 426.
[82] R. Taylor, *The Chatham, Rochester Directory, Family Almanack and Year Book* (Chatham, 1867), 29.
[83] Percy and Co. *Rochester, Chatham, Strood, New and Old Brompton and Gillingham Directory for 1871–2–3*, 137.
[84] Manning and Co., *Rochester and Chatham District Directory* (Chatham, 1877), 82.
[85] Craske, *op. cit.*
[86] *The Builder*, 22 May 1880, 643.
[87] Craske, *op. cit.*
[88] Davis, *op. cit.*, (1943), 99.

[89] Davis, *op. cit.*, (1924), 153.
[90] Craske, *op. cit.*
[91] Davis, *op. cit.*, (1943), 100.
[92] Craske, *op. cit.*
[93] Davis, *op. cit.*, (1943), 17.
[94] *The Builder*, 28 February 1880, 246.
[95] Davis, *op. cit.*, (1943), 17.
[96] *The Builder*, 28 February 1880, 246.
[97] Bowley, *op. cit.*, 90.
[98] Craske, *op. cit.*
[99] Information from Mr Parker.
[100] E. J. March, *Spritsail Barges of the Thames and Medway* (Newton Abbott, 1970), 34–5.
[101] *Post Office Directory of Kent* (1874), 1699.
[102] Information from Mr Parker.
[103] K.A.O. U565 T93. Lease Darnley to Weekes 1876.
[104] K.A.O. U234 T4 Aylesford Mss Letter F. Dollman to Lord Aylesford, 1 August 1872.
[105] K.A.O. U234 T4 Letter C. Baylis to Bennett, Dawson and Bennett, 11 August 1876.
[106] K.A.O. U234 T4 Letter C. Baylis to Bennett, Dawson and Bennett, 16 February 1877.
[107] K.A.O. U234 T4 Lease Aylesford to West Kent Gault Brick and Portland Cement Co. Ltd. 31 May 1877.
[108] Information from Mr Parker.
[109] E.C. 47386, Letter, Jenning, White and Buckton to Secretary of Ecclesiastical Commission 9 July 1877.
[110] E.C. 47386, Letter, Gush, Phillips, Walters and Williams to Globe, 9 April 1897.
[111] E.C. 47386 Letter, Bridge Co. to Ecclesiastical Commission, 19 April 1893.
[112] Bridge Warden's Records, Register of Leases 1876–1906, 214.
[113] *Ibid*, 251.
[114] E.C. 47386. List of firms April 1893.
[115] Bridge Warden's Records, Register of Leases 1876–1906, 250.
[116] K.A.O. U565 Addnl E175 Bundle I Lease Darnley to Adams 19 November 1881.
[117] K.A.O. U565 Addnl E175 Bundle I Mortgate Indenture 20 January 1885.
[118] Smetham, *op. cit.*, 246.
[119] K. R. MacDonald, *The Isle of Sheppey and the Swale* (London M.A. thesis, Geog., 1949), 80.
[120] B. Stoyel and R. Kidner, *Cement Railways of Kent* (Lingfield, 1973), 56, 59.
[121] *1907–1957 A History of the Queenborough undertaking of Settle Speakman and Co. Ltd.*, (Published by the firm, Queenborough, 1957), 8.
[122] Information from Mr Parker.
[123] K.A.O. U565 E176 Lease Darnley to Cummin 1883.
[124] Information from Mr Parker.
[125] *Chatham News*, 29 January 1887, 8.
[126] K.A.O. U565 Addnl E175 Bundle I. Transfer of mortgate 1 February 1887.
[127] *Ibid*, Assignment of lease London Agency to Reliance Co. 1 February 1887.

[128] Information from Mr Parker.

[129] Unsourced newspaper cutting, Rochester Library, 15 February 1893.

[130] *Chatham News*, 22 September 1894, 4; 29 September 1894, 4.

[131] *Kent Messenger*, 19 January 1895, 5.

[132] E.C.R. 47386, Memorandum, A.P.C.M. to Ecclesiastical Commission, 13 July 1905.

[133] Information from Mr Parker.

[134] K.A.O. U565 A443 Letter Book, 590. Darnley to Weeks 25 Jne 1895.

[135] K.A.O. U565 Addnl E185 Bundle 3. Assignment of lease to Martin, Earle and Co. 4 February 1895.

[136] Smetham, *op. cit.*, 349.

[137] Marsh, *op. cit.*, 21.

[138] Information from Mr Sibun.

[139] A. G. Munro and Prescott Row, *Rochester and Chatham with their Surroundings —A Handbook for Visitors and Residents* (1905), 85.

[140] *Blue Circle*, July 1958.

[141] Information from Mr Parker.

[142] Smetham, *op. cit.*, 347.

[143] *Blue Circle*, April 1952.

[144] Craske, *op. cit.*

CHAPTER V

Brickmaking 1850–1900

Some idea of the demand for bricks can be gained from the indices of house building[1] and from inter-censal changes in the numbers of houses built and the numbers occupied in the building industry in England and Wales.

INTER-CENSAL CHANGES IN NUMBER OF HOUSES AND BUILDING WORKERS 1851–1901

Census Year	*Persons occupied in Building* No. 000's	*Persons occupied in Building* Inter-censal change 000's	*Inter-censal* increase in numbers of houses, 000's
1851	390		
1861	462	72	492
1871	567	105	596
1881	690	123	698
1891	706	16	606
1901	953	147	886

Taken from M. Bowley, *Innovations in Building Materials* (1960), 50.

However, such figures give no idea of the amount of replacement building which took place, nor of the amount of industrial building which affected brick production. One can only suppose that the persistent increase in building activity lead to a consequent increase in the demand for bricks.

No statistics for brick output nationally or locally appear to be available as a measure of the performance of the Medway brickmakers. Nor is there any real evidence to fit the activities of Medway brickmakers to the indices of the residential house building cycle. However, there is evidence of brick manufacture on a very considerable scale in the area. In 1864 a newspaper report on Rainham said

> 'Much building—principally of small houses—is going on in and about this pleasant village. The large amount of employment in

> brickmaking in the neighbourhood causes such a constant increase in the number of working people at the place that now houses are engaged before they are half built.'[2]

Four years later the inhabitants of Gillingham were described as

> 'agricultural or dockyard labourers, with many brickmakers, whose operations are gradually destroying the magnificent plum and cherry orchards for which Gillingham has been celebrated for years.'[3]

Brickmaking continued in all those riverside areas with suitable brickearth, including Lower Halstow, Upchurch, Newington, Rainham, Gillingham and Brompton, the Luton area of Chatham, Burham, Aylesford, Strood, Frindsbury, and Hoo. Evidence of brick earth digging is still to be seen in many areas where the level of the land is artificially lower than normal, for instance below the Cuxton Road, Strood, or near Otterham Quay, Rainham. Many of the small brickmakers were also farmers who carefully removed the topsoil from areas where clay was to be extracted, removed the six to ten feet of brickearth, and replaced the topsoil and restored the land for agriculture.[4] Some of the better known brickmakers such as Henry Everest at Strood and the Wakeleys at Rainham were farmers.

The fact that many of the brickmakers followed primarily another occupation probably accounts for the fact that before 1890 little is heard of recessions in the industry following the London building cycle. London was the main market for bricks outside the Medway area to which they were mainly carried by barge, although some were despatched by rail.[5] Brickmaking by the smaller manufacturers was carried on by traditional methods, on a seasonal basis, with hand moulding, hack drying and clamp firing, meaning that very little capital equipment was necessary. In hard times the farmers could always fall back upon agriculture, as could the workers. Anyway, the men who could not get work digging clay or sifting 'rough stuff' (ashes) between October and April had to fall back on farm work.[6] In fact much of the labour for brickmaking was recruited from among local agricultural workers. At such places as Burham or Lower Halstow brickmaking provided the only alternative employment. Reference to the Census Returns of 1851 for Rainham and Burham shows that brick workers came from only a few miles radius. When Thomas Cubitt opened the extensive brick works at Burham in 1852 he equipped it with the then most modern brickmaking machinery. This allowed for the use of unskilled labour recruited locally from among agricultural workers, only the foremen, who were skilled brickmakers, were brought from outside the county.[7]

Apart from the obvious London market, there was also a considerable local market for bricks to house the growing local population, and also to build the factories and commercial premises which were springing up. For instance the number of houses in Rochester increased from 3,710 in 1871 to 6,515 in 1901, while in Chatham the number of houses increased over the same period from 7,816 to 15,390.[8] In the villages in the valley increases in the number of houses took place demanding bricks, probably an average of 5,000 per house.

INCREASE IN INHABITED HOUSES 1871–1891

	1871	1891		1871	1891
Aylesford	395	560	Queenborough	149	209
Burham	212	308	Rainham	425	640
Cuxton	79	86	Snodland	347	571
Hoo St Werburgh	236	272	Upchurch	159	228
Frindsbury	608	976	Wouldham	154	258
Halling	154	386			

Compiled from *Census Abstracts* 1871 and 1891.

The cement works alone would have accounted for millions of bricks. The bricks were mostly delivered locally in two wheeled brick carts. Eastwoods at Otterham Quay had at one time stables and 150 horses for this purpose.[9] Sometimes they were also transported short distances by barge, an instance occurring in 1901 when bricks for a contractor were unloaded at a wharf in Canal Road, Strood.[10]

Several of the brickmakers were in business to supply their own needs as builders and contractors. This was the case with Thomas Cubitt, the London builder, who started brickworks and cement works at Burham in 1852. These were extensive works with, when the works were put up for sale in 1857, five Ainslie double brick machines, two steam wash mills, steam driven pug mills and fixed kilns, all the works, pits and wharves being connected by tramways. The machines had each a capacity of about 1,000 bricks per hour. In five years, according to Hermione Hobhouse, Cubitt spent £54,000 on the purchase of land, buildings and machinery,[11] a figure at variance with one given by a descendant, Sir Stephen Tallents who said of Cubitt

> 'One of his last ventures was to buy land on the bank of the Medway . . ., and to spend £80,000 in equipping it for making bricks and the like. These works had just been completed when he died[12] in 1855.'

Brickmaking continued at this site, especially creamy white gault bricks made from clay extracted from a large pit nearby, by Cubitt's successors Webster and Co. (1859). This firm incorporated in 1871 as the Burham Brick, Lime and Cement Co Ltd, continued to make bricks at a rate of about five million a year until its merger with the B.P.C.M. in 1912.[13]

Another brickmaker who was a contractor was J. Foord and Sons of Rochester. The firm acquired the use of Upnor brickfields (Ten Gun Field) so as to be able to meet the requirements of the government departments in the locality with whom they had triennial contracts for maintenance.[14] Records of their net production exist from 1855 to 1864.

1855	2,163,027	1860	562,535
1856	2,073,349	1861	940,676
1857	1,030,340	1862	671,400
1858	417,048	1863	734,267
1859	—	1864	795,000

Taken from D.C.R.C.R. Eb1/39 to Eb1/48 Returns of bricks produced.

Yet another was the firm of Ball and Gammon, contractors, who worked Kingsland Brickfield, New Brompton until April 1889.[15] This particular firm was connected with William Ball who held the lease to all the land containing chalk on Church property at Frindsbury, and who supplied all the cement works on Chatham Ness from about 1881[16] until his death in 1913.[17] Contracts with which Ball had been associated included a considerable part in the construction of Rochester Bridge of 1854–5; Westminster Bridge; Gillingham Pier; Chattenden Barracks (a £25,000 contract); Upnor Magazines; Rochester and Blackfriars Goods Stations; Rochester Banks Station; the branch railway into the dockyard from Gillingham; Victoria Bridge, Gillingham; Deptford and and Lewisham Bridges.[18] Also a contractor was R. West of Strood.[19]

Many of the smaller brickmakers' activities are virtually unknown, their names occurring in directories, or alternatively notices of closing down sales appearing in local papers. More often than not it appeared that the smaller works closed for other than financial reasons. In 1864 John Wyles's Darland Brickfield, Luton, closed 'having worked out the field of excellent brickearth'.[20] The same applied to the Cuxton Brickfield where in March 1867 Richard Badcock gave notice to quit as 'there does not appear to be brickearth enough to go on with'.[21] Production here had reached 2½ million bricks in 1866,[22] but the site was abandoned for brickmaking from 1868. Retirement on the 'expiration of lease' was the reason for the closure of Mr Bullbrook's Navy Row Brickfield, Gillingham in June 1888.[23] The death of the principal seemed also to be a frequent reason for closure. The Brickfield of Mr Butcher of Rainham was closed on his death 1 October 1886, throwing all his employees from work, some of those displaced being 'driven to dishonesty through want'.[24] The plant and equipment of the late T. Honey at Pier Road, Gillingham were sold up in April 1888.[25] George Roots of Gillingham died in 1892, aged 82, having been

> 'one of the most successful brickmakers in the district. His bricks were scarcely equalled, and certainly never excelled by any in the market, and as a consequence, they always commanded a ready sale at the best prices.'[26]

A possible reason for these fields not being taken over as going concerns was that the closures took place at a time when there was a down swing in the building cycle.

Coinciding with the slump in building in the late 1880s and early 1890s there was a technical development which was to have a great impact on the Medway industry—the introduction of the semi-dry pressed clay brickmaking process, producing Fletton bricks from the Peterborough area. This process, instead of using soft plastic clays, enabled hard shales to be used, which were ground to form granules and then forced into moulds in a moist state. This gave bricks stiff enough to be set in the kiln without preliminary drying, any moisture present being expelled in the kiln. A considerable saving was incurred by eliminating the handling from a drier to the kiln. However, the main advantage of using Oxford clay for Flettons and other carboniferous shales was the fuel economy achieved through the carbon content of the clay. Some shales contain so much combustible matter that it is difficult to control the temperature rise, and the amount of coal necessary to complete the burning may be as little as ¼ cwt per ton of bricks compared with 4 cwt per ton of bricks where no combustible element exists in the clay.[27]

Before this technical advance brickmakers, including those on the Medway, had been insulated from competition in local markets, including London, by transport costs. Bricks were of low value in proportion to their weight and bulk which made carriage over long distances uneconomic, especially to areas where there were local producers. The cheapness of production by the new methods wiped away this advantage, and during the 1890s Fletton bricks were offered for sale in the south east of the country cheaper than locally made bricks despite a 100 mile train journey.[28]

Geological limits on the size of the firms in the area made the introduction of labour saving brick making machinery or fuel saving Hoffman kilns uneconomic.

Evidence of the effects of the building slump and new competition is found in 1890 during a dispute between the brick makers and the bargemen over higher freights. The brickmakers said

> 'Having regard to the depressed state of the brick trade, the fall in price, and competition from Foreign and Midland counties bricks, it was considered that there was no justification for any advance in the freights.'[29]

The dispute resulted in a lock out of 5,000 brick workers. In March 1890, the *Chatham News* reported that

> 'Peterborough bricks are now being sent into London in large quantities. The masters assert that owing to keen competition with which they have to contend from machine made bricks they are positively unable to give the bargemen what they ask for—viz. a rise of 10% to 20% on old freights. At present there are in stock in the Kent, Essex and Middlesex areas supplying the London markets with stock bricks, 210 million as compared with 150 million at this time last year—that is to say an increase in stock of 60 million and the greatest increase is in the Kent district.'[30]

The effect of competition and depression on individual firms is not clear. Obviously many of the small manufacturers could withdraw from the business to concentrate on their other activities such as farming. The Burham Company had its extensive cement and lime works, although these were also vulnerable to the building cycle, to fall back upon. The neighbouring West Kent Gault Brick Co. at Aylesford had practically ceased making bricks by 1889, concentrating on its new cement works,[31] where previously in the 1860s the field had a capacity of about 10 million bricks per year.[32] There was no spate of bankruptcies, although there were two early in the slump in 1887. One was of Harry Burr who had set up at the Friars Brickfield, Aylesford in 1880.[33] Judging from the equipment sold from the site in November 1887, this was a well appointed works with steam washmill and slurry pump, four pug mills and four brick making machines.[34] The other bankruptcy was of Joseph William Chalmers, who carried on business at Upchurch with John Barton.[35]

The firms that survived best were the large ones who were prepared to produce on a large enough scale to overcome high lease and royalty charges and the high cost of installing modern equipment. One firm dominated in size at the end of the nineteenth century, this was Eastwood and Co. Ltd. Eastwoods were long established builders' merchants at Lambeth, who owned their own fleet of barges for the collection of materials from the Medway and Thames. In the 1880s a merger was arranged between Eastwoods and five brickmaking firms: Edward Quilter of Suffolk; Joseph E. Butcher of Frindsbury; Josiah Jackson of Shoebury; Charles Richardson of Vauxhall and John Woods of Singlewell. Joseph Butcher owned brickfields at Rainham and John Woods at Lower Halstow.[36]

Woods' works at Lower Halstow in the 1880s turned out 12½ million bricks per annum from 18 wash backs and 12 hand moulding berths. In 1900 they also took over the small Ten Acres Field, Halstow which had a capacity of 3–4 million bricks per year. At Rainham they took over from Butcher three fields on the site of the present Redlands works, which contained a total of 19 wash backs and 12 hand berths for moulding bricks. About 1900 they also absorbed Leeneys brickfield adjacent to Otterham Quay which had been owned by a Charles Eltham, and which had a capacity of 2½ million bricks per annum from 3 hand berths.[37]

In South Western Road, Strood, R. West, contractor and brickmaker, had established a business in 1861. In 1891 the 'extensive premises' covered 'an area of about three acres, comprising clay pits, kilns, moulding sheds, grinding and pug mills, replete with modern steam-powered machinery capable of producing an immense output of manufactured bricks' including stock bricks supplied by the proprietor 'to the leading contractors and builders within a radius of many miles, and are in well established demand for their superior and reliable qualities'. The works were said to employ 'a large number of hands'.[38]

By 1900 brickmaking on the Medway was in decline. Many of the small, seasonal fields had disappeared in face of competition from the cheaper Fletton bricks. Brickmaking was then left to a greater extent in the hands of the bigger firms. However, the decline was likely to affect more than just employment in the brick works. It would also have lead to a decline in the demand for barges, and also for the products of local engineering works who were dependent to a very large extent upon brickworks in the area for their livelihoods. The problems of the latter industries would have been aggravated by the large quantities of secondhand equipment available from closure sales.

[1] See above 81.

[2] *Chatham News*, 17 December 1864, 3.

[3] Rev. J. H. Leach, '*Memoirs of the Church and Parish of Gillingham*' (1868), quoted by C. S. Leeds, *Chats about Gillingham* (Gillingham, 1906), 28.

[4] Information from Col Dean.

[5] Information from Col Dean.

[6] F. G. Willmott, *Bricks and Brickies* (Privately published, Rainham, 1972), 30, 39.

[7] H. Hobhouse, *Thomas Cubitt, Master Builder* (1971), 312.

[8] Figures taken from the Registrar General, *Census of 1871, Tables of area, houses and inhabitants in 1871*, Division II (Surrey, Kent, Sussex, Hampshire and Berkshire) (1872) and Registrar General, *Census of 1901*, County of Kent, Area Houses and Population (1902).

[9] Willmott, *op. cit.*, 6.

[10] Rochester, *Chatham Journal and Mid Kent Advertizer*, 1 February 1901, 5.

[11] Hobhouse, *op. cit.*, 310, 312, 315, 530.

[12] S. Tallents, *Man and Boy* (1943), 35.

[13] Information from Mr Parker.

[14] W. Coles Finch, *The Foords of Rochester* (Rochester, 1917), 7.

[15] *Chatham News*, 6 April 1889, 4b.

[16] E.C. 47386. Map November 1881.
E.C. 47386. Letter, Cluttons to Church Commission, 7 August 1890.

[17] E.C. 47386. Letter, Cluttons to Church Commission, 1 March 1913.

[18] *Chatham News*, 26 July 1913, 10c.

[19] See above 97.

[20] *Chatham News*, 6 February 1864.

[21] K.A.O. U565 E10 pt. II, Letter Badcock to Darnley, 19 March 1867.

[22] *Ibid*, Letter J. Crosse to Darnley, 9 February 1867.

[23] *Chatham News*, 9 June 1888, 4c.

[24] *Chatham News*, 29 January 1887, 2.

[25] *Chatham News*, 31 March 1888, 4d.

[26] *Chatham News*, 2 March 1892, 5.

[27] B. Butterworth, *Clay Building Bricks*, National Building Studies Bulletin No. I (HMSO 1948), 3–4, 5.

[28] Bowley, *op. cit.*, 69.

[29] *Chatham News*, 22 February 1890, 3.

[30] *Chatham News*, 22 March 1890, 6.

[31] K.A.O. U234 T4. Legal opinion R. Jones Bateman, December 1889.

[32] K.A.O. U234 T4. Letter Rixon and Sons—to Earl of Aylesford, 2 March 1861.

[33] K.A.O. U234 L2. Lease Aylesford to Burr, 28 July 1881.

[34] *Chatham News*, 5 November 1887, 4.

[35] *Chatham News*, 15 January 1887, 4.

[36] Willmott, *op. cit.*, 1–2.

[37] *Ibid*, 25, 26–8, 29.

[38] *Industrial Great Britain*, Part II. (1891), 126b.

CHAPTER VI

Barge and Boat Building 1850–1900

After 1850 a great stimulus to barge building was the expansion of the Portland cement industry. Millions of tons of cement had to be carried from the Medway and Thamesside factories to markets in London and to the London docks. Stumpy barges were popular for this task, having to work up the Thames to higher reaches, and contend with congestion on the river and bridges over it. The barges also serviced the cement industry by bringing on the return trip cargoes of coal, coke from London gasworks such as Fulham or Beckton and staves for barrels. The brick industry flourished over most of the 1850–1900 period, giving work for many 'brickies'. Barges for agricultural and general cargoes were still in demand, as were specialized barges constructed for instance with low sides to facilitate loading with mud dug from the Medway marshes for the cement industry.

The number of vessels registered as belonging to Rochester showed a healthy upward trend to 1881.

NUMBER OF VESSELS REGISTERED AS BELONGING TO ROCHESTER

Sail		*1853*	*1859*	*1865*	*1881*
Below 50	No.	324	370	573	1,007
tons	Tons.	10,091	12,114	19,848	38,159
50–100	No.	62	65	80	103
tons	Tons.	7,745	8,020	9,914	5,540
100–300	No.				14
tons	Tons.				2,433

Taken from H. Rees, *The Medway Towns, Their Settlement, Growth and Economic Development* (London Ph.D. thesis, 1954), 203.

Likewise the number of vessels entering the Port of Rochester in coastal trade appears to reach a peak in the 1880s.

NUMBER OF VESSELS ENTERING THE PORT OF ROCHESTER IN COASTAL TRADE

1877	4,492	1885	4,573
1880	3,835	1888	9,360

From Rees, *op. cit.*, 204.

E. J. March estimated that in the 1880s and 1890s 'more than 100 [barges] a day entered and left the Medway on every tide'.[1] However, not all the barges in use on the Medway would have been built there. Many were constructed on Milton Creek and at Conyer, others on the east coast at such places as Maldon, Essex and Ipswich. Some figures for launchings at Rochester are available.

NUMBER OF VESSELS LAUNCHED AT ROCHESTER 1877–1900

Year	*Number of Ships Launched*	*Tonnage*
1877	23	1,039
1878	20	853
1879	15	633
1880	18	780
1881	14	590
1882	13	591
1900	22	995

Taken from Rees, *op. cit.*, 218.

The average size was just under 50 tons, one favoured by the cement and brick makers.

Apart from barge owners who specialized in the carriage of other firms' produce, most of the cement manufacturers and many of the brickmakers owned their own fleets. William Peters of Wouldham Hall Cement Works, for instance, was reputed in 1881 to have a fleet of 80 barges,[2] while William Lee, Harry Margetts of the West Kent works and Eastwoods all had sizeable fleets. Some of these owners also ran their own barge yards.

The Burham Brick Lime and Cement Co. built barges at Burham named after the seasons and days of the week. These included *Spring*, 1879; *Summer*, 1879; *Autumn*, 1881; *Winter*, 1881; *Monday*, 1882; *Tuesday*, 1882; *Wednesday*, 1885. William Lee and Son of the Lime Dock, Halling built barges at least between 1863 and 1869, when the following were constructed: *Superb*, 1863; *Defiance*, 1865; *Renown*, 1866; *Invicta*, 1867; *Monarch*, 1867; *Swiftsure*, 1867; *Victory*, 1869.[3] Lee's barges were distinctive. Instead of the usual russet-brown sails, Lee's 'stumpy' barges carried black sails with white jibs on bowsprits, with a white rampant horse on the mainsail.[4]

At least two barges were built at Cuxton. In 1861 a racing barge *Agnes* was launched.[5] Then in 1888 it was reported

> 'A barge launch was successfully accomplished on Saturday afternoon last from the barge-building establishment of Messrs. T. and W. Weeks, Cuxton, the foreman of the works Mr J. Weekes superintending her launching upon the bosom of the Medway without a hitch. The event being the leading topic of the village gossip for weeks past, from the fact that the launch from the particular establishment was the first of its kind.'[6]

and in all probability the last.

At least one mud contractor had his own yard. This was Solomon J. Brice of the Point Yard, the Esplanade, Rochester, who at one time owned over 40 barges.[7] The Point Yard, which was essentially a repair yard, was described by Edwin Harris

> 'at the junction of the land wall with the bottom of the Backfields was a picturesque old barge building establishment, with its smithy, its sheds, its long wooden arrangements for steaming the planks, all of which were shaded by the large trees that formerly grew along the river side of the field.'[8]

Here were constructed at least the *Miranda*, 1883; *Santry*, 1899; *Busybody*, 1905 and *G.C.B.*, 1907.[9]

John Woods, brickmaker of Lower Halstow, had a barge yard which was taken over by Eastwoods in 1880. Woods built *Director*, 1863; *Sophia*, 1866; *Fanny*, 1867 and *Father James*, 1878 among others.[10] Eastwoods initially bought barges from Currells of Frindsbury, but around 1889, Ambrose Letley, who had built barges at Lower Upnor,[11] went to Lower Halstow to build barges as foreman shipwright. Before leaving in 1898, Letley built *Grebe*, in 1890; *Gamma*, in 1891 and eight others named after birds. His successor, Archie White, between 1898 and 1901 built *Theta* and eight other barges.[12]

Apart from the above, barge builders were to be found from Queenborough to Aylesford with again the largest concentration in the Medway Towns area. Acorn Wharf continued to be used by several barge makers. E. G. Watson, the sail maker, used to launch from a site near Rochester Bridge till the yard was taken over in 1876 by G. Gill and Sons. George Gill had operated the Medway Patent Slipway at Chatham since 1858[13] and had been involved with George Cheetham in the business of Cheetham, Gill and Co., Canal Shipyard, Frindsbury.[14] The Chatham yard was probably given up in 1900, one of the last barges to be built there being

Centaur in 1899.[15] The Chatham yard was referred to as the lower yard, and Acorn Wharf as the Bridge Yard.

Some idea of the scope of the work undertaken by the Gills can be gained from newspaper reports for the year 1887. The barge *A.B.C.* was built for Ald. Craske for the cement trade on Regents Canal.[16] A barge yacht *Dinah* was launched at Rochester to be used for cruising. This was about half the normal size of a barge at 45 feet long. A barge, *Arthur,* which sank at Gillingham after a collision was raised and taken to the Rochester yard for repair,[17] and a sloop *Emma* grounded at Sheerness was brought to the lower yard for repair.[18] A stack barge *Partridge* was launched from the Bridge yard for Messrs Tuff and Miskin,[19] and a topsail barge *New Trader* from the lower yard for Messrs Woodham and Levy for the London to Rochester hoy trade.[20] A barge made for a customer away from the Medway was the *Maid of the Mill* launched March, 1887 from the Bridge yard for Messrs Marriage and Sons of Colchester for use in the corn trade. This barge was 'fitted with sails and gear complete, made on Messrs Gill's premises'.[21]

Not all the barges launched were for local customers. It is perhaps indicative of the quality of the barges that, for instance, Gills were able to launch in 1892 a stack barge for T. Keeble of Maldon, Essex, an order coming from another barge building area.[22] However, judging from newspaper reports of barge launchings, the barges built at Gills and other yards on the Medway were mostly for local owners. These owners were particularly engaged in the cement and brick trades.

The extent of Gills construction may be gauged from the fact that when the topsail barge *Dinah* was launched from the Bridge yard in 1894 it marked the completion of 51 vessels constructed by the firm on this site.[23] The firm, about 1900, shifted the centre of their activities to their Central yard at Frindsbury.[24]

Among other firms to use the Acorn yard were Wakely Bros. the farmers, brickmakers and barge owners of Rainham, Ambrose Letley and A. J. Knight.[25] Another who operated from the area was Mr F. Sollitt who was in business in the 1890s.[26]

Another well-known barge builder at Rochester was William Higham. He had a barge building yard, 'with many tarred sheds and workshops' at Blue Boar Hard, where the barges were built on a wharf 'two or three feet above the ordinary high tide' and 'when a barge did drop into the river, it gave a mighty splash'. He was reputed by Edwin Harris to have built and launched over one hundred barges.[27] He was active throughout the 1890s, launching at least four barges in 1890 alone.[28]

The oldest barge building firm, Curels, remained in production till at least the mid 1890s. They were operating by then two yards, one adjoining the 'Railway Tavern' in Canal Road,[29] the other next to the Phoenix Cement Works where all the repairing work was 'promptly and efficiently despatched'.[30] George Curel Jnr according to Rochard had in 1894 'for a considerable period—had both yards in full work'. He went on to describe the firm

> 'Barge building constituted a staple branch of business and this is carried on at the principal yard (Canal Road), a very frequent occurrence being for two or three new barges to be lying off the wharf to receive the finishing touches at the hands of the skilled painters and shipwrights, of which a full staff is always employed by the principal, who, by the way, is a practical master of the trade in all its branches. A large stock of sound, well-seasoned English timber is always on hand and to give a vague idea of the magnitude of the work and the size of the spars used, it may be stated that we saw one which measured 3 feet in circumference at the butt, and was 92 feet in length and 2 feet square at the top. Then, too, the sheds, slips and workshops are provided with every requisite, a large number of experienced men are employed, so that orders can at all times be promptly taken in hand and completed without delay. All the hands in the yard appeared to be occupied to the fullest extent, but although exceedingly busy laying down the keel of a new barge, the organizing arrangements of the place are so good that perfect order reigns supreme, and nothing like confusion can be noticed in any department.'[31]

Reports of launchings were frequent in the local papers, includfour in 1891.[32] The Frindsbury yard, however, was relinquished by 1900 when it was taken over by Gills.

At the barge yard in Lower Upnor, vessels were constructed by W. B. Little, and before 1889 by Ambrose Letley.[33] Letley launched at least the *Maid of Kent* and the *City of Rochester* from the yard in 1881.[34]

A new, and not altogether welcome newcomer to the barge building industry arrived on the scene with the setting up of the 'Medway Ship, Barge, Yacht and Boat Building and Repairing Society Ltd' as a co-operative enterprise in May 1892. The venture had apparently been promised work by the Thames Lighterage Co. among other boat owners, quite possibly because the Society would undercut other yards prices by an undertaking to pay a dividend to customers of 40 per cent of profits if bills were paid within 31 days of receipt.[35] A set of blocks for barge repair were under construction at the Tower Works below Fort Clarence by January 1893.[36]

> In the half yearly report, August 1894, it was stated 'we were giving our customers faithful work at practically cost prices'.

which resulted in work for the nine months of operations in 1893 of one new barge and three boats built and repaired nineteen barges, three boats, one ketch and one yacht. The

> 'diffidence and reluctance of owners in placing their work with us is rapidly being removed, and increased confidence will tend to secure for our Society a larger share of patronage and support.'

This was to an extent borne out in that in the first six months of 1894 they had launched one barge, nearly built another, and repaired eighteen barges, one schooner, two lighters, two yachts and two boats. They had also managed with the aid of a loan, to build a shed over the building slip and also to build a large boat building shed and workshop.[37] It was also proposed to set up a barge owning co-operative,[38] for which the Society would construct.

The Society continued to prosper up till 1900 by which time they had constructed at least six barges.[39] The chairman's report in that year showed that they had managed to purchase the freehold of the land on which their slipways were built, and obtained an option to purchase an adjoining plot.[40]

The barge building industry continued to prosper as long as there was an expansion of trade on the Medway, accounted for largely by the brick and cement industries. Trade expansion was necessary as the barges were quite durable having lives if kept in good repair of perhaps 40 or 50 years. There was probably something of a replacement market for vessels lost in accidents. Reports of losses appear quite frequently in local newspapers, especially in winter when there were fog or storms. For instance, in 1891 under the headline 'Barge run down in the Medway'

> 'On Friday A.M. at 5.30, the barge "Frindsbury", one of the fleet of the Formby Cement Co., was run down in Chatham Reach by the screwsteamer "Kron Princesse Victoria". The barge was at the time lying at anchor, and the master and mate escaped a watery grave by climbing into the rigging.'[41]

There was however usually something of a second hand market in barges which would have limited replacement or new buying. Sometimes numbers of barges were put up for sale as in April 1857 when 'six well built fast Sailing Barges with all stores and tackle' were offered,[42] or in early 1872 when 18 barges and 2 schooners were offered,[43] other times single vessels as in December 1868, when Mr Lilley of Strood was giving up the barge business and selling his 'fast sailing barge, *Ebenezer*, 65 tons.'[44]

A few other craft apart from barges were built on the river. Although the fishery was in decline between 1850 and 1900 some dobles and bawleys were still being built. One well-known builder was Alexander Ring of Canal Road. Strood,[45] whose business passed into the hands of E. Lemmon in 1864.[46] Lemmon made dobles, which at a price of £1 per foot were a cheap boat. He also made the dinghies most favoured by the 'hufflers' at Rochester Bridge.[47] Bawleys were built by George Gill at Rochester. The *Iverna* was built about 1893 for £140, and remains the last working bawley on the Medway.[48] Curel's yard at Canal Road also repaired, if not built, fishing boats. [49]

Allied to fishing boats in size of vessel was yacht making. Alexander Ring was known to have built one such boat the 'fine schooner yacht *Santa Caterina*.'[50] One firm that specialized in yacht and dinghy building was Messrs. Abbot Bros, boat builders and ship chandlers, near Ship Pier, Rochester.[51] The firm started about 1870 with a capital of £100,[52] and had built up a considerable reputation locally and farther afield for the construction of racing yachts.[53] Among the less conventional boats built by the firm were in 1887 a 21 foot steam yacht 'built entirely of oak with mahogany and polished brass fittings'[54] and in 1892

> 'a yacht that is likely to revolutionize the style of building of yachts . . . what is known as double hulled'.

This catamaran had an overall length of 46 feet, each hull having a beam of 7 feet.[55]

However, the firm had little opportunity to exploit their new design. The brothers Abbott appeared to have little business ability, failed to keep proper accounts, and appeared to have been insolvent for some time before bankruptcy in Autumn 1892.[56]

A small number of steam-driven vessels were built on the Medway, but the river was really completely insignificant as far as this type of construction was concerned. The Thames on the other hand was by far the most important centre of steamboat construction in southern England.[57] Those that were built included the *Queen of the Isles* 65 tons, a wooden boat of 111 feet, constructed in 1853, and the *North Kent* 46 tons, also a wooden boat of 94 feet, launched in 1863. Both were said to have been built at Rochester for the Woolwich Steam Packet Company.[58] The constructor was probably E. W. Gill who also built three boats for the Medway Steam Packet Company which ran services to Sheerness and Southend.

These included the paddle steamer *City of Rochester*,[59] 73 tons, of 123 feet and 40 n.h.p. built in 1849. The *Alma*, 69 tons built in 1855 and the *Lady of Lorne*, 59 tons built in 1871. All were launched from the lower yard.[60]

Gill also launched from the lower yard in 1872 a screw steam yacht, the *Elaine* of 25 tons and 16 n.h.p. which was modelled on the *Lady of Lorne*.[61]

These other craft were really of little significance to boat building on the Medway. The main business and speciality of the Medway was barge building and repairing which was sufficient to keep the yards on the river busy until 1900.

[1] E. J. March, *Spritsail Barges of the Thames and Medway* (Newton Abbott, 1970), 87.

[2] R. Marsh, *The Conservancy of the River Medway 1881–1969* (Rochester, 1971), 21.

[3] *Barge Yards Around Rochester*, Mss., Rochester Museum.

[4] F. G. Carr, *Sailing Barges* (1951), 180.

[5] *Barge Yards Around Rochester*, MSS.

[6] *Chatham News*, 5 May 1888, 2a.

[7] March, *op. cit.*, 77.

[8] E. Harris, *The Riverside* (Rochester, 1930), 28.

[9] *Barge Yards Around Rochester*.

[10] J. Willmott, *Bricks and Brickies* (Rainham, 1972), 2.

[11] *Barge Yards Around Rochester*.

[12] Willmott, *op. cit.*, 4–6.

[13] Harris, *op. cit.*, 4, 15.

[14] *Post Office Directory of the Six Home Counties* (1852), 1147.

[15] *Barge Yards Around Rochester*.

[16] *Chatham News*, 18 June 1887, 8c.

[17] *Ibid*, 2 April 1887, 5c.

[18] *Ibid*, 9 April 1887, 8.

[19] *Ibid*, 27 August 1887, 5.

[20] *Ibid*, 12 November 1887, 5a.

[21] *Ibid*, 10 March 1887, 2.

[22] *Chatham News*, 26 November 1892, 5.

[23] *Chatham News*, 25 August 1894, 2.

[24] *Rochester and Chatham Journal*, 10 May 1901, 5.

[25] *Barge Yards Around Rochester*, MSS.

[26] *Chatham News*, 8 March 1890.

[27] Harris, *op. cit.*, 8, 9.

[28] *Chatham News*, 8 November 1890, 4.

[29] Harris, *op. cit.*, 40.

[30] J. Rochard, *Historical Chatham and Rochester* (Chatham, 1894), 48.

[31] Rochard, *op. cit.*, 48.

[32] *Chatham News*, 10 January 1891, 6; 11 April 1891, 5; 1 August 1891, 6.

[33] *Barge Yards Around Rochester*.

[34] *Kent Life*, Vol. 7, No. 3, March 1968, 35.

[35] *Chatham News*, 14 May 1892, 5.

[36] *Ibid*, 21 January 1893, 5.
[37] *Chatham News*, 21 January 1893, 5.
[38] *Ibid*, 11 August 1894, 8.
[39] *Rochester and Chatham Journal*, 9 June 1900, 1a.
[40] *Rochester and Chatham Journal*, 23 June 1900, 3.
[41] *Chatham News*, 24 January 1891, 5a.
[42] *Maidstone and Kentish Journal*, 18 April 1857.
[43] *Chatham News*, 23 March 1872, 4.
[44] *Ibid*, 19 December 1868, 1.
[45] *Chatham News*, 3 April 1909.
[46] *Ibid*, 25 June 1864, 3.
[47] *Kent Life*, February 1970, 55.
[48] March, *op. cit.*, 20.
[49] *Chatham News*, 21 May 1892.
[50] *Ibid*, 3 April 1909.
[51] *Ibid*, 9 June 1888, 4c.
[52] *Ibid*, 26 November 1892, 2.
[53] *Ibid*, 18 June 1887, 8.
[54] *Ibid*, 12 November 1887, 2b.
[55] *Chatham News*, 9 April 1892, 2.
[56] *Ibid*, 9 April 1892, 2.
[57] See P. Banbury, *Shipbuilders of the Thames and Medway* (Newton Abbott, 1971).
[58] F. Burtt, *Steamers of the Thames and Medway* (1949), 40.
[59] W. Coles Finch, *The Foords at Rochester* (Rochester, 1917), 8.
[60] Burtt, *op. cit.*, 114–15.
[61] *Chatham News*, 13 May 1872, 3.

CHAPTER VII

Engineering 1850–1900

Engineering and founding grew up in the second half of the nineteenth century as essentially a Medway Towns industry. The industry grew to fulfil the growing demand for machinery for the expanding cement and brick industries, with their need for steam engines and boilers, grinding machines, pumps and other paraphernalia. The large number of barges needed to carry away the cement and bricks added a demand for gear such as windlasses, pumps and steering gear. The Medway Towns were also the centre of an agricultural area, and as a result were a centre for the repair and manufacture of farm implements and machinery of all types. The Medway Towns were also a centre of expanding population and therefore also satisfied demand for domestic goods such as fire grates and kitchen ranges, gates and locks, and for retailers equipment such as beer engines.

One firm came to dominate in size of output and number of employees, Aveling and Porter of Strood. This firm also came nearest to having a specialized product in producing steam locomotives, particularly steam rollers. There were apart from Aveling and Porter a number of smaller firms who manufactured a whole range of products.

Quite a well known firm in Rochester in the 1850s and 1860s was W. and H. Spencelagh founded in 1850.[1] The firm operated the Vulcan Iron Works, Rochester, occupying a site near Bath Hard on the corner of William Street, where there

> 'was a large private house, next to the railway arches, used as a shop for ironmongery for some years by Spencelagh, together with the railway arch adjoining as a forge and engineering workshop.'[2]

The firm also had premises at 16 and 159 High Street, Chatham and traded as the 'Medway Iron and Brass works'. In 1858 they advertised themselves as

> 'Ironmongers, Iron and Brass founders, Engineers, Millwrights, machinists and smiths, lathe and tool makers, Coppersmiths and

gas engineers, Steam boilers and tanks, Iron roofing, Locksmiths and Bell hangers, Agricultural implements repaired.'[3]

In 1859 the Medway Works were described as being near the Ship Hotel, Rochester, and 'Balconies and Palisading' had been added to the list of products.[4] By 1865 the firm's Medway Waterside Ironworks were described as

> 'Government Contractors, Manufacturers of High and Low Pressure, Vertical and Horizontal Steam Engines, also Pumping and Donkey Engines, Double and Single Purchase Crabs, Ship Windlasses and Pumps and Steam Engines and Machinery of every description made and repaired.'

Spencelagh's were also 'Wholesale and Furnishing Ironmongers, Stove and Range Manufacturers' as well as manufacturers of an 'Improved Beer Engine'.[5] The firm had obviously expanded its range of activities to meet the needs of the local brick, cement and barge building industries. The firm as Spencelagh and Archer[6] continued in business until the early 1880s, when the iron works were taken over by the firm of Taylor and Neate, and the rest of the business by J. Carter Linay.

The firm of Taylor and Neate concentrated on equipment for the brick, cement and barge industries. One of the partners Percy Neate, had at one time an interest in the Borstal Cement Works,[7] the other, W. R. Taylor was an engineer. They were particularly known for their cement grinding mills. The introduction of these mills was heralded by the following headline in September 1887, 'A New Departure in the Manufacture of Cement', and the following report,

> 'a test of cement grinding machinery took place at Messrs. Booth's Cement Works (Borstal), where Messrs. Taylor and Neate gave a display of their new patent grinding mill which produced good, well ground and perfectly good cement which was turned out of the mill at a rate of almost exactly four tons per hour, with an expenditure of only 46 actual horsepower, or about one third of that required to perform the same work with mill stones.'

This type of mill was extremely important as can be seen by the list of those attending the demonstration which included

> Messrs. Barron of Rainham Cement Works, Cheffins of Gillingham, Cooper of Wexford, Hollick of Greenwich, Courtney of Sittingbourne, Skelsey of Hull, and Johnson of Greenhithe, and representatives of Coles and Shadbolt of Uxbridge, Sussex Port-

> land Cement Company of Newhaven, Wouldham Cement Company and Formby's.[8]

and was favoured by the Thames and Medway cement manufacturers.

The firm also made slurry pumps—another speciality—from at least 1882 onwards in sizes from 5 to 12 inch diameter, one, two or three throw. A 12-inch set weighed as much as 8 tons. These pumps could be used for pumping brick or cement slurry, especially needed as deposits near the works were gradually exhausted and supplies of clay or chalk needed to be transported on occasion several miles. An alternative use was for sewage disposal.[9] Washmills were also supplied by the firm.[10]

Taylor and Neate's equipment was used by many of the cement manufacturers and particularly by the brick makers of Kent including Smeed Dean and Co. Ltd, of Sittingbourne who were the biggest brickmakers in England with an output of one million bricks per week, and by Wills and Packham of Sittingbourne.[11] This success led to a contract with the Hennigsdorf Brickworks near Berlin in June 1887 for

> 'a complete plant of their slurry washing and pumping machinery with about four miles of pipe. The contract is noteworthy as being for the first machinery of this kind yet erected in Germany and also for the fact that the slurry has to be pumped a much longer distance than has yet been attempted either in this country or elsewhere.'[12]

The partnership was dissolved in 1888, W. R. Taylor firstly becoming receiver and manager,[13] then taking over the business and continuing to trade as Taylor and Neate. Under Taylor the firm continued to make much the same sort of equipment at the works which were described in 1888 as a collection 'of numerous wooden buildings adjoining the [Cook's] wharf'.[14]

Advertised in 1888 was a range of barge equipment including: the iron mast case, which had 'now become a necessity on all modern barges', offered at £8.10s.od.;[15] the Double Purchase Windlass in sizes from 26 inch wheel at £6.15.od. to a 34-inch wheel at £10.os.od.;[16] deck capstans in pairs, two sizes 18 or 24 inches high;[17] a new steering gear designed and patented by the firm (Patent 9280).[18]

A complete range of Taylor's products was on display at the 1890 Agricultural Show at Rochester. The *Chatham News* reported

> 'Among their exhibits we notice a set of their improved mill for grinding cement clinker and a somewhat lighter set for grinding

cement slurry; one patent compound rotary shifter for cement etc; one set each of 8 inch and 5 inch, three throw slurry pumps, one set of their patent screw steering for barges, which is now being adopted by most of the principal barge builders in this district, also several of their improved mast cases, deck capstans, windlasses, leeboard and main brail crabs, screw conveyors, elevator chains, deep well pumps, pug mills, Dean's patent brick moulds, Bower's patent solid corner brick moulds, and adjustable bed plates and the Cyclone Pulverizer. This pulverizer is a novel one, it will pulverize to an inpalpable powder the lightest to the hardest substances, by means of two opposite currents of air moving at great velocity causing attrition of the substances to be ground.'[19]

In 1891 Taylor had taken out patents for improvements in cement manufacture with a view to utilizing the CO^2 gas driven off in firing which accounted for a 40 per cent weight loss. The gas was to be liquified and used for aerated mineral waters, freezing purposes, fire extinguishers, and medical purposes.[20] The process was demonstrated in February 1893. Taylor had produced a cement slurry brick making machine which corrugated and perforated the bricks for better burning. Bricks were used in the semi-continuous kilns. After drying the bricks were put in a retort and the gas driven off by surplus kiln heat at 900°F., after which it would be collected for purification. The *Chatham News* stressed the importance of innovation as cement was the biggest employer in the area, and engineering the second biggest. In this case it was hoped to cheapen cement by selling byproducts.[21]

The firm continued in business till after 1900. Meanwhile the other former partner in Taylor and Neate, Percy J. Neate, set up as an engineer a short distance from the Medway Iron Works at St Margaret's Bank, Rochester. He too displayed at the 1890 Agricultural Show, the main item being

'the set of three throw pumps, pumping 10,000 gallons per hour. The speciality about this is the self-contained frame, which is made to bear a much heavier pressure than usual. Another set of three throw pumps is built especially for South African use, the lightness of its frame affording special facilities for export. Mr Neate has taken out a patent for an improved sifter of cement, which supercedes the original patent . . . The sifter has removable internal protecting screens and is rendered especially amenable to the processes of cleaning and repairing. There was also on view a new mill stone of great durability, which is

> Adair's patent. A new pattern of composite steel mast case for 100 ton barges, a pair of reversible lee board capstans and a set of windlass gear completed the list at the stand.'[22]

The firm most noted for cement grinding mills, apart from Taylor and Neate, was Collis and Stace of Strood. The firm originated about 1777 as retail ironmongers with premises in Strood High Street.[23] In 1865 the firm was still described as

> 'Joseph Collis; Wholesale and Retail, General and Furnishing Ironmonger; Stove, Grate and Kitchen Range Manufacturer; Zinc, Iron and Tin Plate Worker; General Smith, Locksmith, Gasfitter and Bellhanger.'[24]

However, by the 1870s Stace had been taken into partnership and its products considerably changed. It also appears that the firm had taken over the Pelican Foundry vacated by a Mr H. Hollingsworth in 1868.[25] In the early 1870s the firm described itself as

> 'Ironmongers, Iron and Brass Founders, Engineers and Millwrights—Manufacturers of improved and other Ranges, Horizontal Engines, Wash Mills, Drying Plates, Bone Crushing Mills, Barge Pumps and Windlasses, Iron Grates, Hurdles, etc.'[26]

The firm had expanded to meet the new demands from the brick and cement industries. The foundry also supplied structural ironwork for buildings and bridges, lavatory cysterns,[27] together with manhole covers.[28]

The firm's important cement machinery was exhibited at the 1890 Rochester Agricultural Show, when among their implements

> 'the most noteworthy of which are an ordinary cement grinding mill, a new cement grinding mill, and a wharf crane for loading barges.'[29]

The Pelican Yard and Foundry, which incidentally had access to the Medway via a wharf with cranes to receive scrap iron and coal from barges in Janes Creek,[30] were acquired by Aveling and Porter in 1895.[31] Cement machinery manufacturing was then added to the range of activity of Avelings. Collis and Stace retained a small amount of foundry work by making closed-fire ranges, reverting for the main branch of their business to being wholesale and retail ironmongers, and agricultural machinery merchants.[32]

There were other small engineering and iron works in the Medway Towns before 1900. The bigger of these, about which little information is forthcoming, included Cuthbert Russell of the

Equipment Produced by Collis and Stace for the Cement and Brick Industries

Centre of the picture features the grinding mill which was popular with the cement manufacturers of the Thames and Medway. The machine on the right is a double throw slurry pump and on the left a small hand crane and burr stones.

The original of the picture is in the hands of Joseph Collis Ltd., Rochester, and was taken on the occasion of the 1890 Agricultural Show at Rochester.

Eagle Iron Works, Strood. He was operating in the 1860s when he was a stockist for a wide range of agricultural equipment.[33] He was described in 1865 as

> 'Engineer, millwright, iron and brass founder, manufacturer of High and Low Pressure Steam Engines and Boilers. Steam and Hand Cranes, Pumps, and every description of Machinery. Casting of every description. Patentee and manufacturer of improved brickmaking machinery. Agricultural implement maker.'[34]

Here was another engineer profiting from the brickmaking boom. There is no information to indicate the scale of his business.

Another firm about which there is no information was the Frindsbury Ironworks carried on until his death in 1888 by Mr W. R. Curel.[35] In the same year Messrs Hall and Sons established an engineering and iron founding works beside Blue Boar Creek.[36]

With a great deal of machinery in use in the area at least one consulting engineer, James Butchart, of Canal Road, Strood, was at work. His business was established about 1881. He had a store and warehouses which stretched to wharfage on the river, where he stocked engine packings, mountings, boiler tubes, belts and other components. He acted as a consulting engineer with special reference to steam engines and boilers, which he inspected and prepared estimates for all kinds of machinery.[37]

Below this level of operation were businesses which were basically ironmongers. This class can be represented by such people as Mr George Udal of 174 High Street, Chatham, who manufactured 'in the most well-equipped workshops, stoves and ranges'.[38]

Finally among the small producers, there was an agricultural implement maker who was little more than a blacksmith. This was Joseph Simmonds of Rainham, who in 1851 was described as a 'Wheelwright Smith, master employing five men and one boy'.[39] He displayed his products at the Royal Agricultural Society Show at Canterbury in 1860 when his speciality seems to have been ploughs. He won a third prize of £10 out of twenty-four entrants for 'ploughs on the turn-wrest principle, or otherwise adapted to turn the furrow slice according to the Kentish system of ploughing'.[40] He would have been unable to compete with the big agricultural implement makers such as Ransomes, and is later in business as a blacksmith.

By far the most outstanding firm in the Medway Towns was Aveling and Porter. The firm started in 1850 when Thomas Aveling who farmed at Ruckinge set up a small engineering works at Rochester to repair agricultural machinery.[41] Aveling began experimenting with steam cultivation in 1852,[42]and by 1856 had produced a steam plough which was sufficiently successful for Kent farmers to present him with an award of 300 guineas.[43] However, his first great achievement was when Aveling became the 'Father of the Traction Engine' by making portable engines self-propelling.[44] The first machines adapted in 1858 were Clayton and Shuttleworth portables, which were chain-driven to a cog inside the offside rear wheel.[45] This spared horses the killing labour of dragging engines from site to site, although they were still required for steerage purposes.[46]

In 1858 Thomas Aveling was established in premises at 24 High Street, Rochester with workshops 27 Edwards Yard, near the Corporation Street end of Free School Lane, and a foundry at Strood, later the Invicta Works.[47] These did not give him the manufacturing resources required when he designed his own traction engine in 1859. This '8 h.p. Patent Locomotive engine', which incorporated pilot wheel steerage, was built for him by Clayton and Shuttleworth at Lincoln.[48]

Thomas Aveling's 1860 Catalogue shows that he was an agent for a wide range of other manufacturers' goods. He supplied Clayton, Shuttleworth and Co's portable steam engines and horizontal fixed steam engines, and Clayton threshing tackle and straw elevators. He was agent for Fowlers steam ploughing sets, Burgess and Kay's reaping and mowing machines, Ransome and Sims of Ipswich crushing mills, Richmond and Chandlers chaff cutters among other items. Aveling only appears to have manufactured the Beverley Roller (self-cleansing clod crushers), iron land rollers with balanced shafts, circular saw benches, and a portable grinding mill. However, pride of place was given to 'Aveling's Patent Locomotive Steam Thrashing Train' consisting of an Aveling 8 h.p. engine, thrashing machine and patent straw carrier, with a total cost of £475,[49] and presumably all made by Clayton and Shuttleworth.

It is thought that the main works were established in Strood in 1861 to enable Aveling to commence construction of his own engines,[50] 34 being built in 1861,[51] according to Hughes. To provide extra capital for the firm Richard Porter was taken into partnership in 1862, the firm becoming Aveling and Porter.[52] At this time Thomas Aveling was taking out patents for improvements to steam locomotives. These included in 1859 devices for varying chain tension and for disengaging the drive to allow a traction engine to be used as a stationary engine; pilot wheel steering 1860; the steam jacketed cylinder 1861 and two speed gearing in 1863.[53]

The appearance of Aveling's traction engines excited the local people, the engines being generally approved as this report of 1862 shows.

> 'On Tuesday last a trial of one of Aveling's patent road locomotive engines was made in Rochester in the presence of several foreigners of distinction. The engine manufactured by Messrs. Aveling and Porter was one of 10 h.p. and had behind it a load of 21 tons on five carriages, which it took up Star Hill, along the New Road to the Station, returning through the narrow streets of Chatham with the greatest facility. We understood that the visitors were much astonished at the rate with which the heavy mass moved up and down hill and the manner in which the long train turned the sharp corners of the streets. They appeared to be well pleased and altogether favourably impressed with the application of steam to common roads.'[54]

Foreign visitors must have been adequately impressed for orders to be forthcoming. In November 1862 there appeared a report of an engine being exported to Prussia.[55] By 1863 when 97 engines had been completed,[56] orders from Australia were received, an engine built for Queensland being tested on Frindsbury Hill with a 45-ton load in May 1864.[57] The engines built for Australia were much heavier than those for Britain, designed to haul six waggons each of five or six tons laden weight, and costing £530. In South Australia they reduced the cost of transport from Port Royal to the Yudanamutana copper mines from £10 to £2 per ton.[58]

However steam traction engines were not welcomed everywhere. There was strong opposition to locomotives from those using horse-drawn vehicles for the transportation of goods,[59] and also from Highway Boards who complained of the damage done to road surfaces by these heavy machines. At the end of 1863 Aveling opposed a proposal by Faversham Highway Board to ban steam locomotives. His case rested mainly on the financial saving to be gained from the use of steam power over horse power. He used the example of moving 12 tons over 10 miles with wagons returning empty. The capital cost involved he reckoned would be:

STEAMPOWER		HORSEPOWER	
One 10 h.p. locomotive engine	£420	4 teams of horses and harness	£560
Three waggons (6 inch wheels) at £45	£135	Four waggons at £30	£120
Total for steam power	£555	Total for horsepower	£680

Working expenses per day	£	s.	d.
Coal 8 cwt at 1/-	0	8	0
Oil etc.		2	0
Engine Driver		5	0
Steersman		3	0
1 Labourer		2	6
Wear and tear at 20% p.a. for 250 days		9	0
Interest on capital for one day at 3% p.a. for 250 days		2	3
Total....	£1	11	9

	£	s.	d.
Keep of 4 teams stabling and wages of 8 men per day	2	12	0
Waggon grease			3
Wear and tear at 10% p.a. for 250 days		5	5
Interest on capital for one day 3% p.a. for 250 days		2	9
Total....	£3	0	5

Cost by horsepower would be 6d. per ton mile.

Cost by steampower would be 3d. per ton mile.

The total saving on such journeys over 250 days would be in the order of £358.[60]

However, opposition was strong enough to ensure the passing of the Locomotive Act, 1865 which stipulated a speed limit of 2 m.p.h. in town areas and 4 m.p.h. in the country. Three men were also required, two to work the engine, one to walk in front with a red flag. On top of this was a clause designed to make the use of road locomotives virtually impossible by stating that locomotives should be constructed to consume their own smoke.[61] Despite these hindrances Avelings continued to develop locomotives.

One of Aveling's most important inventions was the horn plate, an extension of the fire box to carry the crank shaft and gearing. This gear had previously been carried on brackets rivetted or bolted to the top of the boiler. The stress involved had an obvious effect on the boiler which was now avoided. The first to carry this invention also incorporated a geared drive instead of chain drive, with one gear ratio of 15:1, and also modern front wheel steering. This engine was exhibited at the Royal Show, Oxford in 1870.[62]

There were several variants of the road locomotive made at Strood. Among these was the 'Steam Sapper', introduced in 1871 as a light military engine. It was used by the British army for hauling guns and supplies, and for pumping water to camps. It was also purchased by the governments of France, Italy and Russia.[63] A number of Aveling and Porter engines were to see service in the Boer War.[64] Another variant was the locomotive fitted with a crane. One such locomotive was awarded a gold medal at the Paris Exhibition of 1889.

> 'The engine is an improvement on their road locomotive crane engine which was awarded a special gold medal by The Royal Agricultural Society in 1876, and a gold medal by the Minister of Agriculture at the Paris Universal Exhibition of 1878. By this arrangement the crane is made to slew at right angles.'

The firm also showed a small engine fitted with an electric generator at Paris.[65] This engine was basically a single cylinder locomotive with a platform erected over the front of the hornplates carrying the generator gear which was driven off a cast iron gear ring bolted to the flywheel spokes.[66] Some of these machines with generators were used by the army.[67] However, Avelings only built two of the 411 showman's engines built in Britain. Leaders in this field were Burrells of Thetford, Fowler of Leeds and William Foster of Lincoln.[68]

Another important variant was the steam ploughing engine, of which 328 were made[69] before production ceased in 1921 in face of the motor tractor. Aveling's plough sets closely followed Fowler's designs, using the two engine system, with rope drums slung under the boilers with the front wheels protruding to allow a wide angle forward for working the rope, although Aveling engines were usually smaller than Fowler's.[70] In this specialized branch of locomotive building there were few competitors, notably Burrells, Fowler, J. and H. MacLaren of Leeds and John Allen and Sons of

Oxford.[71] These firms had developed like Avelings at market centres, although there was a greater number of locomotive and implement makers in the southern and eastern arable farming areas of England. Some such as Ransomes of Ipswich and Bentalls of Maldon, Essex remained purely implement manufacturers.

Aveling plough sets were being exhibited in the late 1860s. A gold medal was won at Ailly sur Noyes (Somme), France in June 1868,[72] and success in plough trials held at Beauvais in 1869 lead to orders from Napoleon III. However, after 1881 and after the depression in arable farming set in, home sales were very few, what production there was being for export to developing countries. Avelings ploughs were exported to South Africa, Australia, France, Greece, and Egypt.[73] Apart from the depression sluggish home sales were due to plough sets being very durable with a very small replacement market. Plough sets were also very expensive, and, in a country of small farmers, beyond the reach of all except the larger farmers and estate owners. This led steam ploughing to become mainly a contractor's business. Avelings made not only the engines, but a full range of ploughs, harrows, water carts and sleeping vans which made up a plough set.[74]

However, the variant of the locomotive and the product for which Aveling and Porter were most famed was the steam roller. Of the 12,700 steam engines constructed by Aveling and Porter, 8,600 were steam rollers.[75] A large number of components, for example cylinder blocks and gearing, were common to all machines constructed.[76] Aveling's first attempt at a steam-roller did not appear until 1866 and this was only a converted steam traction engine with rolls instead of wheels.[77] The idea was not original, steam rollers already having been built in France and England.[78] But

> 'just when he first turned his thoughts to road rolling will never be known, but taking produce to market from his farm at Ruckinge, bordering on Romney Marsh, and travelling to and from his foundry and engineering works he had established at Rochester, the parlous condition of the roads must constantly have been forcibly impressed upon him.'[79]

The difficulties Thomas Aveling suffered with the authorities over damage caused by his locomotives must have also brought the problem of road surfaces before him.

Aveling's first real roller came into being in 1867 when he placed the two steering wheels together to form a roller which left no unrolled space between the driving wheels. In the 1867 engine Aveling 'turned the engine around' so that the driving wheels were at the front, after the designs of F. W. Batho of Birmingham of 1863, which probably resulted from some connection with Batho. The 1867 machine secured for Aveling his first order for a steam roller from a city corporation, Liverpool. It weighed 30 tons and was of 12 h.p. Aveling had about twenty enquiries to purchase rollers in 1867 which prompted him to set up a production line.[80]

The 30-ton roller proved too heavy, crushing instead of interlocking the road materials. The result was a lighter machine of 15 tons. By the end of 1869 ten had even been exported,[81] these machines going to France, India and including the first two rollers to work in the U.S.A.[82] The testing of one of these machines for America was reported in September 1868.

> 'Yesterday morning the powers of one of Messrs. Aveling and Porter's powerful and ponderous steam road rollers were exhibited by Mr Aveling on Military Road, Chatham. . . . The roller acted admirably, rolling new-made parts of the road smooth very quickly. . . . This machine has been constructed for use in the city of Philadelphia.'[83]

New lighter and more manoeuvrable models followed after 1871, and although they had the disadvantage of conical front rolls which skidded, the machines won the Order of Franz Joseph at the Vienna Universal Exhibition in 1873. Improvements and innovations continued to take place, including the introduction of a compound engine, which was more efficient, on the 1881 models. With the improvements in efficiency orders increased and the factory had to be retooled.[84]

Another variant was the tram engine. The first was constructed in 1866 for a chalk quarry at Grays, Essex. This was a 10 h.p. locomotive, with a single cylinder three-shaft engine driving 4-foot diameter wheels, and carrying 350 gallons of water in two tanks. Engines could be made to almost any gauge, usually 3 feet 6 inches, being really traction engines with flanged wheels and buffers at each end. These engines had an advantage over railway type locomotives in that their flywheels could be used to drive machinery when they were not in use as locomotives.[85] These engines found a market locally in the chalk quarries and brickworks. Among the local users were the Nine Elms Cement Works, Cliffe who purchased six engines before 1900, Lees Lime Works who purchased five, and Wouldham Hall Cement Works which also purchased six.[86] Engines were also sold farther afield to customers in Vancouver and Russia.[87] One of these tram engines was described by visiting *Public Health Engineer* journalists in 1900.

> 'This locomotive, which weighs 12 tons, has wrought steel brackets flanged upwards and outwards above the fire box thus giving ample room for the gear, which is all within the brackets, the eccentrics being next to them, and the valve faces of the castings contain the high and low pressure cylinder, being thus very accessible. The engine has a short wheelbase, all four wheels coupled, driven by a large steel idle wheel on the offside. She is capable of a speed of 16 m.p.h. and ascends a gradient of 1 in 15 with a load of 30 tons with ease, passing also with smoothness the sharpest of curves. We think there should be a large field of use for this engine in quarries, docks and for contractors and municipal yard use, as the cost is only two thirds that of the ordinary contractors whilst there is the advantage not possessed by the ordinary locomotive of an engine with accessible crank-shaft and flywheel for belt driving of pumps, of stone breakers, circular saws and other fixed machines.'[88]

After the works of Collis and Stace were acquired in 1895 the range of products included cement making machinery, while the foundry acquired was used for castings for the firm's range of concrete mixers, for casting lampposts and girders.[89]

Expansion was rapid after the establishment of the main works at Strood in 1861. Henry Smetham observed in 1899 that

> 'the increase in the works has hitherto been to double their size about every six years.'[90]

By 1872 the firm employed 400 men at the Invicta Works. Extensions were made in 1886, and by purchase of Collis and Stace in 1895, the new site being known as the North End Works. At this time 750 men were employed.[91] It was in this year that Aveling and Porter was incorporated as a Limited Company with a capital of £110,000.[92] In 1897 the factory was described by Edwin Harris as

> 'the largest works in the district . . . the number of hands employed by this firm is close upon 1,000.'[93]

At this time, apart from producing 'one large road engine per day', the firm was distributing more than £70,000 per year in wages in the Medway Towns, the sum

> 'is not merely collected and turned over in the place, but is drawn from abroad and distant parts of Great Britain.'

The amount of fixed capital in the enterprise must have been considerable, but the figure is not available. However, Smetham estimated in 1899 that there were alone '220 lathes and other tools'. The works were conveniently situated to receive supplies of coal and iron from vessels alongside its own wharves, and also had their own sidings from the South Eastern Railway.[94]

Although Aveling and Porter were the largest local works, and the largest manufacturers of steam rollers in the world, their overall size when measured in terms of employment was small compared with some other leading engine and agricultural machinery manufacturers. Marshalls of Gainsborough appeared to be the leading firm, starting up in 1856, employed 500 by 1870, 2,000 by 1892 and 5,000 by 1913. Clayton and Shuttleworth who in 1842 established a general ironfounding business in Lincoln employed 1,400 in 1885 and 2,300 in 1907. Ransomes of Ipswich grew from 1,500 employed in the 1880s to 2,500 in 1911. Rustons of Lincoln, founded in 1857, employed 5,000 in 1911.[95]

A complete description of these important works in 1900 was reprinted from the *Public Health Engineer* in *The Rochester Journal*

> 'On approaching the works . . . a long level frontage of windows, which pertain to the office, stores and drawing office and pattern shop faces one. On entering the main office door, which is appropriately surmounted by the circular smoke box door, with the brass horse and motto "Invicta" from the engine which took a prize at the Canterbury Show of the R.A.S.E. in 1861 or London International 1862 we first enter the time-keepers office, where all the tickets and time sheets of the men employed on these works are dealt with. Adjacent to this is the prime cost office, where every item of expenditure whether it be labour, material or stores is charged to its proper account; here also rates of work are fixed. On this same floor is the forwarding and receiving department for light goods arriving or leaving by railway vans, or which require to be sent by passenger train. This last was a common practice in the earlier days of traction engine building, when, from immature design and defective materials, breakdowns were a frequent occurrence necessitating immediate despatch of spare parts by passenger train to prevent serious loss. By the modern system of improved design, ample surface of working parts, and materials as perfect as money can buy, the need for sending off spare parts by passenger train has practically ceased.
>
> On this same floor, further on, is a mess room seating about 300 men, with a suitable hot plate for warming their food. The remainder of the men live sufficiently near to the works to go home for their meals.
>
> On the first floor are the offices of Mr T. L. Aveling,[96] and

Mr Porter, the managing directors. The back windows of all these offices and of the manager's office next to the drawing office command a view into the works, particularly over the turning shop, in which modern American automatic machinery is rapidly replacing the older forms of lathes and shaping and planing machines. Many of these machines are worked three each by one man or lad; all that he has to do is to see that the bar of steel or gun metal as the case may be, is properly fixed and the right speed given to the tool. The machine itself continues the work and turns faced bolts, pins, studs, bushes, or the various parts of the brass mountings of the boiler with scarcely any need for an attendant's skill or attention.

Further in we came to the crank shaft lathes, slotting machines, key seating and cylinder boring machines, the lathe so arranged that when the casting to be bored is for a double cylinder or compound engine, both faces can be bored at one time.

Grouped all near together and within the reach of powerful cranes are the big wheel lathes, five in number; these lathes are always occupied in turning up the edges of wheels, whilst simultaneously boring out the centres and facing up the bosses. Even the steel plate built up wheels are thus treated to ensure their running with absolute truth; whilst in the cast iron wheels of steam rollers it is necessary that one edge be turned because it is invariable practice of Messrs Aveling and Porter Ltd, to cast the rollers wider by some 3in or 4in than their intended ultimate width so that the completed wheel shall be entirely free from cinder, slag, or blow holes or scab; the extra width afterwards turned off forms what is called the head, into which dirt rises as the molten metal flows into the mould, leaving the wheel or roller absolutely solid and free from defects of any kind.

Cylinders are similarly cast with big heads on, but a more recent practice has been to cast them with saddle (which is afterwards planed to fit the boiler) upwards, because in this way there is less risk of air blow holes in the cored passages of the steam chest.

After leaving the turning shop, we next visited the erecting shop. Here, under the present regime of Mr T. L. Aveling, the engines remain but a few days, for all the parts, boiler, cylinder and mountings come from the boiler and stores so complete and so accurately machined that, as the foreman of the boiler shop observed "You have merely to throw the cylinder on the top and drop the boiler on the wheels and away she steams."

Thence to the smithy, which is replete with all necessary

appliances, including a specially designed turbine actuated stamping press, which stamps at one beat the joints of eccentric rods and slide valve rods, stop valve levers etc. with such accuracy that a subsequent cut on the milling machine of 1.32nd of an inch suffices to clean up completely.

In the boiler shop are plate bending rolls, plate edge planing machines, multiple drills, vertical standard radial drilling and screw staying machines, hydraulic flanging machines.'[97]

These hydraulic presses to turn the flanges were introduced in 1893 in an attempt to speed up production to meet demand for rollers. This work had previously been done by men with large hammers.[98]

The report continued
'It is now the practice of Aveling and Porter to hydraulic flange everything which required to be made of curved plates, consequently not merely the fire boxes, tube plates and smoke boxes are so treated, but even the tenders and water tanks, which instead of being mere rough tank work, are now finished in a style equal to that of the boilers, and leaky tenders are a thing of the past.

We next see the hydraulic rivetting plant, which is very complete, both fixed and portable rivetting on Tweddell's system being installed, so that there is hardly a hand driven rivet in a recent Aveling and Porter boiler. The firm adopted hydraulic rivetters in 1872, in consequence of an ill advised strike.

We next visited the No. 1 Foundry, which is a large and lofty building, well lighted and thoroughly water-tight as to roof. Here we were glad to see the same foreman we knew in 1872, Mr George Neave, engaged at the moment of our entry in pouring a roller hind wheel. Already this year, he informed us, nearly 1,000 tons of iron had passed through the foundry.

In the new North End works purchased from Collis and Stace, an equally large foundry exists; this is used for constructional iron work; cement mill machinery and repairs generally. Attached to it is a large machine erecting shop, where large marine engines could, if desired, be built. But for the most part cement machinery and mills were built here. In this part of the works reclamation from the river is taking place by the aid of piles moored below by chains and blocks of concrete and being filled in with foundry refuse, and borings and clinker etc. which accumulates at 60–100 tons per week. Here we saw powerful steam wharf cranes and a very well designed

> and strong tramway engine, constructed on a special system patented by the firm some years ago.'[99]

The large and heavy components were moved around the factory by 'powerful travelling cranes'. Steam hammers were also employed in the works.

> 'The motive power for driving all this network of ingenious appliances, many of which have been specially designed for the particular work, is derived from main engines of about 200 h.p. but there are other smaller engines utilized in various parts of the works for specific uses.'[100]

The firm of Aveling and Porter continued to expand, was extremely well-equipped and presented a picture of prosperity in 1900.

One last business which showed some originality was that of J. Carter Linay which became involved with electrical engineering. Carter Linay took over possession of premises at 119 High Street, Chatham and the Vulcan Iron Works, Rochester from Spencelaghs in 1878.[101] At Chatham he continued the business as a wholesale ironmonger, engineer, iron and brass founder. The premises, site of present day Swears and Wells, had workshops at the rear.[102] In September 1887 Carter Linay was forced to dispose of the Vulcan Iron Works due to the extension of the South Eastern Railway at Rochester, the equipment of the works including lathes, drills and a planing machine being sold.[103]

In 1891 J. Carter Linay was described as a

> 'Contractor to Her Majesties Government, wholesale ironmonger and Iron merchant, manufacturing electrician, smith and stove and range manufacturer, 119 and 225 High Street, Chatham.'

According to the book *Industrial Great Britain* of 1891 the firm was 'one of the most extensive and important undertakings of its kind in the south eastern counties, and one of the principal industrial concerns in Chatham'. The firm was

> 'associated with iron and metal trades, and handicrafts such as smith work, gas and water engineering, and brass founding.'

Carter Linay had developed the business with particular attention to the electrical department. He manufactured ranges and stoves and had been successful in pewterers work, including making improved beer engines and patent extractors. His shop stocked a wide selection of hardware, ironmongery, tools and hearths. At the rear of his premises were 'extensive and perfectly equipped' workshops and facilities for making

> 'electrical appliances, pewter pots, beer engines, and stove ranges and kitcheners and general orders in copper, zinc and tin, locksmithing, gasfitting and bell hanging.'

Carter Linay was especially known for electric bells 'for all domestic purposes' and 'for signalling, for alarm purposes'. He had fitted them in 'a great many public and private establishments'. Carter Linay brought 'electric bell communication up to a state of the highest perfection, great utility and marked economy in cost'. He was 'contractor to H.M. convict prisons, the War Department and the Dockyard, to the Royal Engineers, the Electrical School, Submarine mining etc.' He had fitted at least H.M.S. *Triton* with electrical communication. In 1887 Carter Linay had won a contract for connecting 'cable boxes etc. for submarine mining defences for Madras'. All this needed 'the services of a numerous staff of assistants and experienced workmen'.[104]

Until 1900 the engineering industry showed a great deal of expansion. It had been created to a large degree as a result of demand from the cement, brick and agricultural industries and from local authorities for road building and maintenance and had developed not only to fulfil the local needs but had managed to export its products all over the world. At that date, 1900, the industry was the second most important on the Medway after cement manufacturing.

[1] *Industrial Great Britain*, Part II, (1891), 118.

[2] E. Harris, *The Riverside* (Rochester, 1930), 5.

[3] J. and J. F. Phippen, *A Directory of Rochester, Chatham, Strood and their vicinities* (Rochester, 1858).

[4] *Chatham News*, 15 October 1859.

[5] Simpson's, *Rochester, Chatham, Strood and Brompton Directory* (1865), reverse of 2nd page.

[6] Percy & Co., *Rochester, Chatham, Strood, New and Old Brompton and Gillingham Directory for 1871–2–3*, 48, 50.

[7] Information from Mr Parker.

[8] *Chatham News*, 24 September 1887, 2.

[9] *Ibid*, 7 November 1888, 3; 24 November 1888, 3.

[10] *Ibid*, 5 January 1889, 3c.

[11] *Ibid*, 24 November 1888, 3.

[12] *Chatham News*, 2 July 1887, 8.

[13] *Ibid*, 11 August 1888, 6.

[14] *Ibid*, 12 May 1888, 7c.

[15] *Ibid*, 20 October 1888, 3a.

[16] *Ibid*, 3 November 1888, 3a.

[17] *Ibid*, 27 November 1888, 3.

[18] *Ibid*, 10 November 1888, 7a.
[19] *Chatham News*, 7 June 1890, 5.
[20] *Ibid*, 25 July 1891, 5.
[21] *Chatham News*, 11 February 1893, 6.
[22] *Ibid*, 7 June 1890, 5.
[23] *Medway Chamber of Commerce Journal*, Summer 1972, 6.
[24] *Simpson's op. cit.*, 48a.
[25] *Chatham News*, 7 November 1868. 1.
[26] Percy and Co. *op. cit.*, 124.
[27] *Medway Chamber of Commerce Journal*, *op. cit.*, 6.
[28] Information from Mr Stacy, Managing Director of J. Collis Ltd.
[29] *Chatham News*, 7 June 1890, 5.
[30] *Chatham News*, 21 October 1893, 6.
[31] Information from Aveling Barford.
[32] *Medway Chamber of Commerce Journal*, *op. cit.*, 6.
[33] *Chatham News*, 14 May 1864.
[34] Simpson's *op. cit.*, 49a.
[35] *Chatham News*, 14 July 1888, 5.
[36] Harris, *op. cit.* 8; *Chatham News*, 11 January 1913, 6.
[37] *Industrial Great Britain* *op. cit.*, 125.
[38] J. Rochard, *Historical Chatham and Rochester* (Rochester, 1894), 22.
[39] 1851 Census Enumerators return for the Parish of Rainham.
[40] *Journal of the Royal Agricultural Society of England*, XXI, (1860), 511.
[41] W. Hughes, *A Century of Traction Engines* (1959), 58.
[42] H. Bonnett, *Saga of the Steam Plough* (1965), 68.
[43] Hughes, *op. cit.*, 58.
[44] Aveling Barford Ltd., *A Hundred Years of Road Rollers* (Grantham, 1965), 5.
[45] Hughes, *op. cit.*, 58.
[46] R. Clark, *The Development of the English Traction Engine* (Norwich, 1960), 17.
[47] Information from Aveling Barford.
[48] Hughes, *op. cit.*, 59.
[49] Thomas Aveling 1860 Catalogue.
[50] Information from Aveling Barford.
[51] Hughes, *op. cit.*, 63.
[52] Information from A veling Barford.
[53] *Hundred Years of Road Rollers*, *op. cit.*, 6.
[54] *Chatham News*, 30 August 1862.
[55] *Ibid*, 15 November 1862.
[56] Hughes, *op. cit.*,
[57] *Chatham News*, 28 May 1864.
[58] Hughes, *op. cit.*, 65, 67.
[59] E. West, 'Traction Engines in Kent', *Kent Life* (April 1965), 42.
[60] *Chatham News*, 2 January 1864.
[61] West, *op. cit.*, 43.
[62] Clark, *op. cit.*, 36; Hughes, *op. cit.*, 120.
[63] Hughes, *op. cit.*, 123–5.
[64] Clark, *op. cit.*, 91.
[65] *Chatham News*, 5 October 1889, 8.
[66] Clark, *op. cit.*, 75.
[67] Hughes, *op. cit.*, 179.
[68] H. Bonnett, *Discovering Traction Engines* (Tring, 1969), 15.
[69] Bonnett, *op. cit.*, (1965), 71.

[70] Bonnett, *op. cit.*, (1965), 68–9.
[71] Bonnett, *op. cit.*, (1969), 20.
[72] *Chatham News*, 20 June 1868, 4.
[73] Bonnett, *op. cit.*, (1965), 63, 71.
[74] Information from Aveling Barford.
[75] Bonnett, *op. cit.*, (1969), 14.
[76] Clark, *op. cit.*, 114.
[77] Information from Aveling Barford.
[78] Clark, *op. cit.*, 162.
[79] *Hundred Years of Road Rollers*, *op. cit.*, 5.
[80] *Hundred Years of Road Rollers*, *op. cit.*, 8, 10, 12.
[81] Clark, *op. cit.*, 169.
[82] *Hundred Years of Road Rollers*, *op. cit.*, 10.
[83] *Chatham News*, 19 September 1868, 4.
[84] *Hundred Years of Road Rollers*, *op. cit.*, 12, 18, 20.
[85] Clark, *op. cit.*, 193.
[86] B. Stoyel and R. Kidner, *Cement Railways of Kent* (Lingfield, 1973), 62, 76, 81.
[87] Clark, *op. cit.*, 352.
[88] *Chatham News*, 9 June 1900, 5.
[89] Information from Aveling Barford.
[90] H. Smetham, *A History of Strood* (Strood, 1899), 350.
[91] Information from Aveling Barford.
[92] Aveling-Barford Ltd., *The Origin and Development of Aveling Barford Ltd.* (Grantham, 1952), 40.
[93] E. Harris, *A Trip up the Medway* (Rochester, 1897), 1.
[94] Smetham, *op. cit.*, 350.
[95] S. B. Saul, 'The Market and the Development of the Mechanical Engineering Industries in Britain, 1860–1914', *Economic History Review*, 2nd Series, XX, No. I, April 1967, 118–19.
[96] Thomas Aveling died in March 1882, to by succeeded as a partner in the firm by Thomas Lake Aveling, his son. *Maidstone and Kentish Journal*, 9 March 1882, 2.
[97] *Rochester, Chatham and Gillingham Journal*, 9 June 1900, 5.
[98] *Hundred Years of Road Road Rollers*, *op. cit.*, 20.
[99] *Rochester, Chatham and Gillingham Journal*, 9 June 1900, 5.
[100] Rochard, *op. cit.*, 47.
[101] *Industrial Great Britain*, *op. cit.*, 118.
[102] F. Sanders, *A Business History of Chatham High Street*, (MSS Chatham Library, 1961), I, 118.
[103] *Chatham News*, 17 September 1887, 4.
[104] *Industrial Great Britain*, *op. cit.*, 118–19.

CHAPTER VIII

Naval and Military Influence 1850–1900

Apart from the concentration of cement works, engineering factories and barge building yards in the Medway Towns area, the other great influence which added to the predominance of the Towns in the area was the extension of Chatham Dockyard. Certain problems had arisen for the dockyard since the Napoleonic era. J. Presnail said in his work on Chatham that

> 'In the meantime ships of war continued to increase in length and draught of water, and became liable to injury by grounding at low water in places where ships of lighter draught had been able to float at all tides. The river had silted up locally, notably in Sovereign Reach, and rendered certain places no longer safe as mooring ground for larger vessels.
>
> The introduction of steam, involving further lengthening of ships, demanding greater depth of water, and the getting in or out of machinery—an operation attended with great difficulty and risk in an open river—rendered it each year more and more difficult to carry on the work of the yard with safety, speed and economy.'

In 1855, St Mary's Island of 173 acres was purchased for extensions to the dockyard, work on developing the area commencing in 1862. The design of the extension consisting of three large basins—a repairing basin, a factory basin, and a fitting out basin—was settled in 1864.[1] Each basin was to have four graving docks connected to it.[2]

Much of the construction work on the extension was done with convict labour. A convict prison for 1,200 was built on what later was the site of the R.N. Barracks,[3] where the convicts were housed between 1854 and 1898. In 1865 a brickfield covering 21 acres was constructed on St Mary's Island where the convicts manufactured the brick requirements for the extension, which became more necessary with the closing of the Woolwich yard in 1869 and the transference of its plant and machinery to Chatham.[4]

In January 1871 the Repairing Basin was completed. The basin covered 21 acres, was 1,320 feet long and 700 feet wide. The Fitting out Basin had an area of 28 acres and the Factory Basin about 20 acres. The three basins replaced St Mary's Creek in dividing the Island from the land. Also involved in the works was the making up of the whole of the ground for the extensions by an average of 8 feet, and the provision of hydraulic capstans, steam sheers and cranes and pumps to drain the docks.[5]

The extensions were completed in 1885. Presnail commented

> 'It was a great engineering feat to convert this tract of amphibious ground, half land, half water, gradually from a state of chaotic desolation, into a vast, regulated establishment which after twenty years of labour and an expenditure of £3 million was completed . . . bringing the line of wharfage of Chatham Dockyard to 10,000 feet, and an embankment of 4,500 feet in length, enclosing a total area of 500 acres.'[6]

The extension had added 380 acres to the existing 97 acres of the yard.[7]

The type of ship built in the dockyard was changing. On 23 December 1863 the first iron ship built in Chatham, the screw battleship *Achilles*, 9,820 tons was launched. Battleships up to 14,900 tons such as the *Victorious* and *Illustrious*, launched in 1895 and 1896 respectively, were built.[8] With the extensions and bigger ships being built at Chatham employment in the dockyard rose. The number of established hands had fallen slightly from 1,778 in 1855–7 to 1,735 in 1860. By 1875 the numbers had risen to 1,330 established hands and 2,170 hired hands,[9] reaching about 5,000 in 1909.[10]

The expansion of the dockyard is reflected by the developments in building in Lower Gillingham and the Luton area of Chatham where the increased numbers of employees had to find accommodation. Many new streets of working men's terraced houses appeared during the expansion, producing a demand for millions of locally made bricks.

Along with the increased activity in the dockyard, and with the continued naval presence, there was a continuing military influence in Chatham. There were regiments of Royal Marines, infantry and artillery stationed at Chatham. However, the main regiment in the area was the Royal Engineers. They were strengthened in 1856 when the Woolwich depot was abolished and moved to Brompton with 20 officers and 500 recruits of the Royal Sappers and Miners.[11] In 1865 land at Wouldham was acquired for use in connection which pontoon bridging exercises.[12]

Between 1887 and 1905 the Royal Engineers provided coastal defences based upon the Brennan Torpedo. The weapon was used by the Submarine Mining Service of the Royal Engineers, and training was conducted at the School of Military Engineering. Additional employment was created by the production of the Brennan torpedo at Chatham. The War Department initially set up a factory in buildings in front of St Mary's Barracks, the factory working at full capacity to meet War Department demand. In 1896 a new factory was built in the Submarine Mining Enclosure, to the east of Gillingham Pier, on a site now occupied by Novadel Ltd. Louis Brennan himself was superintendent of the factory from 1887 to 1896 after which he was head of the design branch until 1906.[13]

Apart from in housing, and in employment in the various War Department establishments, the naval and military presence had other economic and social effects. Chatham, more than Rochester, catered for the soldiers, sailors and dockyard workers. This was noticeable in the number of public houses and beer shops to be found in such areas as the Brook, and the continued prosperity of brewing in the area. Retailing catered for military needs with such businesses as army bootmakers like J. Turner of 75 High Street, Old Brompton[14] or army outfitters. In 1891 Rix and Co., Ironmongers and Upholsterers, High Street, New Brompton, mentioned particularly the militarymen and officers of the area among their clientel, while Owen J. Carter, Wholesale and Family Wine Merchant, supplied the Royal Engineers and Royal Marine messes.[15] The officers must also have provided a demand for mess waiters and domestics of all kinds.

The maintenance of the numerous War Department establishments in the area must have provided considerable work. The War Department usually put out contracts to tender from builders. For instance in 1860 tenders were sought for the repair of the sea wall at Sheerness,[16] Foords, the contractors of Acorn Wharf, Rochester, Rose Street, Sheerness and 32 Stangate, Lambeth[17] found much of their work in triennal contracts for the upkeep of War Department buildings in the Medway Towns and also at Grain, Gravesend, Maidstone, Woolwich and Shoeburyness. They constructed the officers' quarters at the Royal Marine barracks, Chatham, and had a hand in the dockyard extensions of St Mary's Island. They acquired the lease of Allington Quarries to provide ragstone for the latter work, and had earlier acquired Upnor brickfield to supply bricks for military contracts. These activities were in addition to Foords civil work which included constructing the approaches to Rochester road bridge, constructing Rochester

Esplanade and considerable domestic construction. Repair work was also carried out for the Ecclesiastical Commission and private residents.[18] Describing Acorn Wharf in its heyday Edwin Harris said

> 'It was a busy place. Approaching the wharf one heard the hum of circular saws, and the planing machines at the steam saw mills, and saw the planks as they left the machines right across the road.'

The site was later occupied by the Gas Company stores. Also at the wharf were offices, painters and glaziers shops, a stone mason's shed and a double blacksmiths forge.[19]

Another firm to benefit from the maintenance needs of the military was W. and S. Scott, Timber and Slate Merchants and Importers, Steam Saw Mills, High Street, Chatham. This business founded in 1862, covered two acres of land by the Medway with 'excellent wharfage', including buildings for a sawmill, moulding department, and joinery works, 'all splendidly equipped with the best modern machinery'. Scotts were government contractors and in 1891 held

> 'a three year contract for the supply of materials and labour to the whole of the War Department buildings in the area, besides holding other contracts with the naval and military establishments in the locality.'[20]

While the dockyard at Chatham remained the biggest single employer of labour in the Medway Towns area, and considerably influenced the area, the dockyard was the only source of employment in any numbers at Sheerness. Sheerness was also a minor seaside resort. Samuel Bagshaw had said in 1847 that its beach was 'remarkably clean' making Sheerness 'during the summer months a favourite resort for seabathing'. It had then an 'elegant hotel' and a steam boat connection with London.[21] Items in the Sheerness newspapers mentioned the popularity of Sheerness as a resort in the 1870s. In 1875 the new suburb of Sheerness-on-Sea claimed the largest salt water bath in England, with an area of 11,250 sq. feet in which visitors could bathe at any hour of the day, and had a large ladies' bath under construction. Other attractions included the beach, and walks on the cliffs.[22] Visitors had the choice of seven dining rooms in Blue Town, as well as numerous public houses. Other attractions included donkey rides, pleasure boats and various stalls and side shows. The Whitsun and August Bank holidays were the peak occasions for excursionists, together with Sheerness Regatta in July, and the month of August for visitors in general.

Visitors arrived by train or excursion trips on the boats of the Medway Steam Packet Co. from the Medway Towns or river boats from London. August Bank Holiday 1875 for instance brought six or seven thousand visitors.[23]

However, one problem which occurred in 1877, according to a letter to the editor of *The Sheerness Times*, was that the beach was becoming too steep and narrow for the bathing machines.[24]

Among other employment noted in 1874 was oyster fishing, supplying shipping, and the corn and seed trade.[25] But the main source of employment remained the dockyard with between 2,000 and 3,000 artisans and mechanics employed in 1866.[26] The figure remained within these limits into the twentieth century,[27] the only expansion to take place here being the construction of an iron-framed boat shed in 1861. The dockyard otherwise remained much as planned by Rennie in 1810,[28] with a basin with 26 feet depth of water, two smaller basins, storehouses, victualling storehouse, mast house, rigging-house, sale loft, smitheries and navy pay office. Barracks, some recently built, could in 1874 house between 1,500 and 2,000, some of whom were required to man the town's fortifications which cost more than £100,000 to construct, extended for one and a half miles, and mounted more than 100 guns.[29] Reference to directories show that a considerable number of retailers and suppliers of services such as builders and plumbers were supported by income generated by the dockyard employees.

[1] J. Presnail, *Chatham, the Story of a Dockyard Town* (Chatham, 1952), 216, 217, 219.

[2] J. G. Grace, *Some Notes on the History of Chatham Dockyard* (1946), 16.

[3] Presnail, *op. cit.*, 219.

[4] Grace, *op. cit.*, 16.

[5] Presnail, *op. cit.*, 217, 226, 227.

[6] Presnail, *op. cit.*, 227.

[7] Grace, *op. cit.*, 16.

[8] *Ibid*, 69, 72.

[9] Presnail, *op. cit.*, 216, 217.

[10] J. Whyman, MSS *A Sketch of Economic Development in Kent*, 40.

[11] *Royal School of Military Engineering 1972 Open Day booklet*, 13.

[12] Presnail, *op. cit.*, 228.

[13] *Louis Brennan CB, Dirigible Torpedo*, Gillingham Public Libraries Local History Series No. 5, Part 1 (1973), 7–8.

[14] Simpson's, *Rochester, Chatham, Strood and Brompton Directory* (1865), 45.

[15] *Industrial Great Britain*, Part II (1891), 119, 121.

[16] *Chatham News*, 7 July 1860.

[17] *Post Office Directory of the Six Home Counties* (1874), 1481.

[18] W. Coles Finch, *The Foords of Rochester* (Rochester, 1917), 6–8.

[19] E. Harris, *The Riverside* (Rochester, 1930), 14.

[20] *Industrial Great Britain, op. cit.*, 120b.

[21] S. Bagshaw, *History, Gazetteer and Directory of the County of Kent*, II, (Sheffield, 1847), 504.

[22] J. Whyman, 'Looking at Life in the Island of Sheppey 100 Years Ago,' *The Sheerness Times and Guardian*, 9 May 1975, 44.

[23] *Ibid*, 16 May 1975, 13.

[24] Sheerness Library, Newspaper Cuttings Book for 1877, 20–2.

[25] *Post Office Directory of the Six Home Counties* (1874), 1477.

[26] *Post Office Directory of Kent* (1866), 1118.

[27] Whyman, *op. cit.*, 40.

[28] P. Banbury, *Shipbuilders of the Thames and Medway* (Newton Abbott, 1971), 105.

[29] *Post Office Directory of the Six Home Counties* (1874), 1477.

CHAPTER IX

Seed Crushing, Brewing and Other Medway Towns Industry, 1850–1900

The Medway Towns became a centre of industries, apart from those already described. This was due to two causes. Firstly the location of the Medway providing easy access by water to the London market, to the Continent, and to sources of raw materials and by rail to inland markets. The railway had first come to the Medway Towns in 1845 when a line was laid from Gravesend to Strood via the old Thames and Medway Canal tunnel, and was linked with the London and Greenwich Railway. The South Eastern Railway opened its link btween Strood and Maidstone, thence via Tonbridge to London or Folkestone, in June 1856. The East Kent Railway, later the London Chatham and Dover Railway, opened from Strood, via Faversham and Canterbury to Dover in 1861, having already gained access to Victoria, London, and built a branch line to Sheerness in 1860.[1] Improved transport facilities enhanced the Towns position as a centre for distribution and as the leading industrial area in Kent. The second cause was the growing demand for certain products such as beer, mineral waters and carriages from the expanding population of the area.

One industry which owed a lot to its location and to transport facilities was oil seed crushing which returned to the Medway Towns in 1879, when the firm of Stewart Bros. and Spencer bought a site in Canal Road, Strood. The firm had started business in 1868 by taking over an old mill, Brambridges Mill, at East Peckham on the failure of Boorman, Wild & Co. They modernized the mill, converting it from a stamper to a box press mill, but, because of expanding business, decided to move to a new, better located site.[2] The Strood site had the advantage that vessels of 2,000 to 3,000 tons burden could come direct to the mills laden with seeds from ports in Egypt, India, North and South Russia and from both sides of the American continent. The mill also had a railway siding linking directly with the South Eastern Railway through which it could distribute its products.[3]

The mill was destroyed by fire on 9 November 1884,[4] a common hazard in the oil seed industry, and the entire works on the west of Canal Road were razed in the 'greatest local conflagration in living memory'.[5] The works were rebuilt, and, while construction was in progress, the firm firstly occupied a small mill at Teston which was later burnt out, then hired two mills in London, before restarting operations at Strood in 1885.[6]

The new mill was equipped with the most 'up to date machinery', and an artesian well was sunk to 750 feet to ensure an abundant supply of pure water. In 1890 a refinery was erected for the purification of cotton seed oil. It was fitted

> 'with every modern appliance and includes a completely fitted laboratory which is under the supervision of resourceful and skilful chemists.'[7]

In 1894 it was stated that the oil mills were the largest of their kind in the district with

> 'brands known throughout Britain and in the various foreign markets for their sterling character and uniformly reliable quality.'

It was

> 'an important and useful industry, which, whilst furnishing employment for many skilled workmen, also exercises a most beneficial effect on the agriculture of the home counties and the general trade of the Medway ports.'[8]

The firm's products for agriculture were exhibited at the Show held at Rochester in June 1890, and included

> 'linseed cakes of guaranteed purity, cotton cakes, rape cakes and the Thomas Phosphate Powder, which is said to be the cheapest and most lasting phosphatic manure.'[9]

Cattle cake was in demand to feed the increasing number of cattle kept in the country which rose from 4,993,000 in 1867 to 5,912,000 in 1880 and 6,805,000 in 1900.[10] The increase in numbers was due to the greater demand for meat products including good quality home produced beef with rising real wages especially after 1873. There was also a buoyant market for liquid milk.[11] Kent would only have produced a small market for cattle cake, the number of animals being kept in the county being relatively few, 63,087 in 1868 rising to only 77,037 in 1898. Commenting on the figure in 1899, Sir Charles Whitehead said

> 'Of the increase in cattle it would be expected that dairy cattle would form a large portion, although Kent is by no means a

> dairy county. Accordingly, the number of cows and heifers in milk show a difference of 6,257, the figures being 26,919 in 1868 and 33,176 in 1898.[12]

Of dairying in general he said

> 'Herds of dairy cattle are kept in various parts, especially near London in the district between Gravesend and Bromley, and near the large seaside towns. In the Isle of Thanet there are several herds of very useful cows near Margate, Ramsgate, Broadstairs and Westgate for supplying milk and cream to visitors; also round Folkestone and Dover, Tunbridge Wells and Sevenoaks. Comparatively little milk is sent to London. Butter is not a speciality of the county.'[13]

The bulk of the market for cattle cake must have been outside the county.

The cattle cake was made from the residue after oil had been extracted from cotton seed, rape seed or linseed by means of hydraulic presses. Refined cotton seed oil from the mill was used largely as a substitute for Olive Oil for the table for salads and for cooking.

> In 1894 the most recent addition to the mill was a soap factory, 'established for the production of a novelty in soap making, a pure vegetable oil-soap, possessing remarkable detergent qualities, the unpleasant associations attaching to the use of animal fats being avoided.'

The soap was apparently not made by any other soap maker in Britain, and was gaining a market with wool-scourers, launderers and dyers. Besides having the latest equipment in the line of crushing mills and hydraulic presses, there were other conveniences such as a coopering plant, and stores extending to the river for loading barges at their own wharf.[14] The refined cotton seed oil was mostly exported to the continent where it was chiefly used in the manufacture of margarine. By 1899 the firm was employing about 200 people and the machinery in the factory was run day and night from Monday morning till Saturday evening. The property now covered about four acres on either side of Canal Road, connected by a bridge between buildings. The firm also had a large mill and office in the City of London.[15]

In 1899 the five partners in the firm, Messrs Halley Stewart, Ebenezer Stewart, Percy Stewart, Reginald Stewart and Knowles Spencer first of all suffered a serious setback in April when fire destroyed the refinery, soap and bleaching rooms together with machinery valued at £10,000 (although not many jobs were lost).[16]

Then they merged the firm with the new British Oil and Cake Mills Ltd,[17] The British Oil and Cake Mills merger dates from July 1899 when seventeen of the leading firms in oil and cake manufacturing and oil refining amalgamated, in an industry of generally small units. The company aimed to take advantage of an expanding market for cattle cake, for linseed oil for paint, varnish, soaps, oil and floor cloth, and cotton seed oil for soap and edible purposes, by having 28 mills and 12 refineries with a capacity of 500,000 tons of seed per year, more than half the total importation of seed, under its control. The combine had an issued capital of £1,750,000 and looked forward to a dividend of 8 per cent which was not immediately achieved.[18]

Stewart Bros. And Spencer's Oil Seed Mills, Canal Road, Strood.

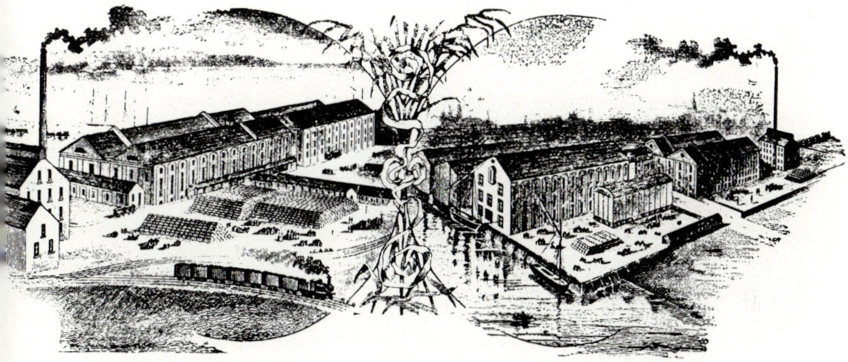

from an illustration in H. Smetham, *History of Strood* (1899)

It was in 1899 that the works first produced compound cattle cakes. In these the contents of the cake were mixed to ensure a more balanced feed.[19] Smetham claimed at that time that the works were producing '1,000 tons per week of its various manufactures' which were distributed by rail and water.[20]

The oil mill owed its existence to its location in relation to its sources of raw materials and markets and the availability of transport facilities. Its future was ensured as part of a large combination, which would mean its continuation as an important source of employment.

One other oil seed crushing business was operated by Mr W. J. Mackay as the 'Kent Cattle Food and Spice Company', Brompton Mills, Mill Road, New Brompton. He also was trying to profit from the demand for cattle feed, producing 'Prize winner' cattle spice and fattening meal and all varieties of compounded meals. The Mills which were housed in a three storey double fronted building with engine house and chimney shaft at the rear,[21] were partially destroyed by fire at the end of October 1895 when damage exceeding £1,500 was sustained.[22] Soon after this event the business was transferred to Maidstone.[23]

Strood Dock 1906

Used by Stewart Bros. and Spencer to import oil seed

The trade in alcoholic drinks continued mainly on the basis of a growing market in the Lower Medway Area itself with its expanded dockyard, and expanding cement and brick industries. Distilling did not prosper. The distillery of Richard Winch and Son at St Margaret Banks, Rochester, finally closed in 1890, when the utensils of the trade including '40 spirit vats holding from 60 to 30 gallons each' were sold.[24] Locally, it is probable that gin made at Maidstone distillery was more in favour.[25]

Beer brewing continued to prosper, the number of publicans in Rochester and Chatham increasing from 138 in 1831 to 195 in 1871.[26] However, certain changes took place which were consistent with trends nationally. Firstly, there was the decline of the small brewer/retailer and the concentration of production of beer in the hands of bigger breweries, a process largely resulting from the economies of scale resulting from the employment of greater capital.[27] The bigger brewers not only had an advantage over price but they could also produce a beer with less variation of quality between brews.[28] After 1850 brewing in the Medway Towns was slowly concentrated into the hands of five brewers. Probably the last of the publican brewers to disappear in the Medway Towns was T. Francis of the 'Bee Hive', Henry Street, Chatham. He had advertised 'Home Brewed Ales—Families supplied in small casks with real Home Brewed Ales' since at least 1860.[29] In 1881 this free beer house was put up for sale when it was suggested that the small brewery at the rear with its equipment of

> 'coppers, mash tuns, malt mill, coolers and all necessary plant for a small trade . . . could at very little cost be converted into a mineral water factory.'[30]

Conversion to ginger beer factories would appear to have been the fate of many small breweries.

A second change to affect the area was increased competition from industrial brewers such as Guinness, Allsopp, Bass and Worthington. With the growth of the railways their bottle beers were sold on a national scale at competitive prices.[13] In 1892 the range of bottled beers from outside the Medway Towns offered by R. J. Passby of High Street, Chatham, included those from Bass and Co., Guinness of Dublin, Shepherd Neame, Fremlins, Combe and Co. of London, Allsopps and Whitbreads.[32] With railway and water transport facilities an area of growing population like the Medway Towns was not neglected by brewers, especially when bearing in mind that average annual consumption of beer per head had risen from under 20 gallons in 1850 to 30 or more between 1875 and 1900.[33] Several stores and depots for the distribution of beer were set up in the area. In the 1880s Messrs Truman, Hanbury, Buxton and Co., Black Eagle Brewery, Spitalfields had a depot at Chatham. Alfred Barnard noted in 1889 that the brewery had

> 'At Chatham, . . . a wharf and an extensive store; the central depot for the large trade done by the firm in that neighbourhood.

Their own sailing barge '*Black Eagle*' makes two voyages to Chatham every week loaded with beer.'[34]

It would appear that Simmonds of Reading Brewery also had a depot at Chatham.[35] Jude, Hanbury and Co. of Wateringbury had a depot at London Wharf, High Street, Chatham and advertised weekly in the 1890s.[36] Fremlins of Maidstone were little represented through public houses in the Medway Towns,[37] but had a branch at Eastgate, Rochester whence pale ale in casks and bottles was widely marketed.[38] Yet another competitor from nearby was Shepherd Neame of Faversham.[39]

Thirdly, most of the beer and public houses were tied in by 1900. This was due to the restrictions placed on the issue of licenses after 1869, and the need of bigger beer brewers for reliable exclusive outlets. As beer was a perishable commodity this would give an accurate measure of demand, and stop over brewing.[40] By 1851 Bests brewery already controlled 90 freehold and leasehold beer or public houses and rented four more.[41] Some houses were acquired by breweries from outside the Medway Towns adding to competition and limiting outlets for local brewers. The Medway Brewery, Maidstone under Mr A. F. Style particularly followed a policy of acquisition in the Lower Medway area. Some of his acquired houses included: the 'Walnut Tree', Eccles, leased in 1866;[42] the 'Three Mariners', Rainham, leased March 1868;[43] the 'Man of Kent', Luton Lane, Chatham, bought for £250 in September 1874;[44] the purchase for £2,000 of the 'Foresters Arms', Wouldham, in December 1883;[45] and the lease of the 'Jolly Gardeners', Lower Rainham, in October 1896, a house next door but one to the 'Three Mariners'.[46] The position of the Medway Brewery was considerably strengthened by its merger with E. Winch of Chatham in March 1899, making the new firm Style and Winch Ltd,[47] the dominant brewery in the Maidstone and Lower Medway areas. Apart from local and Kent brewers, at least one London brewer took a house at Chatham, Meux and Co. of Horse Shoe Brewery, Tottenham Court Road, leased the 'Navy Arms', Chatham in 1887, almost certainly cashing in on the naval and dockyard trade.[48]

Of the five breweries to survive till the end of the century the biggest was Bests, Chatham. The family gave up personal involvement in the brewery in 1851 when it was leased to Edward Winch at a rental of £5,375 per annum.[49] Winch eventually bought the brewery for £150,000 in December 1894,[50] only to merge with Medway brewery in 1899. Soon after the brewery at Chatham was closed in line with company policy to concentrate all production at Maidstone.[51]

Another brewery survived until after 1900 in Chatham. This one, set up by James Hulkes, previously a brewer at St Margaret's Banks, Rochester, stood on the site of Featherstones at Commodore Wharf, High Street. According to Edwin Harris, the brewery had an extensive wharf, formerly a coal wharf, stables, brewhouse and stores. On the opposite side of the High Street is a castellated building which was the water works for the brewery.[52] By 1877 the brewery, renamed the 'Lion Brewery', had been bought by Charles Arcoll and Co.,[53] who continued to brew until after 1900.

Troy Town brewery in Victoria Street, Rochester, another long standing establishment survived past 1900. Under Tomlyn Shepherd the brewery was modernized about 1860 after which he traded (in 1861) as the Troy Town Steam Brewery.[54] After 1865 the brewery changed hands several times between the Woodhams and Levy families before becoming a private limited company in 1895 as Woodhams and Co. Ltd.[55]

Budden and Biggs Brewery circa 1900.

(by courtesy of Rochester Museum)

The fourth brewery, Biggs Brewery, was situated in Strood and would appear to date from the 1850s. An advertisement appeared in 1859 for 'Strood Steam Ale Brewery, Strood, Jonathan Biggs Brewer of XXX, XX and X Ales'.[56] The firm became Biggs Bros in the 1870s,[57] and appears to have supplied domestic requirements as well as the trade, as a 'Family Ale and Porter Brewers' advising

'Persons wishing for a supply of our October brewings should forward their name and address to the brewery at once'.[58] In the 1890s the firm became Budden and Biggs Brewery Ltd,[59] and in 1900 moved into a new brewery in High Street, Strood, where they brewed their 'Body Building Beverages'.[60]

The fifth brewery was the Frindsbury Brewery of Mr H. L. Dampier which is described enthusiastically in *Industrial Great Britain* in 1891 in the following terms—

> 'Mr Dampier brings to the scientific process of brewing the results of a ripe experience, acquired, not in a small country brewery having a mere local connection, but in the great and world renowned establishment of Messrs. Bass and Co. of Burton on Trent . . . he may well be expected to produce ales of excellent quality . . . (and the products) are in no way disappointing.'

The brewery itself was a 'commodious structure' well fitted with the 'approved appliances.'

> 'Pure water—a highly important element in brewing—is plentiful, and the greatest care is exercised in the selection of malt and hops, which alone form the constituent ingredients.'

The brewery adjoined chalk cliffs in which caves were used for storage purposes. At the rear of the premises were extensive workshops for repairs to the firm's 'numerous houses' and for repairing casks. Dampier's brews included Quadruple X Ales, Old Stock Ale, Treble and Double X, Stock Ales, Mild Ales, Pale Ales, Bitter Ales, Double and Single Stout and London Porter.[61]

However, brewing in the Medway Towns was overshadowed by two bigger breweries in Maidstone. Firstly, the Medway Brewery established in 1806. The brewery was enlarged and its business expanded particularly under the ownership of Mr A. F. Style who assumed complete control in 1881. This brewery shared similar advantages with its near neighbour, Fremlins, in that its situation was very nearly ideal, being well supplied with spring water, and situated in the middle of a hop and barley growing area. Communications were also good, Maidstone being the hub of the road network giving access to most towns and villages, linked with the South Eastern Railway network, and having water communication to Rochester and London. The breweries also had the advantage of being centrally situated in their operating area.[62] Fremlin Bros were one of the leading brewers of Pale Ale in the south of England, employing 'upwards of 300 hands' in 1891. The radius of the firm's operations was described in *Industrial Great Britain* in the following terms

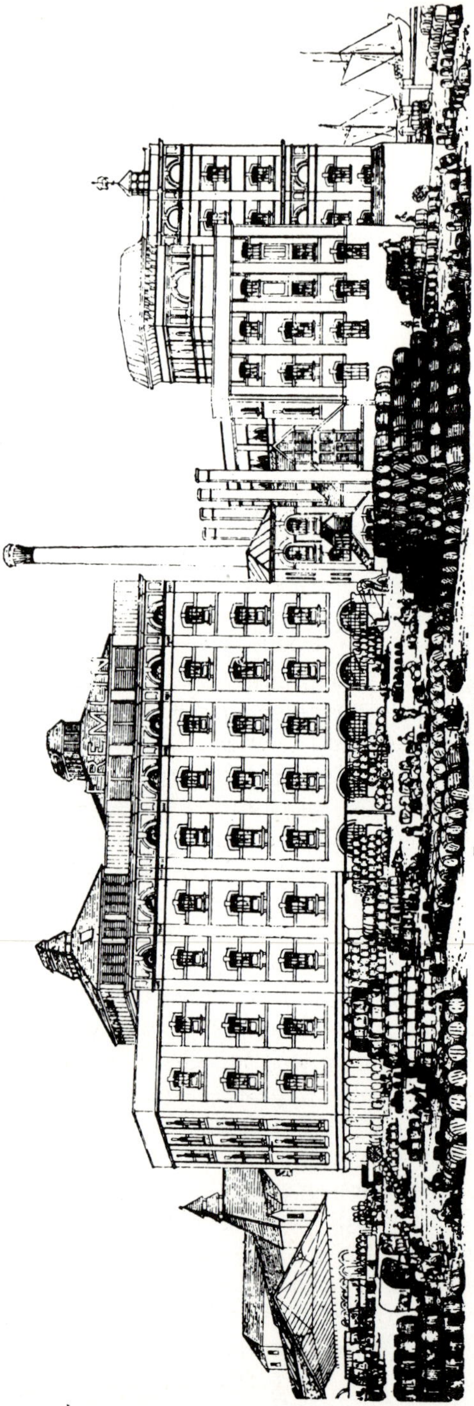

Fremlin Brothers' Brewery, Maidstone.

1890.

> 'it is of great magnitude and widespread influence, and probably no house in the southern brewing trade maintains a more valuable or more substantial connection than the thoroughly representative concern . . . . Fremlin Bros have as perfect a system of delivery as can be conceived and they keep in constant touch with a very large section of the public by means of the many agencies they have established throughout the country'

as far north as Scarborough, and at Buckingham Palace Road S.W.; Camberwell; Brighton; Croydon; Eastbourne; Guildford; Hastings; Eastgate, Rochester; Tunbridge Wells; Woolwich and Tottenham.[63] Between 1886 and 1903 Fremlins supplied Courages Brewery, Shad Thames, London with some 32,000 barrels of pale ale per year, the water at Maidstone being more suitable than London water for this product. The ale was sent by barge from wharf to wharf which cut handling costs.[64] This trade in itself was a solid base for operation. The expansion of these breweries and their greater strength from a wider radius of operations boded ill for the future of brewing in the Medway Towns.

The production of mineral waters developed between 1850 and 1900. Mineral waters became popular in the nineteenth century because they were a healthy drink, the carbon dioxide in them having a germicidal effect, an important consideration in the days of uncertain water supply and cholera. As a result mineral waters were often manufactured by chemists and sold retail through chemists. At least one example of a chemist manufacturer occurred at New Brompton in 1894 where Mr Walter Stokes, chemist and photographer, also carried on manufacture

> 'in works at the rear of the premises. Here an improved modern plant has been put down, power being supplied by a steam engine of 1½ h.p. This plant is capable of turning out a large daily supply of pure sparkling beverages.'[65]

There was a growing domestic market for mineral waters with the rising living standards of the second half of the nineteenth century. However, changing drinking habits were a major factor in encouraging manufacture, either as a result of the temperance movement requiring an alternative to alcoholic drinks, or of it becoming fashionable to dilute or kill the taste of whisky or gin with mineral water. The result of the latter was that some wine and spirits merchants made mineral waters. One example is E. A. Stewart and Co., Bank Chambers, Gillingham, who ran a drinks store, but who in 1894

> 'have now made arrangements for the supply of superior mineral waters of all kinds, of their own manufacture, for which they have a large and extending connection.'[66]

The two most important manufacturers in the Medway Towns were the Phillips and Walter Dove. George Phillips, a clay pipe maker started by making ginger beer for his own consumption in 1848, at John Street, Chatham. The only equipment required would have been a bucket and a few bottles for the gallon or so he made per week.[67] As a result of gifts to friends he gathered together a clientele, and set up in business making his own ginger beer and selling other brands of mineral water. [68]In 1870 he sold the business to his son Benjamin, who moved to larger premises at 25 Jeyes Street, Chatham.[69] After acquiring still larger premises in Frederick Street, he finally moved to Railway Street,[70] where he most likely occupied the 'Invicta' Mineral Water Works, which was occupied between 1877 and 1889 by George Ayres[71] and which were for sale in December 1894 following the bankruptcy of David Whiffen.[72]

Walter Dove started a small business in 1877 operating from the basement of a building adjoining Rochester Post Office. With gradual expansion of his trade Dove moved to bigger premises firstly to a mineral water manufactory formerly carried on by a Mr Ray behind the 'George', High Street, Rochester, and then to a factory at Eastgate, Rochester.[73] At Eastgate the factory was a two storey building with the syruping room on the upper floor, and all the plant on the lower floor including

> 'All latest appliances for washing, bottling and corking . . . driven by steam power.'

Dove had developed a trade in the area with hotels, public houses and shops, and his specialities, Lemonade made with Messina lemons and ginger beer, were used largely 'for blending with spirits'. In the summer hundreds of dozen crates of mineral waters left the works, delivered in his own horse vans.[74]

> In 1894 Mr Dove, due to continued expansion of business 'bought a freehold site under St Margarets Banks where a commodious factory was erected'.[75]

Here he installed a Riley steam bottling machine, and ordered a second due to the rising demand for his drinks which apart from lemonade, ginger beer and soda water included a range of winter drinks; gingerette, pineapple, raspberry, blackcurrant, cloves, spruce and peppermint.[76] Two years later, 1896, the works had to be enlarged to keep pace with demand. About 1,000 dozens were stocked in the summer. The average employment was probably in the region of 20 people.[77]

Here there was obviously an expanding market which was being catered for by a variety of small manufacturers in the Medway Towns area.

Demand for personal and business transport was met in the Medway Towns by a number of carriage, coach and cart builders. Very few details are available for coach makers, who received little attention in the local papers. Among those operating in the area was Mr Butcher of 189 High Street, Rochester, who was 'relinquishing the business' in August 1868, and was putting up for auction his coach maker's stock-in-trade and effects including 30 modern carriages.[78] The landlord of the 'Coachmakers Arms', 335 High Street, Chatham, Mr A. Attwood had a coach works and yard at the rear from at least 1877 to 1890.[79] Perhaps a more important business was that established in Railway Street, Chatham in 1827 by Jesse Catt, Snr, who died January 1860,[80] to be succeeded by his son Jesse Jnr, who enlarged the business by the acquisition of a shoeing forge in 1885. In 1888 the business was taken over by Mr J. B. Martin, a veterinary surgeon and later partner in the Wickham Cement Works, who carried on the business as a coachbuilder, wheelwright and general smith. The premises in Railway Street had showrooms for landaus, phaetons and 'other modern vehicles'. At the rear 'extensive workshops are devoted to the manufacturing departments, and a spacious shoeing forge is also in operation'. The business required the 'services of a numerous staff' for the 'production of the high class vehicles supplied by the firm'.[81] Another builder was Mr Frederick Clark of the Medway Carriage Works, 17 High Street, Chatham. In 1894 it was stated that his works

> 'are well provided with a good stock, and are calculated to meet the requirement in the way of carriage building. The proprietor, who has the advantage of a sound practical knowledge of all branches of the trade, personally superintends the operations of a staff of skilled workmen, thereby securing proper attention to all details. The vehicles turned out by Mr Clark are light yet perfectly strong and all parts are carefully tested before being put together.'

Clark built all kinds of covered and open carriages and trade vehicles.[82]

A new demand arrived late in the century with the growing popularity of the bicycle. The development of specialist component makers in the Midlands allowed small businesses to undertake cycle ment from 1862 wanted '100 good male and cloth finishers and a few good Lancashire Machine Hands' for W. B. Black's Sewing Machine Establishment, Rochester Common.[87]

The best known of the clothing firms was the Axe Brand Machine Sewing Works. This firm was originally established at 305 High Street, Chatham, but moved into the buildings formerly occupied by the Old Union workhouse (built 1726) when the workhouse was removed to new buildings (now All Saints Hospital) in assembly.[83] In 1890 there was one bicycle maker in Rochester, George Robins of St Margarets Banks.[84] By 1898 the number for the Medway Towns had risen to five, including Bember and Lewis, Railway Street, Chatham; Charles Barnes, 41 High Street, Strood; William Hodshon, Bridge approach, High Street, Rochester; Robins and Day, cycle works, 230 and 256 High Street, Rochester; and Henry Taylor, musical instrument dealer and cycle manufacturer of 7 and 9 High Street, Chatham.[85]

The last activity worthy of note in the Medway Towns was the existence of clothing factories. By 1860 the sewing machine was finding wide distribution in Britain, revolutionizing the production of clothing. Factories for the production of clothing with the aid of machinery were set up in the area. Advertisements appeared in the local papers for 'hands for sewing in machine clothing' factories such as that of J. Johnson, Chatham Intra.[86] Another advertise-Magpie Hall Road, Chatham. The move allowed for an expansion of the business, and created new employment possibilities for women, who previously could find few 'respectable' opportunities in Chatham.[88] Some details of the works appeared in a newspaper of November 1872. The Axe Brand Works were then in the hands of Messrs. Cooke, Son and Co., of St Pauls Churchyard, having acquired the Chatham premises from Messrs. Farell and Bousfield who were retiring from the trade. Cooke's had obtained additional space to the south by leasing four houses and turning them into workrooms. They had also improved the ventilation and sanitation, and added a chimney shaft and a 15 h.p. steam engine from Misto, Unity Ironworks, Mile End. The engine was used to drive two cloth cutting machines, propulsion being by means of under-floor bands and shafts. It was proposed in the future to carry the bands to the upper floor to work sewing machines which at that date were still of the treadle variety. The cutting machines were equipped with an endless steel blade travelling at 3,000 feet per minute, and which were first used to cut 20 thicknesses at a time of moleskin for Australian miners' trousers, but which could cut 120 thicknesses of calico. One room was equipped with machines for button holing. 'An army of women at sewing machines turned out 6,000 garments per week.'[89] The actual scale of employment is not clear, but a report of the works day out July 1889 stated 'over 100 female employees of the Axe Brand Works' were involved.[90]

The scale of employment in the sewing machine works was far greater than the direct employment produced by the breweries, ginger beer works or carriage makers, and although the bulk of the work was for women, must have been a valuable asset to the area.

[1] C. F. Dendy Marshall, *History of the Southern Railway* (Revised by R. W. Kidner, reprinted 1968), 287–8, 296, 326–30.

[2] H. W. Brace, *A History of Seed Crushing in Great Britain* (1960), 153.

[3] H. Smetham, *History of Strood* (Strood, 1899), 351.

[4] Kelly, *Directory of Rochester, Strood, Chatham* (1890), 46.

[5] Smetham, *op. cit.*, 351.

[6] Brace, *op. cit.*, 156.

[7] Smetham, *op. cit.*, 352.

[8] J, Rochard, *Historical Chatham and Rochester* (Chatham, 1894), 45.

[9] *Chatham News*, 7 June 1890, 8.

[10] B. Mitchell and P. Dean, *Abstract of Historical Statistics* (Cambridge, 1962), 82.

[11] S. B. Saul, *The Myth of the Great Depression 1873–1896* (1969), 35.

[12] C. Whitehead, *A Sketch of the Agriculture of Kent* (1899), 3.

[13] *Ibid*, 56.

[14] Rochard, *op. cit.*, 46.

[15] Smetham, *op. cit.*, 352.

[16] Unsourced newspaper cutting, Rochester Library.

[17] Brace, *op. cit.*, 156.

[18] H. W. Macrosty, *The Trust Movement in British Industry* (1907), 314–16.

[19] Brace, *op. cit.*, 156.

[20] Smetham, *op. cit.*, 351.

[21] *Chatham News*, 29 December 1894, 8.

[22] *Ibid*, 2 November 1895, 6.

[23] Brace, *op. cit.*, 105.

[24] *Chatham News*, 4 October 1890, 4.

[25] J. W. Bridge, 'Maidstone Geneva, An Old Maidstone Industry', *Archaeologia Cantiana*, LXV, (1952), 84.

[26] *Abstract of Answers and Returns of Census*, 1831, 1871.

[27] J. Vaizey, *The Brewing Industry 1886–1951* (1960), 3.

[28] J. Vaizey, 'The Brewing Industry', in Ed. P. Lesley Cook, *Effects of Mergers* (1958), 400.

[29] *Chatham News*, 14 January 1860.

[30] *Maidstone and Kentish Journal*, 6 January 1881, 1.

[31] Vaizey, *op. cit.*, (1958), 398.

[32] *Chatham News*, 23 July 1892, 2.

[33] A. E. Dingle, 'Drink and Working Class Living Standards in Britain, 1870–1914', *Economic History Review*, 2nd Series, XXV, No. 4, Nov. 1972, 609.

[34] A. Barnard, *Noted Breweries of Great Britain and Ireland*, I, (1889), 206.

[35] *Ibid*, IV, 24.

[36] *Chatham News*, 20 February 1892, 5.

[37] Information from Whitbread Fremlin Ltd.

[38] *Chatham News*, 2 April 1892, 1.

[39] *Ibid*, 30 April 1892, 7.

[40] Vaizey, *op. cit.* (1960), 3.

[41] KAO U480 B536 Lease Bests to E. Winch, 1851.
[42] KAO U612 T96 Conveyance to A. F. Style, June 1898.
[43] KAO U612 T54 Lease to A. F. Style, March 1868.
[44] KAO U612 T26 Conveyance to A. F. Style, 30 September 1874.
[45] KAO U612 T67 Conveyance J. Peters to A. F. Style, December 1883.
[46] KAO U612 T47 Lease to A. F. Style, October 1896.
[47] Information from Courage (Eastern) Ltd.
[48] KAO U612 T45. Lease to Meux and Co. 1887.
[49] KAO U480 T42. Lease Bests to E. Winch, 1851.
[50] KAO U480 B536. Conveyance Bests to E. Winch, 27 December 1894.
[51] Information from Courage (Eastern) Ltd.
[52] Harris, *op. cit.*, 3.
[53] Manning and Co., *Rochester and Chatham District Directory* (Chatham, 1877), 6.
[54] *Chatham News*, 30 March 1861.
[55] *Chatham Observer*, 22 March 1913.
[56] *Chatham News*, 24 December 1859.
[57] Manning, *op. cit.*, 6.
[58] *Maidstone and Kentish Journal*, 3 January 1881, 2.
[59] *Kelly's, Directory of Rochester Strood Chatham* (1898–9), 204.
[60] *South Eastern Gazette*, 12 December 1961.
[61] *Industrial Great Britain, op. cit.*, 125a.
[62] Information from Courage (Eastern) Ltd.
[63] *Industrial Great Britain, op. cit.*, 1131.
[64] G. N. Hardinge, *The Development and Growth of Courages Brewery* (privately published, 1932), 17, 18.
[65] Rochard, *op. cit.*, 32.
[66] Rochard, *op. cit.*, 29.
[67] *South Eastern Gazette*, 12 December 1961.
[68] *Chatham Standard*, 8 September 1859.
[69] Manning and Co. *op. cit.*, 111.
[70] *South Eastern Gazette*, 12 December 1961.
[71] *Chatham News*, 30 November 1889, 4.
[72] *Chatham News*, 14 January 1893, 4; 29 December 1894, 4.
[73] *Rochester, Chatham and Gillingham Journal*, 24 May 1901, 7.
[74] *Industrial Great Britain, op. cit.*, 122a.
[75] *Rochester, Chatham and Gillingham Journal*, 24 May 1901, 7.
[76] Rochard, *op. cit.*, 62.
[77] *Rochester, Chatham and Gillingham Journal*, 24 May 1901, 7.
[78] *Chatham News*, 22 August 1868, 1.
[79] F. Sanders, *A Business History of Chatham High Street*, IV, (MSS, 1961), 30.
[80] *Chatham News*, 21 January 1860.
[81] *Industrial Great Britain, op. cit.*, 121.
[82] Rochard, *op. cit.*, 24.
[83] S. B. Saul, 'The Market and the Development of the Mechanical Engineering Industries in Britain, 1860–1914', *Economic History Review*, XX, No. 1., April 1967, 125.
[84] Kelly, *Directory of Rochester, Strood and Chatham* (1890), 63b.
[85] Kelly, *Directory of Rochester, Strood and Chatham* (1898–9), 202, 213, 221, 224.
[86] *Chatham, News*, 16 June 1860.
[87] *Ibid.*, 4 October 1862.
[88] *Ibid.*, 16 June 1860.
[89] *Chatham News*, 9 November 1872, 2.
[90] *Ibid.*, 27 July 1889, 5.

CHAPTER X

Industries Outside the Medway Towns not Typical of the Area, 1850–1900

While the bulk of activity was concentrated in the Medway Towns, there was a scattering of industries in the valleys which were not typical of the area as a whole. These industries were based mainly on two factors, firstly the historic location of a factory site, and secondly, the availability of raw materials, as well as considerations of transport.

The copperas works at Queenborough were working till at least 1872[1] if not later, but production was only on a limited scale due 'to the dearth of material'.[2] The works had been in the hands of Josiah Hall since 1847.[3] The manufacture of copperas was perhaps not his primary occupation since he was described in 1866 as being 'a manufacturer of the patent gas purifier, surveyor, valuer, auctioneer and engineers' and builders' estimator'.[4] In 1886 the site of the works was taken over by Stevens Chemical Manure Co., who had produced superphosphate from bones in London since 1847.[5]

As early as 1861 plans for a new factory at Queenborough had been rumoured. A report in *The Chatham News* said

> 'It is rumoured that an artificial manure factory is to be erected near the pier; it would give much employment. Whether it would be in good odour with the inhabitants generally is another matter.'[6]

The manufacture of artificial fertilizer had been given a great boost by the work of Liebig, especially through his book *Chemistry in its Application to Agriculture and Physiology*, published in 1840. He had suggested that bones and sulphuric acid should be mixed together to make the phosphate in bones more easily available to plants.

The works in 1887 were named 'The Sheppy Glue and Chemical Works Ltd', the new firm being under the control of William Carr Stevens. All manufacturing by the Stevens firm was now concentrated at Queenborough. By the end of the nineteenth century the firm were in full production of superphosphates from mineral phosphates, manufacture of compounds and potash salts from kelp, the salts being a byproduct in the manufacture of iodine. It is interesting to note that the sulphuric acid used at the factory was being manufactured from pyrites stones obtained from Minster beach,[7] in a three chamber absorption plant.[8] Glues were also produced from bones.[9] The firm had the advantages of an existing factory site with good communications by water and rail to its main markets, London for glue, Essex and Kent for fertilizers. It was also suitably sited in relation to its raw materials, bones which could be collected from London as well as locally, kelp and pyrites for acid found locally. Linked with the constant demand for its products the firm prospered.

A small industry incidental to the presence of gas works occurred at two places on the Lower Medway. This was tar distilling which took place at Queenborough and New Hythe. Using a still and a condenser a range of different products could be obtained from tar at various temperatures. Up to 170°C, light oils, benzene and naphtha were obtained. Benzene had uses in dry cleaning and dyes, light oils as a solvent in varnish and naphtha for flares for lighting. Between 170°C and 230°C phenol used in dyes, carbolic acid for antiseptics, disinfectants and soap, and naphthalene also used in dyes and insect repellents were obtained. Above 230°C creosote for wood preserving or burning for blacking was obtained.[10]

The tar distillation works at Queenborough were set up by Josiah Hall in 1876. His aim was to produce pitch and dyes, the latter probably to replace the obsolete copperas produced dyes. The tar for the enterprise was obtained from Sheppey gas works at West Minster (between Sheerness and Queenborough) being brought to the works by barge. The business closed when Hall died in 1900.[11]

The other firm was Johnson Bros, tar distillers of New Hythe, Ditton which was in business at least by 1874.[12] By 1891 the firm in the hands of William Johnson Jnr was situated at Mill Hall, Ditton (later included in the parish of Aylesford). Here he was described as a

> 'coal, oil and soda merchant, and manufacturer of tar, pitch, creosote, naphtha, benzole, asphalt, black varnish, wagon grease, sulphate of ammonia, disinfecting powder, lubricating oils, etc.'[13]

The Medway Chemical Works at Mill Hall are marked on the 2nd Edition Ordnance Survey, and show what is probably a small refinery,[14] These works survived into the twentieth century.

The biggest employer of labour of the other industries in the valley was the Snodland paper mill which by 1858 was in the hands of Charles Townsend Hook.[15] The mill was well equipped with modern machinery to produce for established connections in London. It gained an extra advantage in 1859 when the railway was constructed near the factory.

The mill suffered from the general shortage of rags for raw material of 1861. The result was that the mill experimented successfully in making paper from straw. In 1862 a prize medal was awarded to Messrs. Hook & Co. at the London International Exhibition for specimens of paper made from straw.[16] By 1866 esparto grass was also being used at the mills,[17] at which time it employed 'about 120 persons'.[18] The employment was small compared with at about that time 350 employed by Balston at Springfield Mill, Maidstone, and 630 by Joynson at St Mary Cray.[19] In 1876 the products of the mill were given as esparto and straw writings, printings and web news, and cartridges from three machines of 51, 60 and 80 inches.[20] By 1881 Hook's were described as 'one of the most prominent centres of industry' in the prosperous village of Snodland, where

> 'the mill has been considerably enlarged, and machinery of the most approved construction is about to be added, which when in proper working order will enable the proprietors to produce 100 tons per week.'[21]

In the 1880s there were four paper machines at work.[22]

The year 1887 saw several developments. The major one was the conversion of the firm into a public company with the issue of 8,000 ordinary shares at £10 and 5 per cent Debenture stock to give a total issued capital of £130,000. Of this sum £100,000 was the price paid to the Misses Hook for the whole property covering 9½ acres, the works covering 4½ acres freehold, and included the goodwill of the paper business, plus a gas works which also supplied Snodland generally.[23] New plant for the latter, including seven coke ovens, was erected in 1887.[24] The remaining £30,000 was left for working capital. Profits for the years 1884, 5 and 6 totalled £39,199. 3s. 4d., or an annual average of £13,006. 7s. 9d., or sufficient to pay a 10 per cent dividend on the ordinary shares. An independent valuation of the business had priced it excluding goodwill at £123,000.

Among the regular customers of the firm were H. M. Stationery Office and through them the War Office, Admiralty, Post Office, Board of Trade, the Ordnance Survey, the Local Government Board and other government departments. The firm also had a contract with the Postmaster General for pulping confidential government papers.[25]

The firm's expectations of its profitability were confirmed with a profit of £14,456. 15s. 7d. for the year 1888 and the 10 per cent dividend was achieved.[26] The prosperity of the firm lead to continued expansion, the works covering an area of 13½ acres in 1894,[27] with five paper machines being at work.[28] This expansion gave the works in 1899 an employment level of about 350 people, and an output of 'more than 150 tons of paper' per week.[29]

Although a small mill by the standard of others in the Maidstone paper making area, and compared with Edward Lloyd's Sittingbourne Mills which had eight paper machines working in 1898,[30] it remained an important source of employment in the Snodland area.

Pratling Street paper mill remained in production making mill board till about 1860. It would then appear that the mill, worked in the 1860s and 1870s by John Skelton Isaac, made mill boards and patent carriage panels. He was succeeded by Warwick Isaac and Co. who made patent panels for railway carriages, paper maker's press boards and mill boards. The mill was however demolished in 1889.[31]

Snodland saw attempts to set up industry apart from lime, cement and paper. In 1866 a silk factory was started near the Brook, Snodland, but proved a failure, the works afterwards being converted into a paper bag and printing factory.[32] The firm, James Nichols and Son produced paper bags, as distinct from sacks, for the grocery, confectionery and green grocery trades in the south of England. The paper could, of course, be obtained locally. The firm employed up to 50 hands.[33]

One enterprise at Snodland which was proposed but appears not to have come to fruition was the setting up of the Alkali Chemical Company Ltd, with a capital of £200,000 to produce bleach and caustic soda by electrolysis. Apparently research on the project had been going on at Snodland for some time before 1894, involving a Prof Hopkinson, a Mr Swinburne, and a Mr J. Leith. Snodland was, of course, a suitable place to work on such a scheme having access to brine from the estuary and lime from nearby. The project was criticized by the *Chemical Trade Journal* as being too costly, particularly in electricity input, compared with the Le Blanc soda and Weldon bleach processes.[34] The project was slightly premature. A workable system however was developed in 1897 by Hamilton Castner for making soda by electrolysis,[35] but not used in the Medway area.

There was also a scattering of tile and pottery works in the valley, offering a range of roofing tiles, drainage pipes and ornamental terra cotta work not produced by the brick works. The most important of these was the Aylesford Pottery Company, established in 1836[36] on property owned by E. L. Betts of Preston Hall. The firm originally made Gault bricks, plum roofing tiles and ridge tiles, being known as Pratling Street Brickfield, and is marked on a 1849 map together with kilns, a tramway to the Medway, and stables, covering an area of 12 acres.[37] The name Aylesford Pottery was in use by 1855.[38] The Company had a pavilion at the Rochester Agricultural Show, 1890, which 'was a conspicuous feature of the show', the roof being

> 'tiled with a miscellaneous variety of the company's special tiles, plain and ornamental, and arranged in such a manner as to throw up in the most effective manner the diversified tints and the patterns of these well-known and special articles of the company's manufacture. A distinguishing advantage claimed by the Company for these hip, valley, gable and eave tiles is that the clay having been subjected while in the course of moulding to a pressure of 120 tons renders the tiles impervious to wet and non-liable to vegetable formation, while the holeing and nibbling and the method of treating the curves enable the tiles to be laid more snugly in a more lasting manner than other makes.'

The Company also showed glazed wall and floor tiles, and an assortment of terra cotta, ridge tiles, finials and chimney pots, stoneware, glazed sanitary goods, flower pots, vases, garden edging and agricultural pipes.[39] The works which employed between 100 and 150 men[40] were the only ones large enough and possessing a wharf to enable them to supply outside the immediate area.

Among the other potteries in the area were those of Mr Roberts of Upnor,[41] and Wainscott Potteries run by Charlton and Matthews in 1868 where oven and paving bricks and tiles, pan plain and ridge tiles, sanitary and land drainage pipes, chimney, flower and paint pots and garden edging tiles were made.[42] Another pottery, Hoo Pottery, of Benjamin Baker[43] made chimney pots, socket pipes, flower pots, vases and all kinds of brown ware.[44]

[1] *Sheerness Times Guardian*, 26 October 1872.

[2] W. Miller, *Jottings of Kent, being a series of Historical, Ecclesiastical and Statistical Sketches* (2nd edition, 1864), 131.

[3] S. Bagshaw, *History, Gazetteer and Directory of the County of Kent* (Sheffield, 1847), 511.

[4] *Post Office Directory of Kent* (1866), 1127.

[5] MSS '*Important Dates in the Glue and Fertilizer Trade*', undated, in volume of paper cuttings and photographs, Sheerness Library.

[6] *Chatham News*, 7 December 1861.

[7] *Important Dates in the Glue and Fertilizer Trade, op. cit.*

[8] *Information from Sheppey Glue and Chemical Works Ltd.*

[9] *Important Dates in the Glue and Fertilizer Trade, op. cit.*

[10] W. Campbell, *The Chemical Industry* (1971), 87, 88.

[11] K. R. Macdonald, *The Isle of Sheppey and the Swale* (London M.A. (Geography) Thesis, May 1949), 81.

[12] Kelly, *Directory of Kent* (1874), 1234.

[13] Kelly, *Directory of Kent, Surrey and Sussex* (1891), 209.

[14] O.S. 2nd Series 25″ to 1 mile Sheet 31/9. (1896).

[15] J. and J. F. Phippen, *A Directory for Rochester, Chatham, Strood and the vicinities* (Rochester, 1858), 78.

[16] *Chatham News*, 2 August 1862, 3.

[17] A. Shorter, 'Paper Mills in the Maidstone District', Part I, *The Paper Maker and British Paper Journal*, March 1960, 62.

[18] *Post Office Directory of Kent* (1866), 1, 138.

[19] A. Shorter, *Paper Making in the British Isles—An Historical and Geographical Study* (Newton Abbott, 1971), 158.

[20] Shorter, *op. cit.*, (March 1960), 62.

[21] *Kent Messenger*, 6 June 1881, 6.

[22] Shorter, *op. cit.*, (March 1960), 62.

[23] *Chatham News*, 1 October 1887, 4.

[24] *Chatham News*, 9 July 1887, 3.

[25] *Chatham News*, 1 October 1887, 4.

[26] *Ibid*, 9 March 1889, 8.

[27] *Historical Jottings of the Parish of Snodland* (Snodland, 1894), 10.

[28] Shorter, *op. cit.*, (March 1960), 62.

[29] *Post Office Directory of Kent* (1899), 548.

[30] Shorter, *op. cit.*, (1971), 153.

[31] Shorter, *op. cit.*, (April 1960), 62.

[32] *Historical Jottings of the Parish of Snodland, op. cit.*, 11.

[33] Information from James Nichols and Son Ltd.

[34] *The Chemical Trade Journal*, 10 February 1894, 93–4.

[35] Campbell, *op. cit.*, 60.

[36] *V.C.H.*, III, (1932), 395. E. M. Hewitt, 'Industries'.

[37] KAO U886 P9 Plan of Preston Hall Estate, I. J. West, 1849.

[38] KAO U886 P11 Plan of Preston Hall Estate, 1855.

[39] *Chatham News*, 7 June 1890, 8.

[40] *V.C.H.*, III, 395.

[41] *Chatham News*, 23 August 1860.

[42] *Ibid*, 29 August 1868, 1.

[43] *Post Office Directory of Kent* (1866), 1002.

[44] Kelly's, *Directory of Rochester, Strood and Chatham* (1890), 252.

PART III

Decline and Changes in the Twentieth Century

CHAPTER XI

The Position in 1900, and Decline of the Cement Industry

The area in 1900 projects a picture of relative prosperity. The previous 50 years had seen the rise of the cement industry to its peak, with the greatest number of factories and employees to be found in 1900. The engineering industry had seen a similar rise particularly the firm of Aveling and Porter. Barge building had prospered with the increased carriage of cement and bricks. The brick industry itself had passed its peak and was already facing stiff competition from the Fletton brick industry. Brewing, mineral water manufacture and a number of small industries all continued to prosper.

The area only had one paper mill left in operation by 1900, and another industry to disappear had been copperas. An industry that had been of some importance to Strood and Rochester which virtually disappeared was fishing. This fishery had remained prosperous until the 1860s. A report of the auditing of the fishery accounts in July 1860 stated that 400 persons were involved in it, 120 being freemen. They had expended nearly £9,000 in the previous year and were continuing to make improvements.[1] But all was not well, and by 1864 an editorial in *The Chatham News* could say

> 'the oyster fishery, if not dead, has been in a state of suspended animation. The fishermen have not been employed, the fishing grounds have not been used, and an ancient privilege has been turned to no account.'

It added that an effort was going to be made to resurrect the fishery.[2]

One reason for this sudden decline was a series of severe frosts which had killed off the stock, and had left a debt of £20,000 borrowed in an effort to renew the oyster brood.[3] Another reason was the extension of Chatham Dockyard in the early 1860s which entailed the closing of Swinborough Creek adjoining St Mary's Island, and the building of river embankments, encroaching on the dredgermens preserve.[4] In 1865 to keep the fishery in being the 'Rochester Oyster Fishery Act' was passed which gave the jury of the Admiralty Court the right to grant leases of fishing grounds as long as they had not been dredged in the previous ten years. This freed the dredgers from debt, creditors were only to be paid from income which resulted from the act.[5] Pollution of the river was becoming a hazard to the oyster fishery in the 1880s and 1890s with increasing amounts of sewage and industrial effluent.[6] To prevent claims due to pollution, the jury gave up the right to grant leases to the Main Drainage Board in 1914.[7] By this time there were only five or six boats left and twenty dredgermen.[8] The fishery was eventually closed in 1936 under the Public Health (Shellfish) Regulations of 1934.[9]

As far as floating fish were concerned, up to 1870, twenty or thirty boats with a three man crew seined for white herring at Rochester in October, November and December of each year, but the catches declined and the industry virtually ended.[10] A reason for this decline might be found in the following report of a statement by Councillor Boucher to Rochester Town Council in 1864

> 'the fishery . . . he considered was conducted in such a manner as not only to reflect discredit on the city but also to do injury to the community at large; he had found that smig were caught in large quantities, and thereby the usual increase in shrimps was prevented; soles and plaice were also caught of such small size that the fishery was gradually decreasing in value.'[11]

By 1909 the fishery had largely failed according to A. Bevans Horsnaill and the men had descended to dredging for coal round the collier moorings.[12] There were in 1910 only twenty one boats and fifty two men regularly employed,[13] some perhaps employed in dredging for mussels in the Thames estuary for use as manure.[14] The number of boats had declined to twelve with thirty employed in 1938.[15]

At Gillingham the fishery had all but disappeared by 1868

> 'trade . . . languished of late years, possibly through the tainting of the water by gas-works and sewage.'[16]

The fishery at Queenborough, however, continued, in 1928 the value of fish landed being £3,074. There were still trawlers fishing for soles, dabs and shrimps and seine netting white bait.[17]

Overall at the end of the 1890s and in the early 1900s a picture of great activity is presented by those writing about the Medway scene. A typical comment appeared in *All the Year Round* (1893):

The Changing Scene at Canal Road, Strood and Frindsbury as seen from Rochester Castle.

1. Taken in the 1870s when there was little residential development in the area. The Canal Basin cement works of Lark and Fletcher are clearly visible to the right of the picture.

2. Photograph taken in the late 1880s with the oil seed crushing mills of Stewart Bros. and Spencer dominating the centre of the picture.

3. Taken in the 1890s. The chalk quarry (to the right) is now encroaching towards Frindsbury Church. The development of residential accommodation is now much in evidence.

4. The scene in the early 1900s.
Photographs reproduced from originals by permission of Rochester Museum

> 'As we approach Strood, the fume and incense of kilns, and breweries, and factories come upon us, and it is a busy world we see as we top the hill and look down on the wide Medway, the mingled smoke and steam throwing a haze over the wonderful scene presented by the noble old Norman Keep that still seems to guard the bridge, and the Cathedral all weathered and brown, and the tangle round about of quaint roofs and dwellings, of closes, courts and fair old gardens.'[18]

Edwin Harris commented in 1897

> 'we shall not fail to notice the number of cement works as we proceed up the stream, which while whitening the banks of the river, and casting a smoky atmosphere over the sky, does not fail to bring wealth and commerce to the adjoining towns and gives employment to hundreds of men.'[19]

Approaching Rochester by train was described in 1905

> 'Presently, in a valley ahead, a silvery sheet of water dotted with brown sails, and bordered by chimneys of the cement and brick industries, announces the River Medway and our arrival in Rochester.'[20]

A more graphic description comes from W. and M. Wyllie in *London to the Nore Painted and Described* (1905)

> 'wherever chalk appears near the water there will be found the tall chimneys and jetties and tramways of the cement works; but the biggest quarries of all are on the Medway where men are rapidly changing the surface of the country, boring great gaps and tunnels into the Downs, carrying away hills, and covering the neighbourhood with an impalpable white powder. Through the smoke rises the Norman Keep of Rochester.'[21]

Above Rochester Bridge

> 'at intervals cement works have driven cuttings into the Downs, leaving tall white cliffs. The still air is heavy with the suspended smoke belched from countless chimneys.'[22]

While at Rochester

> 'all around is boisterous merriment. The noise is deafening. Along the shore are barge-builders, slipways and engineers; and there is a forest of chimneys on the north bank. We catch glimpses of grinding wheels and furnaces. Grey men are loading barges with grey bags. The throb of machinery is everywhere.'[23]

Cement is the dominant industry in all the descriptions, and still was to some extent in 1921 when Donald Maxwell described the scene up the Medway

> 'From Halling to Snodland the river is literally walled on one side or the other with kilns and loading barges,[24] the chalk ravines are lighted with arc lamps, and busy little trains can be seen industriously puffing about, and men roped like Alpine climbers, hewing at giddy heights on precipitous cliffs.'[25]

All this had an adverse effect on the valley.

> 'Marred by intruding commerce and stained by sordid manufacture, a lovely valley has become, they say, a valley of desolation—its villages black with smoke of the furnace and its fair hills devoured by the encroaching works.'[26]

But already a decline had set in. At New Hythe there were

> 'the remains of deserted cement works with rows of old fashioned conical kilns.'[27]

and generally by 1921

> 'Ruined kilns and tottering chimneys skirt the river, and quarries abound in which red-rusted machinery and decrepit trains of trucks lie abandoned as by a plague stricken people.'[28]

The Lower Medway area fell into an era of depression soon after 1900 from which it did not fully recover until the 1950s. The major reason for this change about was the decline of the cement and brick industries in the valley, and the subsequent effect on barge building and engineering.

The reason for the decline of the building materials industry in the early years of the century was the state of the market. The increase in the housing stock between 1901 and 1911 was 840,000 compared with 886,000 between 1891 and 1901 while the number of men employed in building fell from 953,000 in 1901 to 887,000 in 1911.[29] The index of residential house building shows a steady decline from 1901 to 1916.

Index of Residential House Building 1900–1916.
(1900–9=100)

Year	*House Building in London*	*In 34 Towns*
1900	116.0	107.0
1901	125.3	107.0
1902	117.5	117.8
1903	121.9	120.2
1904	107.3	104.6

Year	*House Building in London*	*In 34 Towns*
1905	101.3	97.6
1906	98.8	101.1
1907	88.6	92.9
1908	61.7	77.3
1909	61.5	75.7
1910	54.2	65.9
1911	46.2	51.7
1912	36.9	40.9
1913	39.6	41.5
1914	38.3	37.0
1915	25.6	23.6
1916	16.8	13.0

From Weber 'A New Index of Residential House Building'. *Scottish Journal of Political Economy*, June 1955, 132.

Apart from a depressed home market the cement industry had to contend with other problems including drastic technological change, severe foreign competition, as well as locational problems, which helped to completely transform the industry.

The greatest technological change was the introduction of the continuous kiln which could consume up to 50 per cent less fuel than the bottle kilns by eliminating the heat loss incurred by cooling for unloading.[30] Firstly came shaft kilns the most popular of which was the Schneider kiln introduced in 1898.[31] This kiln allowed layers of raw material and fuel to be fed in from the top, firing to take place in the middle third of the shaft, and the cooling clinker to be drawn from the bottom. The kiln consisted of a brick or concrete cylinder usually 16 feet in outside diameter and 40 feet high from the ground floor to the loading floor. The inside diameter was about 9 feet. Once the kiln had been loaded and fired, the clinker appeared in about three days, and drawing and loading then took place once every four hours. The yield of clinker was usually ten to twelve tons per day, which required 28 to 36 cwt of coke for fuel. The Schneider kiln had to be fed with chalk bricks often made from a dry mixing process for clay and chalk, or sometimes if used alongside chamber kilns surplus slurry could be utilized. This had the drawback of necessitating the use of brickmaking machinery and the incurring of extra labour costs. However, raw material and coal could be mixed together in bricks and loaded together. The kiln did have the advantages of not being expensive to build or maintain, of being easy to work, and relatively economic on fuel.[32] Thus it meant a satisfactory, cheap continuous kiln was available to small manufacturers, and its cost reducing effect meant that small firms were able to survive increasing competition in the industry.[33]

The most important innovation was the introduction of the rotary kiln from the U.S.A. The first rotary kiln was installed in England in 1887, but most of the early versions proved to be failures. Rapid application of the kiln began after 1900 when the Associated Portland Cement Manufacturers (1900) Ltd, purchased the rights to the successful American Hurry and Seaman rotary kiln for installation in their Thamesside works.[34] The rotary kiln was essentially an inclined iron cylinder up to 250 feet long, lined with fire bricks, which was rotated slowly. Liquid slurry was pumped in at the upper end, and heated by finely powdered coal blasted into the cylinder by air pressure. The kiln both dried and burned, and the clinker left the bottom end of the kiln ready for grinding.[35] The effect of the kiln was to increase the size of the works, and the output per works rose to something like 2,000 tons per week.[36] It also increased competition through cost reduction, the price of producing a ton of cement falling to about thirteen shillings per ton by 1914.[37]

Competition became intense with the technological changes and increased capacity of the 1890s, and with competition from continental manufacturers. This had lead in the 1890s to the concentration of 89 per cent of the Thames and Medway production in the hands of 31 firms.[38] However, no discussions took place between the manufacturers to come to any price or production arrangements. According to H. O. O'Hagan, who promoted the A.P.C.M. combine, one of the main weaknesses in the cement trade was the

> 'animosity which existed amongst the various manufacturers, who scarcely knew each other, and this could probably only be removed under a powerful combination.'[39]

Combination of the Thames and Medway firms seemed to be the answer to the problems. This after a few tentative approaches was achieved by an outside company promoter, H. Osborne O'Hagan, in 1900. He described the process of amalgamation in his autobiography *Leaves from My Life*

His first contact with the cement industry came in 1896 when

> 'Mr W. Tingley [Tingey], a partner in one of the old cement works established on the River Medway [Crown Works] called upon me to obtain my views as to the conversion of his business into a public company. Nothing came from negotiating in respect of these Medway Works at the time, as I arrived at the

conclusion that with the retirement of the principal men who had been running the concern it was unlikely to be more successful in the future than it had in the past.'[40]

It was at this time that he came to his conclusion about the need for a combination. He was approached in August 1897, when three or four of the largest manufacturers were contemplating amalgamation, but nothing came of it.[41]

In October 1899 O'Hagan was contacted by Martin Earle and Co. Ltd,

> 'It transpired that Martin Earle and Co. were cement manufacturers owning large new works on the Medway, and were regarded as interlopers by the older-established manufacturers. The directors of Martin Earle and Co. had come to the conclusion that what was needed to make cement making a more profitable business was close co-operation between the various firms of manufacturers. They had already sounded a few of the smaller firms; who appeared willing to co-operate. They wished to secure my assistance to bring about an amalgamation of some half a dozen of the firms engaged in the trade.'[42]

O'Hagan there upon sent for his contacts of 1897, which produced contact with Mr Bazley White and Mr Leonard, a former partner and the solicitor of J. B. White of Swanscombe. Their firm had given them six months leave to attempt to amalgamate the cement industry. They had met general approval for the idea, but lacked the figures to put the idea into effect due to the mutual suspicions of rivals. O'Hagan agreed to form a small syndicate called British Incorporators Ltd, which was to purchase all the cement works obtainable and then turn them over to one big concern to be called the Associated Portland Cement Manufacturers, Ltd. Negotiations were carried out by Bazley White. When White had obtained the agreement of a large number of manufacturers 'to secure a practical monopoly, I [O'Hagan] would arrange the financing and floating of the company'.

O'Hagan stated

> 'If the combine could be formed, there should be room for very considerable savings and additional profits with all the works under one management.'

It would allow for economies due to innovations in manufacture being shared, and cut out waste by buying and selling departments being duplicated. Amalgamation also seemed desirable in face of the rotary kiln which was costly to instal, but provided a superior cement at lower cost, and which was already being installed by

J. B. White and Co. at Swanscombe,[43] which would have been the largest works with a capacity of 160,000 tons per year.[44] Negotiations then took place with 'some hundred cement manufacturers'.[45]

After several months, work began to make progress, but O'Hagan had been

> 'obliged to leave out for the time being Martin Earle & Co. and the Wouldham Company (Grays), with both of whom I had been in close negotiation.'

Martin Earle and Co. of Strood

> 'were anxious to have the combine brought about. . . . They were willing to be taken into the combine, but their purchase price was high and they had been so short a time established that a purchase price based upon their average profits of three years would have amounted to far less than they would have been prepared to take. As I had established very close relations with this firm, I was willing to accept their pledge to work closely with the combination and I may say that their pledge was carried out until the concern was subsequently acquired for the British Portland Cement Manufacturers Ltd.'

A working agreement was also secured with the Wouldham Company as Mr J. B. White was chairman, and another of White's directors on the board.[46]

Eventually in July 1900 preliminary notice of the flotation of the company appeared, the company being registered with a capital of £8 million, made up of 250,000 5½ per cent Cumulative Preference Shares at £10, 250,000 Ordinary Shares at £10, and a First Mortgage 4¼ per cent Debenture Stock of £3,000,000. A third of the Debentures and Ordinary Shares was to be issued to the vendors as part of the purchase price of properties valued at £4,642,000. The purchase price was based on the average profits over the past three years of £561,103 for the firms acquired. Profits in the last year had been £658,356, and greater profits were anticipated through economies in manufacturing and distribution.[47]

The flotation took place at an unfortunate time after the reverses in the Boer War and fictitious accounts in the *Daily Mail* of massacres at Peking had shaken confidence. Insufficient capital had been forthcoming, the result being that the vendors had to take up further stocks and shares. A further difficulty had been the increased cost of coke from the London gas works.

The Chairman stated at a Meeting of A.P.C.M. on 13 November 1900 that he had found a wide variation in the cost of production to the extent of 25 per cent. He hoped to introduce rotary kilns as an answer to some of the problems. He also suggested that one solution to their problems was to have a tied trade with distributors.[48] This latter suggestion of tying the trade and ending price competition was not popular with merchants, and an attempted agreement with the London trade broke down early in 1901.[49] The first year of the combine was much worse than anticipated, with profits after debenture interest of only £121,917. This left only £30,704 after paying the preference dividend. At the time £151,101 was still outstanding to the vendors as the balance of the purchase money.[50] However, costs had increased by £200,000 by the increase in the coke price alone.[51]

The problem of the price of coke stimulated the introduction of the rotary kiln which used finely ground coal dust as fuel.[52] It lead to the investment of £550,000 on new plant between 1900 and 1905.[53] It also lead to the closure of obsolete works and concentration of production on plants which O'Hagan considered first-class, that was works possessing; (i) a freehold estate containing large reserves of chalk and clay; (ii) a good situation in relation to disposing of the output, good facilities for railway and water carriage; (iii) modern machinery, and capacity to increase output; (iv) valuable trade connections and well established brand names.[54]

The Scene at the Quarry, Frindsbury in 1907.

The closures were felt on the Medway with three of the A.P.C.M. works being closed in 1901. The Bridge and the Globe works which had been integrated under J. B. White were closed.[55] It would appear that Booth's works at Borstal were closed in the same year.[56] In 1903 the now obsolete factory of Wouldham Cement Works was closed,[57] although the quarry and tramway were said to have been in use as late as 1908/9.[58]

The problems of A.P.C.M. continued to a large degree due to new competition from Germany and Belgium, especially from inferior quality natural cement from the Antwerp Cement Company.[59] European tariff policies inhibited exports. Germany which had expanded its capacity to double home consumption in hope of entering the American market undersold its competitors to dispose of output. German exports to Britain rose from 12,500 tons in 1900 to 36,700 tons in 1903. Belgian cement was used as a cheap substitute for Portland cement, and helped to moderate the price of the latter. Excessive price rises in 1900–1 served to accentuate imports, leading to a fall in price between 1902 and 1905 and which in turn lead to decreased imports. Imports of Belgian cement rose from 104,771 tons in 1900 to a peak of 272,945 tons in 1904, falling to 114,372 tons in 1907. A.P.C.M. was unable to fix prices permanently, only being able to prevent sharp falls by making reduced competition reflect the protection given the home market by freights.[60]

Rose Cottage, Burham, built by Thomas Cubitt for the manager of Burham Brick Works.

Another problem for A.P.C.M. was that three of the thirty firms dropped out of the combine, in one case where members had sat on the Board for two or three months.[61] This left the combine with the ownership of 27 firms and working agreements with four other firms.[62] One of the three was Trechmann Weekes of Halling.[63] Bitter competition was to come from the three on the Thames and Medway who had a combined output of 140,000 tons per year.[64] Among the works on the Medway remaining independent were Peters Bros Wouldham; Lee, Son and Co. Ltd, Snodland; the West Kent Cement Co., Burham; Queenborough Cement Co.; Barron and Co. Ltd, Rainham; and Formby's Cement Works Co. Frindsbury.[65] There was sufficient chalk land sites available on the Medway for new firms to enter the industry. One such firm to be established in 1902 with its registered office at Horrid Hill, Gillingham, was the Sharps Green Cement Co. Ltd. The Works, owned by Cyril Lawrence Cary, managing partner and Bernard Phillipson Cary, were about the size of the Falcon Works at Otterham Quay, and were the last to use static kilns established on the Medway.[66] Competition also came from firms in the Midlands and North who sometimes sold cement below the cost of manufacture to gain customers.[67] With the wide distribution of cement making materials it was impossible for the combine to control prices through a monopoly position, and by 1911 the group had control of only 75 per cent of the market.[68] However, in gaining control of 89 per cent of the Medway capacity in 1900, the combine also gained facilities for making lime, bricks and tiles and some engineering works for renewal and repairs.[69] These subsidiary businesses proved profitable and gave the firm some stability in the early years.

Finding it impossible to maintain prices the only course open was to cut costs. This lead to heavy investment in rotary kilns and the purchase of labour saving machinery to reduce staff.[70] The result of capital investment and integrating the servicing departments (selling, accounts etc.) was a slow improvement in profits, rising from £248,216 in 1901 to £335,462 in 1906. But no dividend was paid on Ordinary shares at this time.[71]

The earthquake on the Pacific coast of the Americas in 1905 had given the market some support, and created a sudden burst of activity in 1906.[72] This was offset by the home trade which in 1906 was 'wretched: very poor demand and miserable prices'. Future prospects were not good, and little further consumption could be expected from America after the rebuilding of San Francisco due to buy American policies and the effect of the McKinley tariff.[73]

However, after a brief boom on the Medway when manufacturers were 'so busy that they will not guarantee the delivery of new orders',[74] the picture again turned gloomy in 1907. Home building demand was still declining and the price of fuel rising.[75] In November 1907 it became known that A.P.C.M. was to immediately close three of its works at Frinsdbury, throwing out of work

300 men. The works involved were the Phoenix, Quarry and Beehive, leaving only the Crown and Beaver working at Frindsbury.[76] These were some of the older works with obsolete plant. But a contributing factor was that A.P.C.M. was having difficulty in obtaining chalk from Church Commission land, and as a result was bringing chalk from its quarries up the river, which was expensive. Anyway the Combine said it had unlimited chalk on land at Northfleet and Swanscombe where it could develop works, better situated for delivery to London especially in foggy or stormy weather.[77]

A further blow came when one of the firms outside the A.P.C.M., Formby's of Whitewall Creek closed sometime after 1908. The firm does not appear in *Kelly's Directory of Kent* for 1911. The firm was killed by its geographical isolation, being well away from the railway, and only approachable by barge. It also had problems obtaining its chalk from Tower Hill which was covered by a thick layer of Thanet sand. When the sand reached a depth of 20 feet digging stopped. Chalk was then brought by barge at considerable expense from the firm's quarries at Halling.[78]

As a result of the situation in the industry, and having got financial backing from a syndicate led by Lord St David, O'Hagan embarked on a second attempt to amalgamate the cement industry.[79] He took steps to purchase Wouldham Cement Company, Grays and Trechmann, Weekes and Co. of Cuxton, Trechmann, Weekes were not prepared to consider another combine, having been one of the three firms to drop out of the A.P.C.M., but would consider an offer to purchase the works.

> 'During a couple of weeks negotiation I led him [Mr Brown negotiator for Trechmann, Weekes] to think that only a third of the purchase money could be paid in cash. We were getting together on a price when I suddenly asked how much the price would be reduced if the payment was entirely in cash. He did not think this a serious suggestion so he named a very much lower price, when I said "Well, we'll make it a cash transaction." I reported this to the board and I carried out the purchase.'

Wouldham Cement Works, Grays were then purchased, where upon O'Hagan set about negotiations with all outside firms to set up the British Portland Cement Manufacturers Ltd (1911), as a subsidiary of A.P.C.M.[80]

The firms in the merger included on the Medway were: William Lee, Son and Co. Ltd, Snodland in 1912, who were one of the firms who already had a working arrangement with A.P.C.M.: Martin, Earle of Strood, although they retained their separate identity until the early 1920s; Queenborough Cement Company; Barrons Cement Co. Ltd, Otterham Quay, Rainham; Sharps Green Cement Co.; and Peters Bros of Wouldham. As to the effect of the merger

> 'The immediate effect on the industry was almost wholly good. The combine was able to reduce the amount of transport costs by confining the sales effort of individual works to smaller areas, and, probably more important, to close inefficient works which had either high costs or produced poor-quality cement. It is said that after the formation of the combine twenty works on the Thames and Medway were closed immediately. This caused ill-feeling and distress, but was nevertheless clearly in the interests of efficiency.'[81]

Gillingham Cement Works as they appeared in 1907.

Among the works now closed were the obsolete Sharps Green works where all work at the factory and quarry ceased in February 1913.[82] Gillingham Cement Works were closed about 1911 although they appear in a directory for that year, as do Borstal Manor Works,[83] which were also closed soon after. The Upnor works of Hilton Anderson and Brooks, had long been closed by A.P.C.M. and replaced by a barge repair yard for the A.P.C.M. fleet.[84]

Despite the wholesale closure of works by A.P.C.M. and B.P.C.M. they were unable to manipulate supply and price because they were unable to control entry to the industry. In 1912 three new firms entered. One of these, the Cliffe works of the Thames Portland Cement Co., was built by Broads, large London builders' merchants. They were insuring their supply and taking advantage of their secure outlet. E. J. and W. Goldsmith, the barge owners, set up works at Motney Hill, Rainham as the British Standard Portland Cement Co., in an attempt to insure themselves against the loss of the cement trade. Formby's Clinkham works at Halling were revived by Albert Batchelor and Co. Ltd.[85] A monopoly position was not yet achieved, but closing so many obsolete works did increase profits, an ordinary dividend being paid for the first time in 1913.[86]

The 1914–18 war further contracted the industry on the Medway, with little building activity and an end to the export trade killing the smaller obsolete works. The Queenborough works were demolished during the war, and the bricks and debris sold to the War Department to improve the roads on Sheppey.[87] Also closed were the Falcon works at Otterham Quay. The West Kent Works at Aylesford were evidently also closed by 1916.[88]

Two works on the Medway had been modernized by the A.P.C.M. before 1914. One of these, the Burham works was decided upon in 1912. It was planned to have four rotary kilns and coolers to give a clinker output of 5,000 tons per week. This was not a logical step to take considering the geographical disadvantages of Burham. Expansion at Lee's or Halling Manor Works was obviously the best alternative considering their railway and water transport facilities. Transport difficulties were overcome to some extent by taking the clinker by barge to the Crown Works, Frindsbury for grinding, and thence on by rail or water, as cement could be shipped by steamer from below Rochester Bridge. The Crown Works were modernized, with the installation of a 1,000 tons per week rotary kiln, and a new grinding mill to grind the product of both works.[89] O'Hagan had a personal reason for wanting to continue the Burham Works in preference to those better situated on the left bank of the Medway. This was due to the financial arrangements he made at the time of the combination. He wrote in his memoirs:

> 'In negotiating for the purchase of [Bevans and Burham] works I had arranged with the vendors that substantial amounts of the purchase monies should be left on mortgage of the properties sold, at a low rate of interest.'

The mortgage in the case of Burham was for £175,000. When the securities of the Company fell and credit was affected, the directors were uneasy that the mortgages might be foreclosed and thus deplete the liquid assets of the company. The mortgages were redeemed by an issue of 5 per cent bonds with the property as security, but as there were no takers, O'Hagan had to 'get friends to join me in taking up the . . . bonds'.[90] So the decision was made to modernize the works because had the Burham works closed down there would have been no security for the outstanding balance of the £175,000 held by O'Hagan and his friends.

There were several reasons for the decline of the cement industry on the Medway in the early years of the century apart from those already outlined. Many of the works suffered from poor communications, especially those on the east bank and above Rochester Bridge which had no railway connections. Not surprisingly the question of a Medway bridge in the Burham or Wouldham area was raised, and discussed in 1901[91] and again in 1906. In 1906 it was stated that not only would the cement trade benefit, but also the 1,400 men who crossed the river to work each day. The main objection to the idea was the possible impediment to navigation posed by a bridge,[92] and plans never materialized. Other factors in the decline included the development of alternative forms of transport to barges which lost the advantage of a return cargo of coke from the London gas works lowering freight costs when rotary kilns used coal dust. The Medway was at a disadvantage compared with Thamesside in that it was further from the London market, and this was reflected in freight costs. Medway barges lost a tide when making the passage into the Thames, and this also was reflected in freights. Rochester Bridge also increased costs by entailing the use of a huffler to help lower the mast and sails which weighed about 5 tons when shooting the bridge, and to help raise the gear afterwards—the cost five shillings for the service.[93] Difficulties at the bridge were increased when the erection of the South Eastern Railway bridge in 1890 increased the velocity of flow.

The Medway also lacked deep water berths. Only at Frindsbury were there alongside berthing facilities, and here only for four vessels of up to 400/500 tons. The Thamesside works were able to load ocean-going vessels alongside their wharves, giving an advantage in the export trade. Exports from the Medway went either by barge to some convenient docks like London involving costly transshipment, or were handled by costly 'over-side' loading from lighters and barges at moorings in the river. All these handicaps lead to the rapid decline of the trade.

[1] *Chatham News*, 21 July 1860.
[2] *Chatham News*, 10 September 1864.
[3] F. F. Smith, *A History of Rochester* (1928), 212.

[4] R. Goodsall, "Oyster Fisheries on the North Kent Coast", *Arch. Cant.* LXXX, 130.

[5] Smith, *op. cit.*, 212.

[6] R. Marsh, *The Conservancy of the River Medway 1881–1969* (Rochester, 1971), 59–60.

[7] Smith, *op. cit.*, 213.

[8] *V.C.H.*, III, (1932), 433. E. M. Hewitt, 'Industries'.

[9] Marsh, *op. cit.*, 14.

[10] Evidence to Sea Fisheries Commission, Rochester 14 November 1878, (quoted *V.C.H.*, III, 430).

[11] *Chatham News*, 13 August 1864.

[12] A. B. Horsnaill, 'Recollections of Old Strood', *Chatham News*, 3 April 1909.

[13] H. Rees, *The Medway Towns—their settlement, growth and economic development* (Ph.D. Thesis, London, 1954), 218.

[14] E. J. March, *Inshore Craft of Britain—In the Days of Sail and Oar* (Newton Abbott, 1970), 238.

[15] Rees, *op. cit.*, 218.

[16] C. S. Leeds, *Chats about Gillingham* (Gillingham, 1906), 28.

[17] *V.C.H.*, III, 431.

[18] Quoted J. Whyman: "The Build-up of Industry", *Medway, The Quarterly journal of the Medway Chamber of Commerce*, Spring 1973, No. 92, 16.

[19] E. Harris, *A trip up the Medway* (Rochester, 1897), 1.

[20] A. G. Munro and Prescott Row, *Rochester and Chatham with their surroundings, A Handbook for Visitors and Residents* (1905), 12.

[21] W. L. and M. A. Wyllie, *London to the Nore Painted and Described* (1905), 192.

[22] *Ibid.*, 227.

[23] *Ibid.*, 222.

[24] D. Maxwell, *Unknown Kent* (1921), 102.

[25] *Ibid*, 101.

[26] *Ibid*, 98.

[27] *Ibid*, 103.

[28] *Ibid*, 99.

[29] M. Bowley, *Innovations in Building Materials* (1960), 50.

[30] A. C. Davis, *Portland Cement* (1943), 101.

[31] A. C. Davis, *A Hundred Years of Portland Cement 1824–1924* (1924), 155.

[32] Davis, *op. cit.*, (1943), 102–5.

[33] P. Lesley Cook, *The Effects of Mergers* (1958), 26.

[34] *Ibid*, 24–5.

[35] *V.C.H.*, III, 398.

[36] Cook, *op. cit.*, 27.

[37] Davis, *op. cit.*, (1924), 225.

[38] Bowley, *op. cit.*, 89.

[39] O. H. O'Hagan, *Leaves from My Life*, II, (1929), 39.

[40] O'Hagan, *op. cit.*, 39.

[41] *Ibid*, 39.

[42] *Ibid*, 40.

[43] O'Hagan, *op. cit.*, 41, 42, 43.

[44] H. W. Macrosty, *The Trust Movement in British Industry* (1907), 108.

[45] O'Hagan, *op. cit.*, 44.

[46] O'Hagan, *op. cit.*, 48.

[47] *Chatham News*, 14 July 1900, 1.

[48] *Ibid*, 24 November 1900, 7.

49 *Rochester and Chatham Journal*, 29 March 1901, 8.
50 *Ibid*, 22 November 1901, 8c.
51 Macrosty, *op. cit.*, 110.
52 O'Hagan, *op. cit.*, 58.
53 Cook, *op. cit.*, 39; Macrosty, *op. cit.*, 113.
54 O'Hagan, *op. cit.*, 42.
55 Information from Mr F. Parker.
56 Unsourced newspaper cutting, Rochester Library, 11 December 1901.
57 Information from Mr F. Parker.
58 Information from Mr and Mrs Sibun, 2 Private Road, Wouldham.
59 O'Hagan, *op. cit.*, 58.
60 H. Levy, *Monopoly and Competition* (1911), 224–5.
61 O'Hagan, *op. cit.*, 59.
62 Macrosty, *op. cit.*, 108.
63 Information from Mr F. Parker.
64 Macrosty, *op. cit.*, 110.
65 Ed. F. C. Boucher, *Rochester, Chatham and Gillingham as an Industrial Centre and as a Residential Neighbourhood* (Chatham, 1908), 51.
66 Information from Mr. F. Parker.
67 O'Hagan, *op. cit.*, 71.
68 Cook, *op. cit.*, 59.
69 Macrosty, *op. cit.*, 109.
70 *Ibid*, 113.
71 Macrosty, *op. cit.*, 113–14.
72 *Rochester Journal*, 1 June 1906, 4.
73 *Ibid*, 31 August 1906, 8.
74 *Ibid*, 25 May 1906, 4.
75 *Ibid*, 4 October 1908, 8.
76 *Ibid*, 29 November 1907, 8.
77 *Rochester Journal*, 20 December 1907, 2.
78 Rees, *op. cit.*, 242.
79 O'Hagan, *op. cit.*, 84–7.
80 O'Hagan, *op. cit.*, 88, 89.
81 Cook, *op. cit.*, 60.
82 *Chatham News*, 8 November 1913, 9.
83 Kelly's, *Directory of Kent* (1911), 966.
84 Information from Mr Parker.
85 Cook, *op. cit.*, 61.
86 J. Clapham, *Economic History of Modern Britain*, III, (Cambridge, 1938), 235.
87 *1907–1959 A History of the Queenborough undertaking of Settle Speakman*, *op. cit.*, 8, 9.
88 KAO U234 E5. Letter G. Webb to Lord Aylesford 1 June 1918.
89 Information from Mr F. Parker.
90 O'Hagan, *op. cit.*, 63.
91 *Rochester Journal*, 22 February 1901, 8.
92 *Ibid*, 7 December 1906, 7.
93 E. J. March, *Spritsail Barges of the Thames and Medway* (Newton Abbott, 1970), 31.

CHAPTER XII

Decline in Other Industries Before 1918

The decline in house building which affected the cement industry also affected the already declining brick industry. This is reflected in newspaper reports for the early 1900s

> 'the Rainham Cement and Brick Industries are just now suffering from the depression that is experienced in the building trade. The employees at the Rainham Cement Works have this week been put on ¾ time, and the same shortage in the hours of labour has been effected in the brickfields.'[1]

The decline in the market reinforced the blow already struck against the Medway brick industry by the appearance of the Fletton. Other problems included the exhaustion of brick earth in some areas, notably the Luton area.

Many small firms had already left the industry by 1900 without being replaced by new entrants. More firms left before 1918. One of the firms to stop production were A.P.C.M. at Burham. A brief description from 1905 stated of Burham

> 'Long avenues, over arched with woodwork, branching off in all directions, tell us that the famous Burham bricks are dried here.'[2]

Brickmaking ceased in 1912. At the Temple brickfields, Strood production was intermittent.[3] The brickworks on West Hoo Creek, which obtained its clay by tramway from a large pit a mile away immediately to the north of Hoo St Werburgh village, and which was marked on the 1898 Ordnance Survey,[4] was apparently closed by 1909.[5] In 1906 Gransden's Brickfield, Luton, Chatham also closed.[6]

The only firm to appear to prosper was the large concern of Eastwood and Co. Ltd, with their brickfields at Rainham and Lower Halstow. The Lower Halstow works were modified in 1906 to meet demand for its bricks. Three German brick-making machines and a patent drier by Muller and Pliffer were installed. By 1912 there were 60 wash backs with 22 brick berths employing

120 men and boys, giving a production of 17 to 18 million bricks per annum. However, Eastwoods closed their Ten Acres Field, works, Breach Lane, Lower Halstow in 1914.[7]

One small works started up in 1906. This was the Newington Brick works whose product was mainly red facing bricks. These were made of clay without the mixture of any other material. At Newington three intermittent kilns were built to allow for flexibility in production. Newington works were further from the river than most producers, but did have the advantage of being situated by the railway.[8]

The decline of the local cement and brick industries had serious repercussions as far as the engineering industry was concerned. Problems of a declining market were compounded by foreign competition, especially from Germany and Denmark, in technically more advanced grinding mills and in rotary kilns. W. R. Taylor of the Medway Iron Works, although listed as a cement machinery manufacturer in 1903,[9] disappeared soon after. The site was described in 1913 as

> 'that eyesore in Chatham Intra—the old iron works and the "Tarter Frigate" public house (premises which have been closed so long that grass and weeds are flourishing on the spot which was for many years a hive of industry), will ere long be demolished.'[10]

Percy J. Neate of St Margaret's Bank, Rochester must have disappeared about the same time.

Another attempt at making cement machinery was the setting up of an engineering works by Martin, Earle and Co. at Wickham cement works. The works were opened on Saturday 17 June 1899 and employed about 100 men. The object was to supply machinery to the Wickham works, and to the market in general.[11] The workshops were to produce a rotary kiln to the firm's design, the first being installed in 1900. After initial difficulties the kiln ran successfully. It had a length of only 90 feet and an output of 200 tons of clinker per week, and served as a pattern for a battery of 16 more erected at the Wickham works.[12] Although the firm made all their own machinery, and carried out their own repairs, they had little success in selling to other manufacturers.

Aveling and Porter, who also manufactured cement making machinery, put most of their efforts into the manufacture of steam locomotives in the years before 1918. Their works were in 1914 the largest and best equipped roller works in the world.[13] Before 1914 the firm was the largest single employer of labour in the Medway area, after Chatham Dockyard, and the 'largest individual industry' in 1908.[14] In 1913 the Pelican Yard Works were built for engine manufacture.[15] Innovation in road rollers was seen in 1913 with the introduction of the motor roller. These were built because they were more useful on asphalt and bituminous surfaces, and also to meet competition from the firm of Barford and Perkins. The motor roller used a four-cylinder petrol engine, which was later used in a range of motor lorries, whereas their rivals used a two-cylinder paraffin engine. Durability was the prime object in these machines, but this resulted in a high price and high running costs.[16] A variant of the steam engine was also to be introduced, the steam road wagon. Aveling and Porter came to build steam lorries quite late compared with other specialist manufacturers, starting in 1909 and offering two models, a three-ton and a five-ton lorry. Versions with tipping bodies followed in 1913.[17] Overall, Aveling and Porter remained prosperous in the years to 1918.

Aveling and Porter Steam Lorry

(Photo by courtesy of Mr O. Wenbourn)

One venture in which the firm was involved proved less successful. This was the Medway Steel Company. On 7 December 1901 an agreement was sealed between Aveling and Porter and Vickers Sons and Maxim for establishing a Company for the manufacture of steel castings on land owned by Aveling and Porter. The capital of the company, which was not to exceed £25,000, was to be equally held by the two firms. A working agreement was reached

The Interior of Medway Steel Works 1907

The Machine Shop of Aveling and Porter 1907

on 5 May 1902.[18] Works were erected for the venture on the far side of the Strood to Maidstone Railway line in 1902.[19] The works were supposed to 'produce material kindred to, or required for Vickers own manufactures'.[20] However, in 1903 the results of Vickers and Maxim were not good in the South, 'where there was a want of orders, especially for field artillery'.[21] On the 1 March 1904 Vickers wrote off a loss of £7,000 in Medway Steel and a decision was made to retire from the Company. On 27 October 1904 the working agreement of 5 May 1902 was cancelled[22] and the works were closed.

These works were let on a 21 year lease in 1906,[23] when it was reported

> 'The Steel Works at Strood are now opened and, although work is resumed, operations are only in the preliminary stages. At present the labour is only of the skilled class but as time goes on, coupled of course with an increase in work, it is said that some 150 unskilled labourers will be required.'[24]

The works were said to be the only ones of their kind south of Birmingham, and to supply the demand for cast steel from 'the large and numerous engineering works on the Thames as well as for the many cement works on the Thames and Medway'.

The Steel Works had good transport facilities with a tidal creek of the Medway on two sides, and a railway siding on a third. Coal ore and raw material could be unloaded from barges close by the gas producer and the furnace. Without easy access to transportation facilities the firm would not have been able to compete with rivals in the Midlands and North.

A description of the plant in 1908 disclosed several buildings

> 'The Foundry, a large building of 150 feet by 100 feet, is exceedingly lofty, well lit and well ventilated. It is divided into two bays, one of which is fitted with a ten-ton three motor Electric Travelling Crane, and the other with a five ton similarly equipped crane. To this main Building there are several adjuncts; one of these is a building, of 150 feet by 27 feet, containing two grinding mills, and is used for the preparation and storing of large quantities of sand and compo etc. used in the moulding of the Castings.
>
> Another erection of 100 feet by 40 feet contains emery wheels and four saws for cutting off the runners and risers from the castings. An electric welding apparatus etc. is used for the dressing and trimming of the castings. The firm has a great reputation for Machine Moulded Wheels; and all sorts of gear-

ing up to ten tons are made on Wheel Moulding Machines. Then there is an Annealing Oven, in which 40 tons of castings at a time may be subject to the annealing process; another Annealing Oven is of a ten ton capacity. For the drying of the moulds there are most capacious ovens, the moulds being run in on large carriages worked with a wire rope from the crane. The furnace, upon which the success of the quality of the castings so much depends, is a ten ton Acid Siemens-Martin type. The gas for the melting of the steel, and the heating of the above-named ovens, is supplied from two 'Duff' gas producers.

The whole of the machinery of the Works is driven by electric power supplied by the Kent Electric Power Co. situated at Strood. The main firm does a considerable amount of railway work, as well as being on the Admiralty list; and recently their engine wheel centres have sustained tests equal to those of any other firm in the country.'[25]

Engineering had the advantage of being able to diversify its products, unlike the barge building industry, which was in decline.

The decline of the Medway brick industry in face of the Fletton, and the contraction of the cement industry as a result of amalgamation were the most important reasons for the problems of barge building. With a durable product with a life of perhaps 40 to 50 years an expanding market was essential to the health of the industry. Immediately after 1900 many second hand barges came onto the market as a result of cement industry mergers. For instance in 1901 Messrs W. R. Craske of Borstal Manor Cement Works sold up their fleet of ten barges which were surplus to the requirements of the A.P.C.M. Five were to remain unsold.[26] Another factor in the decline was the improvement of dock facilities in the Port of London, with ships being able to load and unload direct from the quay instead of into barges in the stream.[27] Even at Rochester a similar move was being made by Messrs Cory, who in 1906 had a 700-foot wharf constructed of ferro-concrete to take ships of up to 4,000 tons displacement, which could unload direct into railway wagons.[28] The number of boats launched in 1901 was 11, in 1902, 10; 1903, 10; 1904, 11; and 1905 only 6.[29] The number of vessels belonging to the Port of Rochester also fell from 922 ships of 51,236 tons in 1909[30] to 880 ships of 47,485 tons in 1911.[31]

When Gill's launched the 'Westwall' for British Oil and Cake Mills in January 1913 it was the 'first [launched] from the port of Rochester for some time'.[32]

Among the few barge builders and barges built after 1900 were

The Brewery of Budden and Biggs, High Street, Strood, built 1900.

The brewery was subsequently the Dove, Phillips and Petts Ltd, mineral water works, Demolished 1974.

The Victoria Street Brewery of Tomlyn Shepherd, and later Woodhams and Co.

S. J. Brice at the Point Yard, Rochester who built *Busybody* in 1905 and *G.C.B.* in 1907.[33] The Barge Co-operative appeared to transform itself into the 'Medway Barge Builders and Carriers Ltd', and remained in business till at least 1913 when they launched the *Mary Graham*.[34] Eastwoods moved their yard from Lower Halstow to Shrubsall's old yard at Milton in 1901. In 1912 they returned to Otterham Quay where a covered slip, workshop, sail loft and blacksmiths shop were erected, but only used for repairs.[35] Short Bros on arrival at the Esplanade Rochester constructed the metal sailing barge *Lady Rosebery* in 1913.[36]

Contraction is seen in other activities in the Medway Towns. Only one brewer was left in the area after 1918. The others were involved in mergers which lead to their being closed down. In 1912 Charles Arcoll and Co. sold the 'Lion Brewery' to Style and Winch who promptly closed it.[37] Dampier's Frindsbury Brewery merged with Messrs Woodhams of Rochester in 1906, the amalgamation dating from 1 October of that year. Mr H. L. Dampier joined the board of Woodhams as a director.[38] The Frindsbury premises were then sold to D. T. J. Lyle Ltd, who were mineral water manufacturers.[39] This merger brought Woodhams 'a considerable number of houses' and meant the firm had quadrupled its business since 1865. In 1913 Woodham's brewery in Victoria Street, Rochester was modernized with the introduction of electric power, but even then at its height the brewery only employed 25 men and women.[40] The business was purchased by Style and Winch in April 1918 and the brewery closed.[41]

Depression even hit the mineral water manufacturers. 'The depressed state of the trade' being commented upon in 1906.[42] This was the probable reason for the merger in 1905 of the two biggest firms, Phillips of Railway Street, Chatham and W. Dove and Co. Ltd, of Rochester. The new firm operated from Dove's premises at 277 High Street, Rochester.[43] In 1909 the merged firm was joined by Thomas Pett Ltd, of Rainham.[44] Some details of the firms at this time emerge from the ledger of W. Dove and Co. W. Dove's firm became a limited company on 9 July 1902 with the issue of 5,993 shares of £1 allotted to the vendors as purchase money, made up of goodwill £2,000, fixed plant £685 and bottles, boxes, horses, vans and the stock in trade the remainder.[45] Dove's wage bill for the year March 1903 to 28 February 1904 was £1,601. The capital of the firm was increased to £9,000 with the merger with B. R. Phillips, whose goodwill was valued at £617. Sales totalled £6,520 in the year to March 1906, £6,971 to March 1907 and £6,267 to March 1908. Profits rose from £102 in 1903 to reach £1,316 in the year to March 1907 falling back to £620 for

1908 and £820 for 1908–9.[46] The price paid to Thomas Pett for his business on 1 March 1909 was £2,000 of which £500 was in shares, the capital of the firm being increased to £9,883. The goodwill of Petts business was valued at £600 and the fixed plant and machinery at £106. 10s. Profits rose from £649 on sales of £7,962 in the year to 28 February 1910 to a peak of £2,294 on sales of £21,648 in the year to 28 February 1916, but fell away sharply thereafter.[47] The firm normally employed 48 people including the principals, B. and P. Phillips, W. and W. J. Dove and T. Pett.[48]

The firm of Dove, Phillips and Pett greatly increased its turnover and profits as an amalgamated concern, but was undoubtedly assisted by the fact that D. T. J. Lyle of Strood, which was a branch of the firm from King Street, Maidstone remained as the only serious competitor. The other firms in the mineral water industry disappeared.

Employment problems were created in other areas. By 1906 the Brennan torpedo was inferior to 9.2 inch guns for coastal defence work. As a result the manufacture of the Brennan torpedo at Gillingham was abandoned,[49] and the works were closed. There was a slowing of construction in Chatham Dockyard. The last battleship to be launched there was *Africa* in 1905, and the only vessel launched in 1906 was the cruiser *Shannon*. There were no launchings in 1907, with a consequent reduction in the work force.

This situation of a general reduction of employment through mergers, closures and a decline in work demanded action, which was subsequently undertaken by the borough councils of Rochester, Chatham and Gillingham.

[1] *Rochester Journal*, 22 November 1901, 5.

[2] A. G. Munro and Prescott Row, *Rochester and Chatham, with their surroundings. A Handbook for Visitors and Residents* (1905), 86.

[3] *Rochester Journal*, 4 April 1901, 4.

[4] Ordnance Survey 1898 Kent Sheet XI·S.E. 6 inches to 1 mile.

[5] Ordnance Survey 1909 Kent Sheet XI S.E. 6 inches to 1 mile.

[6] *Rochester Journal*, 7 September 1906, 1.

[7] F. G. Willmott, *Bricks and Brickies* (Privately published, Rainham, 1972), 25, 29.

[8] Information from Col Dean.

[9] Kelly, *Directory of Kent* (1903), 873.

[10] *Chatham News*, 2 August 1913, 7c.

[11] H. Smetham, *A History of Strood* (Strood, 1899), 349.

[12] Information from Mr Parker.

[13] *A Hundred Years of Road Rollers* (Grantham, 1965), 56.

[14] F. C. Boucher, *Rochester, Chatham and Gillingham as an Industrial Centre and as a Residential Neighbourhood* (Chatham, 1908).

[15] Information from Aveling Barford.

[16] *A Hundred Years of Road Rollers*, *op. cit.*, 34.

[17] M. A. Kelly, *The Overtype Steam Road Waggon* (Norwich, 1971), 20.

[18] Information from Vickers Ltd.

[19] Information from Aveling Barford.

[20] Information from Vickers Ltd.

[21] J. D. Scott, *Vickers, a history* (1962), 82.

[22] Information from Vickers Ltd.

[23] Information from Aveling Barford.

[24] *Rochester Journal*, 9 February 1906, 4.

[25] Boucher, *op. cit.*, 51, 52, 59.

[26] *Rochester Journal*, 20 September 1901.

[27] E. J. March, *Spritsail Barges of the Thames and Medway* (Newton Abbott, 1970), 124.

[28] *Rochester Journal*, 1 June 1906, 4; 15 June 1906, 4.

[29] H. Rees, *The Medway Towns, Their Settlement, Growth and Economic Development* (London Ph.D. thesis, 1954), 218.

[30] Kelly, *Directory of Rochester, Strood, Chatham and Gillingham for 1911–12*, 2.

[31] Kelly, *Directory of Rochester, Strood, Chatham and Gillingham for 1913–14*, 2.

[32] *Chatham News*, 4 January 1913, 7.

[33] *Barge Yards Around Rochester*, MSS Rochester Museum.

[34] *Chatham News*, 11 October 1913, 5.

[35] Willmott, *op. cit.*, 6.

[36] *Barge Yards Around Rochester, op. cit.*

[37] Information from Courage (Eastern) Ltd.

[38] *Rochester Journal*, 27 July 1906, 5b.

[39] *Chatham Observer*, 22 March 1913.

[40] *Chatham Observer*, 22 March 1913.

[41] Information from Courage (Eastern) Ltd.

[42] *Rochester Journal*, 6 April 1906, 2.

[43] *South Eastern Gazette*, 12 December 1961.

[44] *Chatham Standard*, 8 September 1959.

[45] W. Dove and Co. Private Ledger 1 March 1902 to 27 February 1909, 2, 9, 13, 21, 31, 37, 43, 49, 55, 71, 81, 91, 101.

[46] *Ibid*, 2, 9, 244, 251, 252, 329, 333, 157.

[47] Dove, Phillips and Pett, Private Ledger, 1 March 1909 to 28 February 1918, 2, 47–8, 101, 109, 92, 65.

[48] Wage Book 1912.

[49] Louis Brennan, C.B. *Dirigible Torpedo* (Local History Series No. 5, Part 1, Gillingham Library, (April 1973), 8.

CHAPTER XIII

The 'New Industries Committee' and the Coming of New Industry

In view of the lack of employment in the Lower Medway area and the Medway Towns in particular the local councils attempted to attract industry to the area. This was done firstly by the individual councils. Chatham Council wrote on the 28 November 1905 to Bryant and Mays the match manufacturers pointing out that Chatham would be an excellent place to establish themselves if they were, as rumoured, thinking of moving their factory.[1] A similar letter was sent to Messrs. Yarrow and Co. Ltd, of Poplar on 30 November 1905 which pointed out that there was

> 'ample vacant land for large wharves, and building purposes on the river bank, there is water communication by the river Medway, it is near to London, and has fast and frequent train services, there is a large working class population, and low rates.'[2]

The Town Clerk of Chatham was later able to report that both firms had stated that if they decided to move they would 'carefully consider Chatham'.[3] Rochester Council also had unemployment problems, and the City surveyor stated in December 1906 that he had opened a register of the unemployed.[4] The Town Clerk had also written to Yarrows offering them sites either above Rochester Bridge or in Whitewall Creek,[5] but received a reply that the firm had already settled on a site to which they intended to move.[6]

In Gillingham a motion was presented to the council on 3 July 1906 that it was incumbent on the Council to

> 'seek to bring into this area manufacturing and other industry by circulating literature pointing out the many advantages this locality offers as regards cheap land, low rates, electric power, easy access by rail and water etc.'

This led to the appointment of a five man Borough Development Committee on 7 August 1906.[7] The Committee started by resolving to approach the South Eastern and Chatham Railway over railway facilities, and by approaching local landowners to ascertain the amount of land available at what rents or prices.[8]

However, the most important attempt to attract industry was by a joint committee set up by all three town councils. This was the result of an approach by Chatham Traders Association to Chatham Council which had led to a meeting on 1 October 1906. The deliberations led to the view that it would be more practical to have a Development and Industrial Committee made up of delegates from all three councils.[9] Each of the councils then voted the sum of £33. 6s. 8d. to defray the cost of advertising and incidental expenses.[10]

At the first real meeting of the New Industries Committee on 17 December 1906 five resolutions were passed. Firstly, that the Town Clerks prepare a precis of the information already obtained showing the advantages of the area. Secondly, that the Town Clerk of Rochester obtain information about the marshes on the north side of the Medway. Thirdly, that a joint deputation approach the Admiralty to obtain more work for Chatham Dockyard. Fourthly, that the Chairman of the Parish Meeting and the Overseers of the Poor of Frindsbury Extra attend meetings. Fifthly, that the Railway Co. be requested to issue cheap tickets to and from Chatham.[11]

By 25 November 1907, the committee were considering the proofs of a treatise prepared by F. C. Boucher the Town Clerk of Gillingham entitled *Rochester, Chatham and Gillingham as an Industrial Centre and as a Residential Neighbourhood*.[12] At the next meeting on 13 December 1907, the proofs were amended. It was resolved not to carry advertisements, to print the arms of the three towns on the outside, and name Boucher as editor. Tenders for the revised proofs were then to be obtained.[13] It transpired at the meeting of 14 February 1908 that the pamphlet was copied from a similar one published in Harrogate. Also mentioned at the meeting was that the New Patent Act of 1907 required all articles patented in this country to be made here. It was suggested that many continental firms would come to Britain to manufacture their patents and that it would be a good idea to advertise the district as a desirable place for manufacturers. It was resolved to advertise in French, Belgian and German Newspapers.[14] This resulted in a further £33. 6s. 8d. from each council being voted for the cost of the advertisements.[15]

At the next committee meeting on 20 March 1908 it was decided to try to obtain the name of foreign firms affected by the Patents Act. Also it was decided to illustrate the pamphlet, now limited to 5,000 copies, with photographs of the area.[16] On 4 May 1908 advertisements in French and German newspapers were placed to the value of £55 via Sells Advertising Agency Ltd, London.[17] A tender for the printing of the pamphlet from *The Gentlemans Journal* was accepted on 10 August 1908, 2,000 copies being ordered for each council.[18] At the end of August 1908 the councils were again writing to land owners in the area enquiring if they had any land of which they wished to dispose in the prospect of new industry actually arriving. The councils also agreed to co-operate with two London agencies, Leopold Farmer and Sons and Fuller Horsey and Co., on information over available sites. Further and much more important, it was resolved that an arrangement if possible be come to by the three towns for a reduction of the rates for a term of years in respect of new works being erected in the district.[19]

The cost of printing the pamphlet, had been £155. 9s. 5d. and maps from Parrett and Neves and Edward Stanford totalled £33. 19s, the expenditure requiring the vote of a further sum of £33. 6s. 8d. from each council. However, little real progress seems to have been made apart from the distribution of the booklets. The committee was still in October 1909 trying to obtain the names of foreign firms affected by the Patents Act.[20] By March 1909 the interest of the Development Committee seemed to be waning. They resolved not to advertise further in the foreign press, not to advertise in the *Estates Gazette*, deferred consideration of buying lists of foreign owners of British patents at £2. 10s. 0d. per 1,000 from the publisher of *Patents and Designs*, and put up for sale at half-cost price the blocks for pictures in the booklet. The only positive action was to insert a short advertisement in the *Daily Telegraph* once a week for three months.[21] In September 1909 a joint deputation was appointed to press the Admiralty to undertake new construction at Chatham.[22] After this no more mention is made of the Joint Committee, and no appointments were made to it at the first meeting of Gillingham Council on 9 November 1909.[23] By 1914 just after the outbreak of war the problem of new industry is again brought forward, this time by the Medway District Chamber of Trade who suggested a conference on the question of the establishment of new industries in respect of goods hitherto manufactured abroad.[24]

The most important achievement of the New Industries Committee seems to have been the publication of F. C. Boucher's booklet. He outlined the advantages enjoyed by the area

> 'the towns are adapted for almost any form of manufacture, but afford special advantages for Engineering, Ship Building, Portland Cement, Chemical and Paper Manufacture and other kindred industries. Among such advantages the following may be mentioned.

1. Unequalled River Facilities, Low River Dues and Proximity to the Sea.
2. Exceptional Railway Facilities. The towns have seven Railway Stations on the London Chatham and Dover Railway and South Eastern Railway besides many Goods Stations and Sidings.
3. Frequent Fast Train Service to London within the hour.
4. Accommodation for Railway Sidings on Reasonable Terms.
5. An inexhaustible and cheap Supply of Water.
6. Land in Advantageous Positions, at Low Prices, adjoining either Railway or River.
7. Electricity Supply for Lighting and Motive Power at Low Rates.
8. Houses for the Industrial Classes at Low Rentals.
9. One of the Best Health Records in the Kingdom.
10. Exceptional Educational Facilities for all classes.
11. Numerous Recreation Grounds and Parks.
12. Abundance of Cheap Labour, male and female.
13. Cheap Materials for Building.'[25]

Boucher specified the types of industries he thought could be established in the area, including chemical works; paper works; tanneries; boot manufacturies; electric launch building; paint works; soap works; jam factories, motor and cycle works; electrical engineering works; agricultural implement engineering, and artificial stone works.[26]

There is, however, no definite evidence to measure the success of the efforts of the local councils in attracting industry. The most likely answer is that they were completely unsuccessful. There were some new developments in the area, such as the arrival of the British Standard Cement Works, Rainham, and innovations and changes of ownership in some sectors. One change occurred in January 1911 when Martin, Earle severed their connection with the none too successful engineering branch at Wickham Cement Works. The works were leased to a new company, the Rochester Engineering Company, which was to manufacture rotary kilns, tube and ball mills, and cement machinery in general of the type which was imported from Germany and Denmark. There was a hope of exploiting the re-equipment of British cement works to make Rochester the main centre for these products in Britain. In the firm

> 'German cement plant makers will be associated with English. The manager . . . will be an Englishman, but the brains will be partly English and partly German. It is German experience that

> has been wanted all through in the manufacture of this special machinery in this country and this will be supplied by two German experts who are interested in the undertaking.'

It was thought that the new company would only compete with German manufacturers.[27] Whether or not the patent laws or the efforts of the council affected the decision to come to Rochester is not known.

On a smaller scale was the attempt by a local carriage builder to keep pace with the times. Frederick Clark of 17 High Street, Chatham added in 1908–9 a motor works next door at 19 High Street.[28] By 1913–14 the business had expanded with an emphasis on motor vehicles. An advertisement of the time described Frederick Clark and Sons as

> 'Carriage, Van and Motor Specialists, 17 and 19 High Street and 174, 6 and 8 New Road, Chatham. (Midway between Chatham Free Library and St Pauls Church, New Road). Touring Motor Bodies built and fitted up to any chassis. Commercial Motor Bodies specially designed and built to suit all trades. We specialise on the remodelling and renovation of Old Cars.'[29]

The Medway Towns acquired another new industry in 1913 with the setting up of Recess Screw Ltd. The firm with offices at 43 Balmoral Road, Gillingham, was to take over the former Brennan Torpedo Works in Pier Road. The firm had a target production of 5,000 gross of screws per day.[30] The firm was also to carry on the business of tool makers, wire drawers, brass founders and metal workers, iron and steel converters. Its capital was to be £125,000 in £1 shares and the directors included A. E. Gill of the London and Rochester Barge Co., and J. W. Pearson, managing director of British Oil and Cake Mills.[31]

By far the most important new industry to come to the area before 1914 was the aircraft firm of Short Bros, the first British aeronautical engineers. Shorts originally had works at Battersea where they made balloons for the Royal Aeronautical Club. Their connection with Kent resulted from the Royal Aeronautical Club using Shellbeach, Sheppey as a flying field in 1909. Shorts followed the Club, obtained a site at Leysdown in February 1909 and began erecting sheds.[32] An order for six Wright machines was then obtained, this being the first aircraft order given in Great Britain. The engines for the machines had to be obtained from France.[33] By August 1909 the firm had 80 employees on the payroll.[34] Horace Short, about this time, decided to build an all British aeroplane for Mr Moore Brabazon. The machine was completed on 26 September 1909, and a little over a month later, 30 October 1909, this aeroplane won a prize of £1,000 offered by the *Daily Mail* for the first circular flight of one mile in England by a British pilot in an all-British machine.[35] Short's machines were becoming popular by 1910 which necessitated moving to bigger premises at Eastchurch.[36] Military interest was also shown when in 1911 Short's machines were chosen for Lts Samson, Longmore, Gregor and Gerrard, the first naval officers selected for an aviation course.[37]

In 1912 the firm produced the first successful British seaplane.[38] The Eastchurch works were not suitable for seaplane work. What was required were works by the side of a stretch of smooth, sheltered water. The river above Rochester Bridge was fairly ideal for Short's needs, and the move to Rochester made in 1913. The *Chatham News* reported in September 1913.

> 'We understand . . . that Messrs. Short Bros. the world famous manufacturers of aeroplanes, and who have made Eastchurch famous, have entered into negotiations for the acquisition of Tower Field, Rochester, (8 or 9 acres), where almost immediately they will proceed with the erection of aeroplane works. As a matter of fact they are removing almost the whole of their Eastchurch works to Rochester, and this will mean the transference of 200 or 300 mechanics. As Rochester will be Messrs. Short Bros headquarters the whole of the staff will be transferred.'[39]

This was the most significant of the new industries, and destined to become the largest single employer in the area, apart from the dockyard.

New work was also found for Chatham Dockyard. The Admiralty was concerned about having a single source of supply, Vickers, for submarines. The result was that Chatham Dockyard was called upon to supplement construction by Vickers.[40] The first submarine C17 to come from Chatham was launched on 13 August 1908.[41] Submarines then made up the bulk of the output of the yard.

Outside the Medway Towns there were some developments at Queenborough. These were largely the result of improved transport facilities and cheaper coal available from 1908, provided to a large extent by subsidiaries of Queenborough Cement Company. In 1907 E. W. Jaffray, J. E. Castle and W. S. Fenton formed the Queenborough Wharf Company after proposals from Mr Joel Settle and Mr W. Carroll, partners in the firm of Philip Speakman and Sons of Liverpool, and Joel Settle of Alsager, Cheshire, distributors of coal in the industrial area of South Lancashire and Cheshire, and with interests in collieries and washeries in North Staffordshire, to set up a coal washing, grading and distribution point on the Thames estuary. The coal would be shipped from Yorkshire and the North East coast to a suitable wharf in the area. The Wharf Company undertook to acquire land and foreshore rights at Rushenden, erect a 232-foot wharf, acquire rights of way, and construct a railway to the wharf. Philip Speakman and Co. were to construct a washer plant at the wharf capable of handling 500 tons per day. The Wharf Co. was to unload ships and perform all the shunting. The Cement Company then formed a subsidiary, the Queenborough Contracting Company, to construct the railway to the wharf. The wharf and piers were constructed by Robert McAlpine, while Settle built the washer plant. The first ship to discharge coal was the S.S. *Britannia* on 23 November 1908, which brought 1,500 tons of rough slack from Lanarkshire collieries. The result was to greatly reduce the price of coal in the area.[42]

> 'In the years 1908–10 there began a period of industrial development of the area with the building of the Pottery and the Glass Bottle Works, both of which had their services provided for by the Queenborough Wharf and Cement Companies.'[43]

Alfred Johnson and Son Ltd established works in 1908 as a producer of sanitary ware. The works were connected by a narrow gauge line to the Chalk Wharf, to which supplies of china clay and china stone from Cornwall and boulder flints from France were brought by water. Glass manufacture commenced in 1910 with the setting up of the Queenborough Glass Bottle Works to make bottles and jars. Materials were brought to the Chalk Wharf, including amber sand and flint sand and felspar from Belgium,[44] and also sand for amber glass from the Aylesford Sand and Gravel Co.[45] The Queenborough Copper Works were established by a member of the Armstrong Group to meet demand for copper wire for electrical purposes, but the venture was soon abandoned.[46]

Immediately before 1914 there was some recovery in the local economy. Evident is a distinct shift away from the traditional products of cement, bricks and barges to new lighter engineering works and the products such as glass. In the latter industry the Sheppey area was strategically located in relation to raw materials and markets.

[1] Chatham Borough Council, Letter Book 22 June 1905 to 26 February 1906, 664.

[2] *Ibid*, 670.

[3] Chatham Borough Council, Minute Book 1905–6, 56, Highway and Works Committee 28 December 1905.

[4] Rochester Borough Council, Estates Committee Minute Book 21 August 1901 to 7 November 1906, 20 December 1905, 426.

[5] *Ibid*, 6 December 1905, 420–1.

[6] *Ibid*, 20 December 1905, 424.

[7] Gillingham Council, Minute Book November 1905–October 1906, 261, 302.

[8] *Ibid*, Borough Development Committee, 10 August 1906, 308.

[9] Chatham Council, Minute Book 1905–6, 364, 10 October 1906.

[10] Rochester Council, Minute Book 1905–6, 31 October 1906, 344.

[11] Chatham Council, Minute Book 1906–7, 17 December 1906, 51.

[12] Gillingham Council, Minute Book November 1907 to October 1908, 25 November 1907, 17.

[13] *Ibid*, 13 December 1907, 61.

[14] Gillingham Council, Minute Book, November 1907 to October 1908, 14 February 1908, 118.

[15] Rochester Council, Notices 1907–8, Estates and General Purposes Committee, 18 March 1908, 139.

[16] Gillingham Council, Minute Book November 1907 to October 1908, 20 March 1908, 175.

[17] *Ibid*, 235, 4 May 1908.

[18] *Ibid*, 10 August 1908.

[19] *Ibid*, 31 August 1908, 374.

[20] Gillingham Council, Minute Book, October 1908 to October 1909, 31 October 1908, 6.

[21] *Ibid*, 8 March 1909, 162.

[22] *Ibid*, 7 Septimber 1909, 361.

[23] Gillingham Council, Minute Book November 1909 to November 1910, 9 November 1910.

[24] Rochester Council, Notices 1913–14, Estates and General Purposes Committee, 4 November 1914.

[25] F. Boucher, *Rochester, Chatham and Gillingham as an Industrial Centre and as a Residential Neighbourhood* (Chatham, 1908), 3.

[26] Boucher, *op. cit.*, 66.

[27] *Chatham News*, 21 January 1911, 7.

[28] F. Sanders, MSS, *A Business History of Chatham High Street* 1, (1961), 25.

[29] Kelly's, *Directory of Rochester, Strood, Chatham, Gillingham and Villages in the Neighbourhood for 1913–14*, ii.

[30] *Chatham News*, 13 December 1913, 3.

[31] *Chatham News*, 13 December 1913, 9.

[32] *Short Story*, No. 18, November 1947, 4.

[33] *A Royal Visit.* Souvenir of the visit of Their Majesties King George VI and Queen Elizabeth to the Works of Short Bros (Rochester and Bedford) Ltd, Rochester, 14 March 1939.

[34] C. Barnes, *Shorts Aircraft Since 1900* (1967), 7.

[35] Short Story, No. 18, *op. cit.*, 5.

[36] Barnes, *op. cit.*, 8.

[37] Short Story, No. 18, *op. cit.*, 5.

[38] F. F. Smith, *A History of Rochester* (1928), 206.

[39] *Chatham News*, 30 September 1913, 3.

[40] J. D. Scott, *Vickers, A History* (1962), 66.

[41] J. G. Grace, *Some Notes on the History of Chatham Dockyard* (1946), 73.

[42] *1907–1957 A History of the Queenborough undertaking of Settle Speakman and Co. Ltd., Queenborough, Kent* (Queenborough, 1957), 10, 11.

[43] *Ibid*, 12.

[44] *Ibid*, 24, 28.

[45] H. Rees, *The Medway Towns—Their Settlement, Growth and Economic Development* (London Ph.D. thesis, 1954), 278.

[46] K. R. MacDonald, *The Isle of Sheppey and the Swale* (London M.A. (Geography), thesis, 1949), 81.

CHAPTER XIV

1918 to 1946
Continuity of Decline

This chapter is intended to purely sketch the progress of industry in the Lower Medway Valley from the time when difficulties became apparent until the closure of the last of the major pre-1918 civil employers.

The First World War itself, created activity in the area. In the Dockyard employment rose from 9,000 to reach 11,000. With increasing use of military aircraft the new firm of Short Bros were also extremely busy. However, the extra employment created was to some extent balanced by the loss of jobs in the closures of older cement works.

After the First World War ended the process of decline continued. The result was for severe problems of unemployment to be felt in the Lower Medway valley. In the inter-war years employment in the dockyard was run down with the trend towards disarmament, falling to 7,000 in 1933,[1] With the end of the war aircraft orders for Short Bros vanished. It was only the skill of Eustace and Oswald Short in finding alternative products and in reorganizing the works for peace which enabled the firm to survive while many of the aircraft firms which mushroomed during the war disappeared. In the lean years of the 1920s and 1930s Shorts kept their work force together in building power launches and highly successful light weight bus bodies for London General Omnibus Company.[2] Also built at Rochester were pram bodies, bodies for Renault, Fiat and Salmson cars; and paddle boats for boating pools.[3] Three sailing barges were built in the inter-war years at the old barge yard on the Esplanade premises. These were *Lady Jean* 1923; *Lady Daphne* 1923 and *Lord Haigh* 1930, the last barge to be built on the Medway.[4] Complete trolley buses were built until 1933.[5]

Aircraft work at Rochester expanded from 1936 onward with the construction of Empire flying boats.[6] The Esplanade factory was unable to cope with orders which led to the establishment of the Belfast factory in 1938. Land-based aircraft which could not be built at the Esplanade were constructed at a new factory to the east of Rochester airport. These included the Stirling bomber first flown in May 1939. Some of the work at Rochester airport was subcontracted to Pobjoy Airmotors in which Shorts had a holding.[7]

Although Shorts managed to survive, some local products were doomed to disappear completely. Small local cement machinery manufacturers were unable to compete with the large foreign and British engineering groups in the business. Work in Britain for such items as rotary kilns was dominated after 1918 by Vickers who set up a large cement machinery plant at Barrow.[8] Aveling and Porter still the largest engineering works in the area continued to concentrate their efforts on road rollers. In 1920 there was a complete reorganization

> 'No longer could each roller be fashioned individually by highly skilled craftsmen: demand was too great, economic pressures too stringent and craftsmen of the required perfection of skills too few. Thus the factory was completely reorganized to make extensive use of jigs and bring about a standardization of components that would speed manufacture, allow maximum inter-changeability and provide spares "off the shelf".'

A complete new range of single and compound cylinder rollers of six to twenty tons replaced all earlier models, incorporating modern features which were cheaper and easier to produce, for example piston valves replaced slide valves.[9] Some other products were discontinued. The last ploughing engines were made in 1921 after a total production of 328.[10] Steam waggons were discontinued in 1925 after 292 were completed, including 12 assembled by Garretts of Leiston in 1921–3, a member of Agricultural and General Engineers Ltd.[11] New products included petrol engine lorries after 1926 when Aveling and Porter also added a diesel engine to their range of products. This was the 'Invicta' diesel which was made in four and six cylinder sizes, suitable for farm tractors and lorries.[12] The 1930 tractor sported a four cylinder diesel engine of 22/38 h.p. three speed gear box and a price of £525.[13]

Aveling and Porter disappeared during the slump of 1932. In 1921, T. L. Aveling started a move towards amalgamation which resulted in the formation of a group called 'Agricultural and General Engineers Ltd' linking Aveling and Porter, Garrett, Burrell of Thetford, Davey Paxman, Blackstone, Bentall and Peter Brotherhood. The Rochester plant was badly hit by the depression in 1929, and the group which was badly mismanaged collapsed in February 1932. In the meantime in 1931 Barford and Perkins had moved from their Queen Street, Peterborough factory, and took over the idle Pelican Yard Works. Barfords then purchased the roller company from the liquidator of Agricultural and General Engineers to form a new firm Aveling-Barford Ltd. In 1934, the firm left the obsolete plant at Rochester to move to Grantham where Ruston and Hornsby had 30 acres which were formerly a munitions factory where a modern production line could be set up.[14] When Aveling-Barford moved to Grantham, Frank Perkins, a director of Barford and Perkins parted and took over the Invicta Diesel Engine and returned to the Queen Street Works, Peterborough. This was the fore runner of what is now the Perkins diesel engine.

The decline and contraction also affected the barge-building industry. Only eight barges were launched on the Medway after 1918.[15] The cost of spars, cordage and sails rose rapidly making sailing barges an uneconomic proposition.[16] Apart from running expenses, the motor lorry was proving more satisfactory for many goods. It allowed smaller quantities to be moved, cut handling costs which were particularly heavy for goods like bricks, and cut the amount of damage. For the brick industry, the lorry meant safe speedy transport from the brickfield to the building site, and was generally adopted.

Brickmaking on the Medway managed to remain an important source of bricks for the local and London markets till the 1930s. Around 1936, the London Brick Company producing Fletton bricks, engaged in a price war, cutting prices by 10s. 0d. per 1,000. This drove small local producers from the market, including Funton Brickworks which was associated with Newington Brick Company, and Batchelor's of Hoo.[17] Only Eastwoods was left as a large non-specialist brickmaker. They only closed one of their works, Leeney's field at Otterham Quay, in 1932. The site which previously had an output of 2½ million bricks per annum from three hand berths and four washbacks became an ash dump for the other works in the area.[18]

Among various other industries to disappear were the Axe Brand clothing works at Chatham in 1934. This was a considerable blow to female employment in the Chatham area.[19] The Medway Chemical Works of William Johnson can be traced through the directories until 1922,[20] thereafter it disappeared. A new firm set up at Queenborough in 1919, the Medway Glass Works had closed by 1921. The firm anticipated winning large contracts for the manufacture of electric lamps. However there were delays in completing the factory, contracts were lost and the works closed soon after starting production.[21]

The last brewery in the Medway Towns, Budden and Biggs of High Street, Strood finally closed in 1938, when the buildings were acquired by the mineral manufacturers Dove Phillips and Pett.[22]

Further contraction was also seen in the cement industry with the closure of more works. Faced with severe competition in a limited market the works with the worst locations were forced to close. Lees works at Snodland were closed down about 1930 or 1931. Halling Manor Works were closed about 1925. They had operated Hoffman continuous kilns which fired pressed dried slurry bricks. After 1925 the brickmaking machines were dismantled and transferred to Burham Cement Works for use with its Schneider kilns.[23] The British Standard Works at Rainham were acquired around 1928 by the Horne (Red Triangle) Group. They were modernized at considerable expense,[24] including two rotary kilns.[25] Subsequently, they came into the hands of the A.P.C.M. and were closed down.[26] Peter's Works at Wouldham were modernized after the war with two rotary kilns,[27] but in the absence of railway communications it was in an isolated position.

Cement works, fronting the Medway on Frindsbury Ness.

Peters ferried cement by barge across the river, and hauled it by cart to Snodland Station. High handling costs which resulted were prohibitive in the long run.[28] The works do not appear in *Kelly's, Directory of Kent* for 1927. The Burham Works with their four rotary kilns were also geographically isolated on the right bank of the river. They were closed in 1930 at the height of the price war with Mr H. S. Horne's Red Triangle group. They were re-opened for clinker only in 1934, the grinding being carried out at the Crown Works. They were finally closed in 1941. The West Kent (Burham) Works was adapted to produce 'Lightning' Brand High Alumina Cement for a limited market, but closed in 1926.[29]

Gillingham Cement Works as modernized, 1932.

One of the pre-war works, Gillingham, was revived in 1920 by an ex-manager of a B.P.C.M. works, who convenanted not to install a rotary kiln for ten years. At the end of that period a 200-foot Edgar Allen rotary kiln was installed. The firm lost money until 1933 when marketing conditions improved. The firm joined the Cement Makers Federation in 1935 accepting a production quota. From 1 December 1935 to February 1936 the works were closed due to high stocks, and the owners tried to dispose of the works. There followed in 1936 an agreement with the Rugby Portland Cement Co. whereby the Rugby Company purchased all surplus production at cost price, allowing the works to run at full capacity. In 1937 the owners accepted an offer of £100,000 from the Amalgamated Roadstone Corporation. This move ended the agreement with the Rugby Company, and without new outlets profits dropped. Eventually in 1939, the Rugby Company offered £130,000 for the Gillingham works, which was accepted. The works were kept running for only a few months, making it possible under the quota system to expand the sales for the company's new works at Halling. The Gillingham plant was then removed and the site sold. In 1936 the Rugby Portland Cement Company had acquired the Halling works of Albert Batchelor Ltd. This company had two old kilns, and an output of 50,000 tons per year of low quality cement which was disposed of to Batchelor's own particular customers. Batchelor took an independent line and refused to join any form of price agreement. The Rugby Company built new works alongside the old, while building up their share of the local market using Batchelor and Gillingham cement.[30]

The one bright spot as far as the cement industry is concerned was the construction of one entirely new cement works. Major William Lee Henry Roberts who had formerly been part owner of Lees cement works built the Holborough Works at Snodland in 1923. Originally the works had two rotary kilns, but a third was added in 1928. In 1929 the works were acquired by the Red Triangle group, but with the failure and liquidation of the group, A.P.C.M. took control in 1931.[31]

The loss of so much industry was not fully counter-balanced by new industry coming to the area. The situation in the Snodland area was eased in 1928 with the opening of A. E. Reed's paper mill at Larkfield. This was the result of increased demand for packaging paper and the mill particularly specialized in glazed and unglazed kraft wrappings.[32] In the Medway Towns the works vacated by Aveling & Porter in 1932 were taken over by Winget Limited who moved from Warwick in May 1934. The firm was looking for larger premises and was offered the Aveling & Porter site on attractive terms by Rochester Corporation. The firm was also offered housing accommodation on the Temple Farm estate for the substantial number of employees and their families who had moved with them from Warwick.[33]

At that time, the company specialized mainly in the manufacture of equipment for the production and pre-casting of concrete, but its interests were to increase considerably over the next decade or two.

By the time Winget were fifty years old in 1958, these interests had broadened into a variety of industries including Wire Machinery and Refrigeration equipment. It was in 1961, however, that a major development took place when Winget acquired the well known Gloucester Railway Carriage and Wagon Company Ltd at Gloucester.

A holding company—Winget-Gloucester Limited—was formed to develop the organization and the Winget Gloucester Group came into being.

The companies within the group were of high repute both in the original spheres of construction equipment and also in such fields as Chemicals and Plastics, Bulk Materials Handling, Malleable Iron Castings and others. Development continued until 1968 when the Winget Gloucester Group was acquired by the internationally famous Babcock & Wilcox Ltd Group of Companies.

At Queenborough, the Glass Bottle Works was taken over in 1926 by the Canning Town Glass Works, and continued in production. The site of the Copper Works was taken over in 1919 by British Window Glass Ltd, who built a factory to produce sheet glass. Production stopped during the depression of 1924. Sheet Glass Ltd, was then formed and opened the works between 1927 and 1929. The works were eventually re-opened by Pilkington Bros in 1932.[34]

If stock is taken after the disruption of the Second World War the following list of firms presented itself. There were only four cement works left in production: Holborough, Halling, Wickham and the Quarry Frindsbury. Of the brickworks there was only Eastwoods at Lower Halstow and Otterham Quay and Funton apart from the small works at Newington. No barge builders survived, although there were a few repair yards. Of the engineers Shorts and Wingets existed. Sheppey Glue Company still remained along with Johnson's Pottery, Canning Town Glass and Pilkingtons.

The paper works of Townsend Hook remained active. In the 8 years, 1898–1905, profits averaged £6,100 (net),[35] and in the last year production had been over 200 tons of paper per week from a labour force of about 250. On 12 August 1906 the mill was totally destroyed by fire, the damage being estimated at £150,000.[36] Fire insurance provided £106,350 with which the managing director, Col. Holland commenced the reconstruction of the mill.[37] A modern building was erected, a 2,300 h.p. engine installed which not only drove the beaters, but also a 850 k.w. generator which supplied electricity for the rest of the plant. The three new paper machines installed were designed to make best quality newsprint, and high class printing paper.[38] Circumstances had forced the adoption of modern technology and a move into a better class market which allowed the firm not only to recover, but also to prosper. Profits from 1906 to 1908 were nil due to the fire, after which they increased; £1,321 in 1909; £14,813 in 1910; £17,577 in 1911; peak performance being reached in 1912 with £19,535 (net). Continual improvements were made to the mill, with new beaters and other equipment installed, and a fourth paper machine in 1912. The mill was modern and in excellent condition on the eve of the First World War,[39] and was thus able to remain competitive and meet severe competition. It eventually was to become part of the News of the World Organization which ensured the future of the mill.

To see an almost complete disappearance of the pre-1914 structure two more firms, Shorts and B.O.C.M. had to go. The closing of Short's Rochester works was announced in a speech on 12 June 1946 by Mr A. Woodburn, M.P., Parliamentary Secretary, Ministry of Supply. He said the government had to contract the aircraft industry after the war and turn it to civil use. It was decided to move to Belfast where there was a new aircraft works, which had room for expansion.

> 'The buildings here at Rochester are not really worthy of a first class aircraft factory. They were erected at different times and at different standards of efficiency; they represent not a well designed whole but a collection of separate buildings ill-suited for the purpose of an aircraft unit. The airfield also is too small for many modern types of aircraft and cannot be extended. The river facilities which you use are becoming inadequate. As you know it was not possible to build even the Shetland under cover at Rochester; it will be impossible to fly anything bigger above Rochester bridge.'[40]

The site apart from being cramped had poor road and no rail access. The plan was to transfer 300 jobs to Belfast and phase out the rest over eighteen months. The last seaplane to leave Rochester flew out in April 1948 when the works closed.[41]

As the biggest employer of labour outside the dockyard the closure of Short's presented employment problems again. The Chairman of Shorts envisaged that 'factories representing a variety of industries—in place of a single industry—will be established in Rochester in the coming months', and that dislocation would only be temporary due to the demand for skilled labour and factory space in the area.[42]

The oil seed mills of B.O.C.M. in Canal Road, Strood had continued to produce oils and compound cattle cake. The only change in the plant had been the replacement of all compound presses with Schueler nutting machines in 1925. (In this machine meal was fed between the intermeshing teeth of two hollowed out gear wheels, and nuts were formed by the teeth of one wheel forcing meal through ports drilled between the roots of the teeth on the other.) The crushing mills, presses and refinery finally closed in 1949,[43] when this part of the business was concentrated at Erith, Strood being equipped with obsolete intermittent machinery.

A flood in 1953 finally closed the factory, it being uneconomic to replace the compounding machinery there.[44]

In face of these closures Rochester City Council made strenuous efforts to persuade other industrial firms to establish themselves at Rochester. The council was able to offer land at low rents at the Esplanade, Knight Road industrial estate and at the Airport.[45] The efforts were met with some success with Blaw Knox who moved from Watford into part of the Shorts Works. The main range of products of this company included such items as earth movers, asphalt pavers, construction plant, transmission towers and steelworks equipment. In the construction field the company devoted its main efforts to the development of asphalt pavers and finishers for which today they are world renowned. They also retained their position in the spheres of power transmission and steelworks equipment which are still manufactured. In 1969 Blaw Knox were also joined to the Babcock & Wilcox Group of Companies as had Winget Limited a year previously. Burnett & Rolfe (standard steel vat makers), Ozonair Limited, William Palfrey, Berry Eade & White as well as C.A.V. also moved into the esplanade. Elliott Automation took a site at the Airport. The valley has also been favoured with oil installations, Berry Wiggins and Co. who set up a refinery at Kingsnorth in the early 1930s to make tar products[46] increased employment, while the new British Petroleum oil refinery at Grain started up in 1953.[47] Higher up the river the Reed Group have expanded their paper interests giving by 1961 employment to 8,000 people, occupying 500 acres, and importing via the river 500,000 tons of wood pulp, paper, board, coal and china clay. Apart from making newsprint, there was also Reed Corrugated Cases Ltd, and Reed Medway Sacks Ltd, making boxes and sacks. Kimberley-Clark a subsidiary specializes in making tissues.[48]

By the early 1950s a completely new pattern of industry has emerged, which is more appropriate to the location and skills of the area. The character of the area has also altered as a result, not only of local industrial changes, but also of new patterns of work and residence emerging in the inter war years. With relatively fast train services to London the area has gained an increasing commuter population. This is reflected in the development of residential estates at Walderslade, Rainham, Strood, Cuxton and Aylesford. This has brought people with new skills into the area, and a trend towards office and commercial development.

[1] J. G. Grace, *Some Notes on the History of Chatham Dockyard* (1946), 17.

[2] *A Royal Visit.* Souvenir of the visit of Their Majesties King George VI and

Queen Elizabeth to the Works of Short Bros. (Rochester and Bedford) Ltd, Rochester, 14 March 1939.

[3] Information from Mr Steevens, a former employee.

[4] *Barge Yards Around Rochester*, MSS.

[5] C. Barnes, *Shorts Aircraft Since 1900* (1967), 19.

[6] *Short Story*, No. 16, August 1947, 2.

[7] Barnes, *op. cit.*, 28, 29.

[8] J. D. Scott, *Vickers, A History* (1962), 324.

[9] *A Hundred Years of Road Rollers* (Grantham, 1965), 38.

[10] Information from Aveling Barford Ltd.

[11] M. A. Kelly, *The Overtype Steam Road Waggon* (Norwich, 1971), 21.

[12] Information from Aveling Barford Ltd.

[13] P. Wright, *Old Farm Tractors* (Newton Abbott, 1962), 65.

[14] *A Hundred Years of Road Rollers, op. cit.*, 40, 52, 54, 56.

[15] E. J. March, *Spritsail Barges of the Thames and Medway* (Newton Abbott, 1970), 124.

[16] F. S. Cooper and J. Chancellor, *A Handbook of Sailing Barges* (1955), 7.

[17] Information from Col Dean.

[18] F. Willmott, *Bricks and Brickies* (privately published Rainham, 1972), 25.

[19] F. Sanders, *A Business History of Chatham High Street*, MSS, IV, (1961), 30.

[20] Kelly, *Directory of Kent* (1922), 47.

[21] *1907–1957 A History of the Queenborough undertaking of Settle, Speakman and Co. Ltd.*, Queenborough, Kent. (Queenborough, 1957), 29.

[22] *South Eastern Gazette*, 12 December 1961.

[23] Information from Mr Parker.

[24] P. Lesley Cook, *Effects of Mergers* (1958), 75.

[25] Aerofilms, Photograph 32181, 1930.

[26] Cook, *op. cit.*, 89.

[27] Information from Mr Sibun, former employee.

[28] H. Rees, *The Medway Towns—Their Settlement Growth and Economic Development* (London Ph.D. Thesis, 1954) 149.

[29] Information from Mr Parker.

[30] Cook, *op. cit.*, 72, 97, 104–5.

[31] Information from Mr Parker.

[32] A. Shorter, *Paper Making in the British Isles—An Historical and Geographical Study* (Newton Abbott, 1971), 170.

[33] Information from Winget Ltd.

[34] 1907–1957, *op. cit.*, 28, 29.

[35] *Chatham News*, 8 March 1913, 10.

[36] *Rochester Journal*, 17 August 1906, 5.

[37] *Ibid*, 22 March 1907, 7.

[38] *Ibid*, 13 September 1907, 5.

[39] *Chatham News*, 8 March 1913, 10.

[40] *Short Story*, No. 5, July 1946, 1.

[41] Barnes, *op. cit.*, 31.

[42] *Short Story*, No. 6, September 1946, 2.

[43] H. Brace, *The History of Seed Crushing in Great Britain* (1960), 155.

[44] Rees, *op. cit.*, 237.

[45] R. Marsh, *Rochester, The Evolution of the City* (Rochester 1974), 71.

[46] Rees, *op. cit.*, 282.

[47] Marsh, *op. cit.*, 71.

[48] Ed. D. Rand, *An Industrial Review and Guide to the Medway* (*c.* 1961), 34–5.

Conclusions

1. Industry as such did not arrive in the Lower Medway Valley until after what is traditionally regarded as the era of the Industrial Revolution.
2. Until well into the second quarter of the nineteenth century the activities of the area were largely based upon agriculture and fishing in the valley generally. The Medway Towns had achieved some importance from (*a*) the position of Rochester as the lowest crossing place on the Medway, being on the main route to Dover. (*b*) Rochester as a clerical centre, (*c*) in trade as a transhipment point due to Rochester bridge, (*d*) the positioning of the naval dockyard at Chatham, (*e*) the garrisoning of the area with various regiments. The dockyard owed its existence to its proximity to London, and the natural features of a sheltered anchorage, and hard shores in a relatively secure position. Sheerness, the other important town owed its existence to the small dockyard which was convenient for the replenishment and repair of the Nore fleet.
3. Activity increased in the second quarter of the nineteenth century. This was based largely on the demand for building materials for the London Market. The Medway was ideally located, and possessed the raw materials to exploit such a demand, stimulating the barge building and engineering industries in turn.
4. Activity in general relied on the availability of raw materials and the possession of a good means of communication to markets—the Medway and the Thames and later railways.
5. The greatest period of activity occurred between 1850 and 1900. This was lead by the demand for Portland Cement and Bricks. It had in turn the effect of stimulating an engineering industry in the Medway Towns, and keeping the barge building industry buoyant.
6. The growth of population in the area which resulted from the new industries, linked with that drawn in by the expansion of the dockyard, helped to maintain industries which were based on domestic consumption, breweries, mineral water factories, carriage builders and a healthy retailing sector.
7. Untypical industries were scattered in the valley largely as a result of isolated occurrence of raw materials such as iron

pyrites at Sheppey, or tar from gas works, or the location in relation to raw materials and markets, as with the oil seed factories, or the glass works at Queenborough.

8. Depression comes to the area between 1900 and about 1950, with the exception of the World Wars.

   This is due to the decline in the brick industry brought on by technological change and competition from the cheaper Fletton bricks. Decline and contraction in the cement industry is the other major factor. This is again due to technological changes, a declining market, and particularly locational problems with the lack of adequate transport facilities compared with the Thamesside works.
9. With the decline of bricks and cement the barge industry was killed off. It was now more efficient to use either motor or rail transport.
10. Those sectors of engineering which dealt mainly with cement, bricks and barges are eliminated when their markets are lost. This left only agricultural implements, and road rollers at Aveling and Porter, and the fortuitous arrival of aircraft engineering.
11. Eventually, after the closure of Shorts a completely new structure of local industry emerges. This is based on (1) new light engineering industries more suited to the south east of England with its distance from raw materials such as iron and coal; (2) oil imports to the deep water anchorage at the Isle of Grain; (3) paper and paper products for the London and south east of England markets, the plants being on the left bank of the river served by the railway, and fronting the river for pulp imports.
12. Some industries disappear with mergers, and are concentrated in more efficient centres, such as Maidstone for brewing, or Erith for oil seed crushing. Others such as the glue and fertilizer works at Queenborough, and the neighbouring sanitary ware pottery, and glass factory, all strategically located in relation to raw materials and markets have managed to survive.
13. Overall the Medway ceased to have the same importance as a means of communication after 1900, although it was still used to bring raw materials into the area.

Bibliography

MANUSCRIPT SOURCES

At the Bridge Wardens Archives, Rochester—Register of Leases 1876–1906.

At Chatham Town Hall—Council Minute Books 1905–6 and 1906–7.

At the Church Commission, 1 Millbank, London—Files 5815, 37842 and 47386 letters and documents relating to the Manor Farm Estate, Frindsbury.

At Gillingham Council Offices—Council Minute Books, November 1905–October 1906; November 1907–October 1908; November 1908–October 1909; November 1909–October 1910.

At Gillingham Library—Maps.

At Kent Archives Office, Maidstone—Various manuscripts including; Aylesford MSS; Browne; Best MSS; Clayton MSS; Darnley MSS; MSS relating to Snodland Mill, Queenborough Copperas Works, Wouldham Cement Works, Maidstone Brewery. Tithe Maps and assessments. Maps to Preston Hall Estate. Ordnance Survey Maps.

Held at the Archives Office—Dean and Chapter of Rochester Catehdral Records, MSS relating to Manor Farm Estate Frindsbury, including records of brick production.

At the Public Records Office—Census Enumerators Returns for 1851 for parishes of Burham and Rainham.

At the Guildhall Rochester—Estates Committee Minute Book 21 August 1901 to 7 November 1906. Council Minute Book 1905–6; Council Notices 1907–8 and 1913–14.

At Rochester Museum—W. Dove and Co. Private Ledger 1 March 1902 to 27 February 1909; Dove, Phillips and Pett Private Ledger 1 March 1909 to 28 February 1918; Dove, Phillips and Pett, Wage Book 1912.

UNPUBLISHED THESES AND SECONDARY MANUSCRIPTS

Anonymous—*Barge Yards Around Rochester* (Rochester Museum); *Important Dates in the Glue and Fertilizer Trade* (Sheerness Library).

D. C. Coleman—*The Economy of Kent under the Later Stuarts* (London Ph.D. thesis, 1951).

K. R. MacDonald—*The Isle of Sheppey and the Swale* (London M.A. thesis, in Geography, 1949).

V. E. Morant—*The Historical Geography of Maidstone* (London M.A. thesis, 1948).

H. Rees—*The Medway Towns, Their Settlement, Growth and Economic Development* (London Ph.D. thesis, 1954).

F. Sanders—MSS *A Business History of Chatham High Street* (1961). 2 volumes. At Chatham Library.

A. H. Shorter—*The Historical Geography of the Papermaking Industry in England* (London Ph.D. thesis, 1954).

J. Whyman—MSS *A Sketch of Economic Development in Kent.*

Contemporary Printed Sources

Anonymous—*A Catalogue* of the Products of Thomas Aveling 1860; *Industrial Great Britain*, Part II, (1891); *A Royal Visit.* A Souvenir of the Visit of Their Majesties King George VI and Queen Elizabeth to the Works of Short Bros (Rochester and Bedford) Ltd, Rochester, 14 March 1939.

S. Bagshaw—*A History, Gazetteer and Directory of the County of Kent* (Sheffield, 1847), 2 vols.

A. Barnard—*Noted Breweries of Great Britain and Ireland* (1889), 4 vols.

Black's—*Guide to the South Eastern Counties of England: Kent* (Edinburgh, 1861).

Ed. F. C. Boucher—*Rochester, Chatham and Gillingham as an Industrial Centre and as a Residential Neighbourhood* (Chatham, 1908).

W. Brereton—*Travels in Holland, the United Provinces England, Scotland and Ireland* (Printed for the Chetham Society, 1844).

W. R. Craske—'The Cement Industry—Its Rise and Progress on the Medway'', *Chatham, Rochester and Brompton Observer*, 7 May 1898.

D. Defoe—*A Tour through England and Wales Divided into Circuits of Journies* (reprinted from 9th Edition, edited by G. Cole, 1848), 2 vols; *A Tour through the Whole of England and Wales Divided into Circuits of Journies* (Everyman edition, 1962), 2 vols.

S. Denne—*The History and Antiquities of Rochester and its Environs* (2nd edition, Rochester, 1817).

W. Finch—*A Historical Sketch of the County of Kent* (1803).

R. Furley—*A History of the Weald of Kent with an outline Early History of the County* (Ashford, 1871), 2 vols.

L. Fussell—*A Journey Round the Coast of Kent* (1818).

E. Harris—*A Trip Down the Medway* (Rochester, 1897); *A Trip Up the Medway* (Rochester, 1897).

J. Harris—*The History of Kent* (1719).

E. Hasted—*The History and Topographical Survey of the County of Kent* (1st Edition, Canterbury, 1778–1799), 4 vols.; (2nd Edition, Canterbury, 1797–1801), 12 vols.

W. Ireland—*England's Topographer or A New and Complete History of the County of Kent; from the earliest records to the present time, including every modern improvement* (1828), 4 vols.

Kelly's—*Directory of Kent, Surrey and Sussex* (1891); *Directory of Kent* (1903); *Directory of Kent* (1911); *Directory of Kent* (1922); *Directory of Rochester, Strood and Chatham* (1890); *Directory of Rochester, Strood and Chatham* (1898–9); *Directory of Rochester, Strood and Chatham* (1911–12); *Directory of Rochester, Strood and Chatham* (1913–14).

R. Kilburne—*A Topographie or Survey of the County of Kent* (1659).

W. Lambarde—*A Perambulation of Kent* (reprinted from the 3rd Edition, Bath, 1970).

S. Lewis—*A Topographical Dictionary of England* (5th Edition, 1844), 4 vols.

Manning and Co.—*Rochester and Chatham District Directory* (Chatham, 1877).

D. Maxwell—*Unknown Kent* (1921).

W. Miller—*Jottings of Kent, being a Series of Historical Ecclesiastical and Statistical Sketches* (2nd Edition, 1864).

A. G. Munro and Prescott Row—*Rochester and Chatham with their Surroundings: A Handbook for Visitors and Residents* (1905).

O. H. O'Hagan—*Leaves from my Life* (1929), 2 vols.

Percy and Co.—*Rochester, Chatham, Strood, New and Old Brompton and Gillingham Directory for 1871–2–3.*

J. and J. F. Phippen—*A Directory for Rochester, Chatham, Strood and their vicinities* (Rochester, 1858).

Pigot and Co.—*London and Provincial New Commercial Directory for 1823; London and Provincial New Commercial Directory for 1826; Royal, National and Commercial Directory for 1840.*

Post Office Directory of Kent (1852).

Post Office Directory of the Six Home Counties (1852).

Post Office Directory of Kent (1866).

Post Office Directory of Kent (1874).

Post Office Directory of the Six Home Counties (1874).

Post Office Directory of Kent (1899).

J. Rochard—*Historical Chatham and Rochester* (Chatham, 1894).

C. Seymour—*A New Topographical, Historical and Commercial Survey of the Cities, Towns and Villages of the County of Kent* (Canterbury, 1776).

Simpson's—*Rochester, Chatham, Strood and Brompton Directory* (1865).

H. Smetham—*A History of Strood* (Strood, 1899).

R. Taylor—*The Chatham, Rochester Directory Family Almanack and Year Book* (Chatham, 1867).

Universal British Directory (1793).

Universal British Directory (1798).

C. Whitehead—*A Sketch of the Agriculture of Kent* (1899).

William's—*Directory embracing the following towns: Rochester, Chatham, Brompton, Maidstone, Dover, Margate, Broadstairs, Ramsgate etc. giving a complete alphabetical list of all the principal inhabitants in the above towns* (1849).

Wright's—*Topography of Rochester, Chatham and Strood* (Chatham, 1838).

W. L. and M. A. Wyllie—*London to the Nore Painted and Described* (1905).

Parliamentary Papers—*Boundary Reports. Kent to Somersetshire: Reports from Commissioners on Proposed Division of Counties and Boundaries of Boroughs*, II, Part I.

Registrar-General—*Census of 1831, Enumeration Abstract* (1833); *Census of 1871, Tables of area houses and inhabitants in 1871, Division II (Surrey Kent, Sussex, Hampshire and Berkshire)*, (1872); *Census of 1891, Vol. I Area, Houses and Population* (1893); *Census of 1901, County of Kent, Area Houses and Population* (1902).

CONTEMPORARY NEWSPAPERS AND JOURNALS

The Builder, 1880.
The Chatham News, 1859–1913.
The Chatham Observer, 1913.
The Chemical Trade Journal, 1894.
The Journal of the Royal Agricultural Society of England, XXI, 1860.
The Kent Messenger, 1881 and 1895.
Maidstone and Kentish Journal, 1857, 1881 and 1882.
Rochester Chatham and Gillingham Journal, 1900, 1901, 1906, 1907 and 1908.
Sheerness Times, 1872.
Short Story, 1946, 1947.
Unsourced newspaper cuttings at Rochester and Sheerness Libraries.

Secondary Sources

Anonymous—*1907–1957 A History of the Queenborough undertaking of Settle Speakman and Co. Ltd.* (published by the firm, Queenborough, 1957); *Historical Jottings of the Parish of Snodland: forming a complete history of the village from the earliest period to the present time* (Snodland, 1894); *A Hundred Years of Road Rollers* (published by Aveling-Barford Ltd, Grantham, 1965); Louis Brennan C.B.: *Dirigible Torpedo* (Gillingham Public Library Local History Series No. 5, Part I, 1973); *Open Day Booklet* (Royal School of Military Engineering, 1972); *The Origin and Development of Aveling-Barford Ltd.* (Grantham, 1952).

A. A. Arnold—'Quarry House on Frindsbury Hill', *Archaeologia Cantiana*, XVII, (1887).

P. Banbury—*Shipbuilders of the Thames and Medway* (Newton Abbot, 1971).

C. Barnes—*Shorts Aircraft Since 1900* (1967).

H. Bonnett—*Discovering Traction Engines* (Tring, 1969); *Saga of the Steam Plough* (1965).

M. Bowley—*Innovations in Building Materials* (1960).

H. W. Brace—*A History of Seed Crushing in Britain* (1960).

J. W. Bridge—'Maidstone Geneva: An Old Maidstone Industry', *Archaeologia Cantiana* LXV, (1952).

F. Burtt—*Steamers of the Thames and Medway* (1949).

F. G. Carr—*Sailing Barges* (1951).

C. W. Chalklin—*Seventeenth Century Kent—a Social and Economic History* (1965).

R. Clark—*The Development of the English Traction Engine* (Norwich, 1960).

A. O. Collard—*The Oyster and Dredgers of Whitstable* (1902).

P. Lesley Cook—*The Effects of Mergers* (1958).

D. Coombe—'The Medway Doble', *Kent Life*, Vol. 9, No. 2, February 1970.

F. S. Cooper and J. Chancellor—*A Handbook of Sailing Barges* (1955).

A. C. Davis—*A Hundred Years of Portland Cement, 1824–1924* (1924); *Portland Cement* (2nd Edition, 1943).

W. Coles Finch—*The Foords of Rochester* (Rochester, 1917); *The Medway River and Valley* (1929).

Ed. D. Flower—*A Short History of Sir Joseph Williamson's Mathematical School, Rochester* (Rochester, 1951).

R. Goodsall—'The Whitstable Copperas Industry', *Archaeologia Cantiana* LXX, (1956); 'Oyster Fisheries on the North Kent Coast', *Archaeologia Cantiana* LXXX, (1965).

J. G. Grace—*Some Notes on the History of Chatham Dockyard* (1946).

G. N. Hardinge—*The Development and Growth of Courages Brewery* (privately published, 1932).

E. Harris—*The Riverside* (Rochester, 1930).

E. M. Hewitt—'Industries', in ed. W. Page, *The Victoria County History of England: Kent*, III, (1932).
H. Hobhouse—*Thomas Cubitt, Master Builder* (1972).
W. Hughes—*A Century of Traction Engines* (1959).
F. Hull—'A Kentish Historiography', *Archaeologia Cantiana* LXX, (1956).
F. W. Jessup—*A History of Kent with Maps and Pictures* (1958).
J. B. Jones—*Annals of Dover* (Dover, 1916).
R. A. Keen—'Messrs. Bests, Brewers of Chatham', *Archaeologia Cantiana* LXXII, (1958).
M. A. Kelly—*The Overtype Steam Road Waggon* (Norwich, 1971).
C. Knight—*Shipbuilding at Gillingham* (Reprinted from *The Chatham News*, 1938).
C. S. Leeds—*Chats about Gillingham* (Gillingham, 1906).
H. Levy—*Monopoly and Competition* (1911).
H. W. Macrosty—*The Trust Movement in British Industry* (1907).
E. J. March—*Spritsail Barges of the Thames and Medway* (Newton Abbott, 1970).
R. Marsh—*The Conservancy of the River Medway 1881–1969* (Rochester, 1971).
C. D. Marshall—*A History of the Southern Railway* (1968).
P. Mathias—*The Brewing Industry in England 1700–1830* (Cambridge, 1959).
E. Melling—*Kentish Sources—Aspects of Agriculture and Industry* (Maidstone, 1961).
G. S. Minchin—'Population' in *V.C.H.*, III, (1932).
Ed. C. Morris—*The Journeys of Celia Fiennes* (1947).
J. U. Nef—*The Rise of the British Coal Industry* (1966) 2 vols.
J. Presnail—*Chatham: The Story of a Dockyard Town* (Chatham, 1952).
J. M. Preston—'When Medway was cement river', *Medway—The Quarterly Journal of the Medway Chamber of Commerce*, No. 94, Autumn 1973.
Ed. D. Rand—*An Industrial Review and Guide to the Medway* (c. 1961).
S. Robertson—'Quarry House on Frindsbury Hill', *Archaeologia Cantiana* XVI, (1886).
V. Salmon—'Beer Exporting from Chatham in the Eighteenth Century', *Cantium*, Vol. IV, No. 3, Autumn 1972; 'James Best, Brewer of Chatham 1744–1782'. *Cantium*, Vol. 4, No. 3, Winter 1972/3.
S. B. Saul—'The Market and the Development of the Mechanical Engineering Industries in Britain, 1860–1914', *Economic History Review*, 2nd Series, XX, No. 1, April 1967; *The Myth of the Great Depression 1873–1896* (1969).
H. A. Shannon—'Bricks—A Trade Index, in ed. Carus Wilson, *Essays in Economic History* III, (1962).
A. H. Shorter—*Paper Making in the British Isles—An Historical and Geographical Study* (Newton Abbott, 1971); 'Paper Mills in the Maidstone District', *The Paper Maker and British Paper Journal*, March and April 1960.

Singer, Holmyard, Hall and Williams—*A History of Technology* (Oxford, 1957) 4 vols.

F. F. Smith—*A History of Rochester* (1928).

A. D. Spicer—*The Paper Trade* (1907).

B. Stoyel and R. Kidner—*Cement Railways of Kent* (Lingfield, 1973)

E. Straker—*Wealden Iron* (Reprint from 1931 Edition, Newton Abbott, 1969).

J. Vaizey—*The Brewing Industry 1886–1951*, (1960); 'The Brewing Industry' in Ed. P. Lesley Cook, *The Effects of Mergers* (1958).

A. H. Waite—'Great Ships of Kent—H.M.S. *Bellerophon*', *Kent Life*, Vol. 9, No. 7, July 1970.

C. de R. Wall—*Snodland and its History 55 B.C. to A.D. 1928* (Snodland, 1928).

B. Weber—'A New Index of Residential Construction and Long-Cycles in House-Building in Great Britain, 1838–1950', *Scottish Journal of Political Economy*, June 1955.

E. West—'Traction Engines in Kent', *Kent Life*, April 1965.

J. Whyman—'The Build-up of Industry', *Medway—The Quarterly Journal of the Medway Chamber of Commerce* No. 92, Spring 1973; 'A look at Life in the Island of Sheppey 100 Years Ago', *The Sheerness Times—Guardian*, May 1975.

F. G. Willmott—*Bricks and Brickies* (Privately published, Rainham, 1972).

Index